ROBERT BADINTER

FREE AND EQUAL...

Emancipating France's Jews 1789–1791

Translated from French
and with an introduction
by Adam Simms

BEN YEHUDA PRESS
Teaneck, New Jersey

FREE AND EQUAL Originally published as *Libres et égaux...
L'émancipation des Juifs sous la Révolution française (1789-1791)*,
© Librairie Arthème Fayard, 1989. Translation and introduction
©2010 Adam Simms.

Published by Ben Yehuda Press
430 Kensington Road
Teaneck, NJ 07666

http://www.BenYehudaPress.com

pb ISBN-10 1-934730-38-6
pb ISBN-13 9781934730386

Library of Congress Cataloging-in-Publication Data

Badinter, Robert.
[Libres et égaux. English]
Free and equal-- : emancipating France's Jews, 1789-1791 / Robert Badinter ;
translated from French and with an introduction by Adam Simms.
    p. cm.
Includes bibliographical references and index.
ISBN 978-1-934730-38-6
1. Jews--France--History--18th century. 2. Jews--France--Social conditions-
-18th century. 3. Jews--Emancipation--France. 4. France--Ethnic relations-
-History--18th century. I. Title. II. Title: Emancipating France's Jews,
1789-1791.
DS135.F82B3313 2010
305.892'404409033--dc22

                              2010029672

20100712
10 11 12 / 10 9 8 7 6 5 4 3 2 1

To my father,
who chose France
because it was the homeland
of the Rights of Man

The Jews came.
Humiliated annually in Toulouse
by having their ears boxed
or hanged between two dogs,
they came to ask
whether they were men.

JULES MICHELET
Histoire de la Révolution française
Book II, Chapter 2

CONTENTS

ILLUSTRATIONS

FREE AND EQUAL...

Emancipating France's Jews
1789–1791

THE ROAD TO PARIS
RAN THROUGH BERLIN

IF YOURS WERE THE FIRST NATION IN EUROPE TO EXTEND FULL CITI-zenship and equal rights to Jews, it is not unreasonable to think that there might at least be a bookshelf lined with volumes dedicated to the subject. But as Robert Badinter notes in his foreword, Jewish eman-cipation in France has generated remarkably few studies. Perhaps the paucity is due to the fact that emancipation took place in the midst of the French Revolution. Certainly, there were many other and far more dramatic developments—the storming of the Bastille, the Ten-nis Court Oath, the trials and executions of Louis XVI and Marie Antoinette come to mind—than two votes by the National Assembly recognizing France's Jews as free and equal citizens. Or perhaps it is a matter that the nation in question is France. More recent events in French Jewish history, such as the Dreyfus Affair and the Vichy regime's collaboration with Nazi Germany in implementing the Final Solution, tend to cast a pall over any credit or gratitude many might otherwise feel inclined to grant. France is in the eyes of many a nation scarred by anti-Semitism and its history, insofar as many Jews are concerned, is more often than not read through that lens.

All the more reason then to pay close attention to Robert Badinter's *Free and Equal*. Since its appearance in 1989 it has be-come the standard account in France of Jewish emancipation during the Revolution. What Badinter, one of a handful of prominent Jew-ish personalities in French political life, adds to previous scholarship is his training as an attorney rather than as an academic historian. His legal perspective, combined with his legislative experience, has enabled him to resolve a fundamental problem inherent in the two other major English-language studies that touch on Jewish emanci-pation in France. The term "touch" is appropriate because both are studies of French Enlightenment thought about Jews rather than the politics of emancipation per se. Those studies are Arthur Hertzberg's *The French Enlightenment and the Jews: The Origins of Modern*

Anti-Semitism, and Ronald Schechter's *Obstinate Hebrews: Representations of Jews in France, 1715-1815*.

First published forty years ago, Hertzberg's study set the terms for most assessments of Jewish emancipation in France that have followed. It is essentially a critique of liberal thought regarding cultural diversity. In the post-1960s era, it is common to think of liberalism as welcoming and supportive of cultural diversity. But it should be remembered that prior to the rise of theories about multiculturalism the dominant approach toward cultural diversity in liberal thought was assimilationism, best summed up in the trope of "the melting pot." Born in Poland shortly after the First World War and the son of a Hasidic rabbi who emigrated to Baltimore, Hertzberg considered assimilationism to be antithetical to the ability of Jews to survive as a particular, distinct people. *The French Enlightenment and the Jews* (Columbia University Press, 1968, 1990) is a harsh indictment of what Hertzberg contended were the motivations underpinning the French Revolution's decision to enact Jewish emancipation. Its ultimate goal, he posited, was radical assimilation. As evidence he highlighted the National Assembly's requirement that in order to qualify as citizens, Jews, like all other inhabitants of the realm, had to take an oath acknowledging the primacy of French civil law. From 1550, when Henri II issued the first *lettre patente*, or charter, to a community of Portuguese Jewish immigrants in Bordeaux, until the onset of the Revolution, Jewish communities in France were largely autonomous and self-governing. But in the northeastern provinces of Alsace and Lorraine, where scattered Jewish communities came under French sovereignty in the seventeenth century, military governors and the monarchy permitted them the right to maintain a civil and criminal justice system administered by rabbinic courts. These courts' jurisprudence was based on the legal codes of the Talmud, the massive compendium of Jewish religious law. Hertzberg maintained that the requirement that French Jews substitute French civil law for rabbinic law and rabbinic courts was a major assault against Jewish continuity, because in doing so the Revolution struck a subtle but nonetheless major blow against continued Jewish adherence to the Talmud as the religious foundation of Judaism and the distinguishing characteristic of what makes Jews a particular people.

Hertzberg located the origin of the National Assembly's attack on the authority of the Talmud in French Enlightenment thought and, in particular, in the writings of its preeminent *philosophe*, François-Marie Arouet, better known by his nom de plume, Voltaire. Voltaire rarely had anything positive to say about Jews and many of his comments are memorably vile. Nor did he have much, if anything, positive to say about revealed religions, whether Judaism, Christianity or Islam, all of which he regarded as collections of irrational "superstition." Hertzberg argued that Voltaire, in fashioning his assault on the Catholic Church's temporal power in Europe, countered with a theory of "natural" (as opposed to revealed) religion, rooted in conditions specific to various geographic regions and their inhabitants. Having developed in the "Orient," Judaism (as well as its offshoot, Christianity) was suited to the people and circumstances of the desert. Europe's "natural" religion, on the other hand, had best been expressed in Greek and Roman polytheistic civilization. A foreign implant, Christianity was unsuited to Europe and had stunted and distorted native spiritual expression; and if Christianity was alien to Europe, even more foreign and even less adaptable was Judaism. In this construct of geographically determined "natural" religions, Hertzberg detected a precursor of "modernized and secularized anti-Semitism," which in the late nineteenth and early twentieth centuries mutated into the racialist-biological anti-Semitism that reached its apogee in Nazi ideology and the Holocaust.[1]

Hertzberg by no means asserted that French Enlightenment *philosophes* were proto-Nazis. What he posited, however, was that both shared a similar solution to their eras' "Jewish question": the disappearance of the Jews as a distinctive people. The *philosophes* sought to accomplish this goal through religious and cultural assimilation; the Nazis through physical annihilation. The French Enlightenment's "solution" on the eve of the Revolution was couched in Christian rhetoric of "regeneration." For Jews to become full members of the national community, they would first have to be "freed" from their adherence to the obscurantist "superstitions," codified in the Talmud, which set them apart from the societies in which they lived. Regeneration would then proceed as Jews saw the advantages of education in the manual arts, which would allow them to enter a nation-

---

1 Hertzberg, 7. His "Introduction" sets his inquiry about French Enlightenment thought within the context of post-Second World War intellectual inquiries into the origins of modern anti-Semitism. Regarding Voltaire and his influence, see 280-313, and especially 306-307.

al economy based on agriculture and craftsmanship. Once integrated into the economic mainstream, they would abandon their almost exclusive reliance on commerce and money lending as a means of livelihood. The key to regeneration, according to French Enlightenment *philosophes* who supported Jewish emancipation, was citizenship in the national community. But in order to qualify for entry into the national community, Jews would first have to renounce their parallel institutions organized around rabbinic courts and rabbinic law. For Hertzberg, who considered the Talmud the cornerstone of Judaism, emancipation on the terms offered by the French Enlightenment was, however ostensibly benign, at heart anti-Semitic. It aimed to rid France of its Jews by offering a powerful incentive to sever their ties with the religious laws that made them a distinctive people. Once distanced from the Talmud and the observances it prescribed, Jews would be loosened from their moorings, assimilate and thereafter be less likely to remain Jews as generation succeeded generation in a post-emancipation world.

Hertzberg's analysis of Jewish emancipation and the French Enlightenment *philosophes'* role in shaping it has become standard among most scholars of Jewish history. Occasionally one stumbles across a footnote taking issue with his reading of the French Enlightenment. Lynn Hunt, in her collection of documentary readings, *The French Revolution and Human Rights: A Brief Documentary History* (Boston and New York: Bedford Books of St. Martin's Press, 1996), decried " ...Hertzberg's anachronistic way of reading out of historical context; he applies a twentieth-century, post-Holocaust standard of judgment to eighteenth-century writers, making little effort to understand what they might have meant in their own time. By this kind of standard just about everyone writing in the eighteenth century was racist, sexist, and/or anti-Semitic, and thus all distinction between positions is lost."[2] Still, there have been no direct or sustained challenges to the central elements of his thesis.

Hunt's footnote nonetheless points to several paths that may be pursued in testing his negative assessment of Jewish emancipation in France. One path would attempt to determine the degree to which Voltaire's writings about Jews were representative of attitudes expressed by the political actors who supported Jewish emancipation

---

2   Hunt, 31, fn. 9.

on the eve of the Revolution and during nearly three years of debate in the National Assembly. Such analysis is crucial because Voltaire was unavailable to voice his opinions: he had died in 1778, at the age of eighty-three.

Thirty-five years after Hertzberg's study appeared, Ronald Schechter, an historian at the College of William and Mary, utilized an electronic database of French literary and historical works to gather and analyze French Enlightenment *philosophes'* writings about Jews and Judaism. His study, *Obstinate Hebrews: Representations of Jews in France, 1715-1815* (University of California Press, 2003), presents a portrait of French Enlightenment thought that is far more nuanced and far more complex than Hertzberg's. Schechter posited that the *philosophes*, few of whom had any direct or meaningful contact with Jews, French or otherwise, drew upon references to Jews and Judaism in travelers' accounts and theological studies, from which they constructed abstract, speculative models of a "Philosophical Jew" who served as the subject for "thought experiments" about the malleability of human nature. The aim of their speculations was to advance arguments about how reform of various social institutions might promote human happiness. His survey, Schechter wrote, "suggests that there was no single way of portraying Jews in the French Enlightenment. On the contrary, the meanings attached to Jews were plural, fluctuating, and often contradictory."[3] Moreover, he observed that as the High Enlightenment was drawing to a close and Louis XVI was ascending the throne (1775), a shift was under way, veering from philosophical speculation about human nature and its perfectibility toward political speculation about the nature of citizenship and nationhood.

Such musings were by no means solely or even primarily focused on France's Jews; taxation and privileges accorded the nobility and clergy, among other issues, were far higher on the National Assembly's agenda when it proclaimed its existence in 1789. But as discussion turned to who among the realm's inhabitants qualified for the status of citizen and what those qualifications might be, the presence of two large concentrations of Jewish communities—one in the southwest, centered around the Atlantic port city of Bordeaux, the other scattered among cities and villages in the northeastern provinc-

---

3 Schechter, 64.

es of Alsace and Lorraine along France's border with Germany, and both well implanted in the economic life of their regions—suddenly became a political issue of major import. If, as the Declaration of the Rights of Man declared, "Men are born and remain free and equal in rights. Social distinctions may be based only on common utility," and if Jews were part of mankind, several significant questions confronted the National Assembly in the months and years following the charter's adoption: Could some "men" be excluded from citizenship? If so, on what basis? What would such exclusion say about the reformers' claims that the rights recognized as those of French citizens were universal and applicable to all mankind? And could a nation exist and its people attain happiness if some of its inhabitants were citizens and others were excluded from citizenship?

Robert Badinter, by focusing on Jewish emancipation as the intersection of French Enlightenment thought with the political process of republican nation building inaugurated by the French Revolution, rather than trying to trace emancipation's roots solely within the confines of French intellectual history, provides a perspective for understanding how what had been "philosophical" speculation was transformed into a political program. He poses a question that challenges the fundamental assumption of both Hertzberg's and Schechter's studies: What if the intellectual framework for emancipation was *not* a product of the French Enlightenment, but rather had developed elsewhere and was then gradually introduced into French discourse by a younger generation of *philosophes* who became important political actors during the early stage of the Revolution?[4]

The Enlightenment, Badinter reminds us, was a European phenomenon and not confined solely to France. *Philosophes* of different nations corresponded with one another, traveled and sometimes accepted patronage or sought refuge in neighboring or distant countries, and published their writings abroad to evade censorship in their native lands. The Enlightenment was cosmopolitan and its proponents closely followed development of new ideas irrespective of national frontiers. In such an environment the only limit to intel-

4 Hertzberg, in his discussion of Voltaire, noted in passing that toward the end of his life Voltaire's views about Jews were "being stated in a context of debate within the Enlightenment," particularly "in the 1760s, and more especially in the 1770s"; but Hertzberg examined only one exchange between Voltaire and another minor French *philosophe*, and did not further develop the insight. See 307.

lectual interchange was an ability to read or converse in a foreign language, a circumstance which gave translators, interpreters and those who engaged them vital roles in disseminating ideas.

The intellectual framework for emancipation of French Jewry, Badinter demonstrates, developed not in France, but in Prussia. This is an especially notable proposition, coming as it does from someone who has spent his professional career in French law and politics, and who published his study of Jewish emancipation in time to coincide with commemoration of the French Revolution's bicentennial anniversary. It was in Berlin, not Paris, that a Jew, Moses Mendelssohn, established an international reputation by demonstrating that Judaism was not the obscurantist superstition its detractors held it to be, and that a religiously observant Orthodox Jew was fully capable of holding his own as a participant in Enlightenment discussions of human nature, spirituality and the perfectibility of human beings. Mendelssohn had honed his reputation during several well-publicized controversies with anti-Semitic Protestant theologians; and it was to Mendelssohn to whom Cerf-Berr turned, in 1779, during an outburst of anti-Jewish agitation in Alsace, with a request that he write a treatise urging amelioration of the economic and social distress in which the vast majority of Jews in northeastern France lived.

Cerf-Berr, a wealthy military contractor with access to Louis XVI's court and leader of Alsace's Jewish community, led a life guided by the Talmud's precepts. He was far from being a *philosophe,* had little sympathy for "enlightened" criticism of "Talmudic obscurantism," and declined to accommodate his Orthodox Jewish religious observances when he did business with France's aristocracy and military. Badinter provides a brief portrait of Cerf-Berr sketched by a non-Jewish contemporary, who described him as being "a rigid observer of the most meticulous observances dictated by Mosaic law, abstained from prohibited foods, did not eat with any Christian, took care not to engage in the least work on the Sabbath..." Nonetheless he recognized that Enlightenment ideas about religious toleration could be marshaled to create a climate of opinion sympathetic to alleviating the economic and social disabilities that weighed upon his coreligionists.

Responding to Cerf-Berr, Mendelssohn counseled that the proposed treatise would have greater impact were it to be written by a Christian. With Cerf-Berr's assent and financial support,

Mendelssohn engaged Christian Wilhelm Dohm, a thirty-year-old Prussian court official, jurist and professor of public finance in Berlin, to write a riposte based on a memorandum that Cerf-Berr provided about the condition of Jews in Europe. Two years later, in 1781, Dohm's reply, *Ueber die buergerliche Verbesserung des Juden* [On the Civic Improvement of the Jews], proposed that removing economic, political and social restrictions would provide Jews with incentives to abandon their despised role as moneylenders and to engage in more "productive" activities that would contribute to the economic growth of nations that accorded them the same rights as other subjects. Scattered throughout his essay were descriptions of what Dohm deemed to be the Jews' less appealing behaviors and beliefs. Far more important for Cerf-Berr's purposes, however, Dohm also posited that such traits were a consequence of restrictions and exclusion; since human nature was malleable and responsive to changes of social environment, those characteristics would fade as disabilities were removed. Cerf-Berr, realizing that a work in German would have limited impact in swaying political opinion in France, engaged Jean Bernoulli, a member of the Berlin Academy of Sciences and a friend of Mendelssohn's, to translate Dohm's treatise into French. Bernoulli's translation was printed in Dessau in April 1782; but when copies were shipped to France it lacked the required censor's license and virtually all copies were seized and destroyed before it could be offered for sale.[5]

Royal censors barred Dohm's treatise from circulating in a French edition, but they had no power to stop Honoré-Gabriel Riqueti, comte de Mirabeau, from meeting Dohm in Berlin. Nor could the censors keep Henri-Baptiste Grégoire, a young Jesuit-trained priest in France's border province of Lorraine, from corresponding with Dohm and acquiring his two-volume treatise in its original German-language edition.[6] Mirabeau and Grégoire, both in their late thirties when Dohm's work appeared, would adapt its analysis and prescriptions for a French audience and emerge as champions

5 Alexander Altmann provides an extended account of Cerf-Berr, Mendelssohn and Dohm's project in *Moses Mendelssohn: A Biographical Study* (University: University of Alabama Press, 1973), 449–71. A copy of the French-language edition, *De la réforme politique des Juifs*, is in the rare book collection of the Jewish Theological Seminary's library in New York City.

6 Dominique Bourel, *Moses Mendelssohn: La naissance du judaïsme moderne* (Paris: Gallimard, 2004), 304.

of Jewish emancipation when the issue came before the National Assembly. In this circuitous fashion, Cerf-Berr's insight—that the road
to influencing the French Enlightenment regarding Jews ran through
Berlin—eventually bore fruit. [7]

In 1785 Mirabeau visited Berlin and made the rounds of the
Prussian capital's literary salons. As a young hellion he had been
incarcerated at his father's request in the Château d'If—the prison
from which Edmond Dantès escaped in Alexandre Dumas' swash-
buckling novel, *The Count of Monte-Cristo*; later he became, for
historians of the Revolution, an archetype of a younger generation
of France's nobility who, influenced by Enlightenment ideas, did not
hesitate to join commoners of the Third Estate in a program of radical
reform when Louis XVI convened the États Généraux. After returning in 1787 from his sojourn in Berlin, Mirabeau staked his claim
as an Enlightenment *philosophe* by publishing in London—far from
the reach of his homeland's censors—*Sur Moses Mendelssohn et sur
la réforme politique des Juifs* [On Moses Mendelssohn, on Political Reform of the Jews]. Quoting copiously from Mendelssohn's and
Dohm's writings, Mirabeau proposed that France's Jews be granted
not only civil rights, but that they be allowed to maintain their religious customs and retain their rabbinic courts.

As Mirabeau was absorbing new ideas in Berlin, Abbé Grégoire
was preparing an essay to answer the question, "Is there a way to
make the Jews happier and more useful in France?" In 1785 the Royal Academy of Sciences in Metz announced a contest on that topic;
the author of the winning essay, to be determined in 1787, would be
awarded a gold medal and 400 livres in prize money. Essay contests,
sponsored by learned societies in France's larger provincial cities, had
emerged in the mid-eighteenth century as a way to burnish the prestige of the societies' patrons, disseminate "enlightened" discourse,
and establish the reputations of budding *philosophes*. Thirty-four
years earlier, in 1751, Jean-Jacques Rousseau had earned his place in
Europe's intellectual firmament when the Academy of Dijon awarded
him its prize for his *Discours sur les sciences et les arts*. An essayist

---

7 Alyssa Goldstein Sepinwall's intellectual biography of Grégoire, *The Abbé Grégoire and the French Revolution: The Making of Modern Universalism* (Berkeley: University of California Press, 2005), confirms and substantiates Badinter's insight regarding
the debt French Revolutionary advocates of Jewish emancipation owed to the Berlin
Enlightenment. See especially pages 25-34 for her discussion of Strasbourg as a meeting ground for French and Berlin Enlightenment ideas.

who responded to the Metz academy's call for papers could hope to earn similar renown should he win its contest.

Of nine papers initially submitted, Pierre-Louis Rœderer, a thirty-three-year-old counselor of the Parlement of Metz and chairman of the essay jury, announced that Grégoire's was one of three entries which, though promising, did not quite meet the royal society's standards. Grégoire and the two other contestants were invited to revise and resubmit their essays in time for a new deadline set for August 1788. When the revised versions, along with three new entries, were considered, Grégoire, then thirty-seven years old, was chosen one of the contest's three winners, each of whom elaborated upon one or more of the themes Dohm had developed. Five months later his treatise, retitled *Essai sur la régénération physique, morale et politique des Juifs* [Essay on the Physical, Moral and Civic Regeneration of the Jews] was published—with the royal censor's approval—in Metz, Paris and Strasbourg.

Much of Grégoire's essay recounted the history of Jewish persecutions and the prejudices with which Christians justified restrictions of Jews' rights. Grégoire was also harshly critical of the Talmud. One notable passage described the compendium of the Jews' religious and civil codes as a "vast reservoir..., virtually a cesspool in which are gathered the fevered confusions of the human mind." Grégoire castigated the Talmud for perpetuating "superstitions" that had encouraged Jews throughout their exilic history to segregate themselves from the societies in which they lived. Still, for all the stereotypes Grégoire repeated—most often in order to refute them—and despite his denigration of rabbinic law, he argued forcefully and without concession that Jews were more sinned against—especially by his fellow Christians—than sinners, and that their much criticized and feared commercial activities and money lending were rational responses to economic restrictions imposed on them. Once such restrictions were removed by granting Jews equal rights, Jews could begin to participate as members of civil society. Allowed to own land, attend French schools, learn trades and join guilds, they could become farmers and craftsmen like their fellow citizens and abandon reliance on commerce and moneylending. Moreover, granted equal rights and opportunities, Jews would have little or no reason to continue to rely on their religious law as they did when confined to autonomous, self-governing communities within French society. Together France and its Jews would be regenerated: France, by becoming a more just society as it granted citizenship to its most despised minority; its Jews, by participating as full members of the French nation once they grasped opportunities afforded by equal rights.

Soon after Grégoire's *Essai* appeared he was chosen to serve as a member of the Estates-General, representing the First Estate of France's Catholic clergy. There, as one of several priests who were influenced by Enlightenment currents and did not share the conservative outlook and interests of the French Church's hierarchy, Grégoire joined with dissident nobles on 20 June 1789 to take the Tennis Court Oath. Together with the Third Estate of commoners they declared that they constituted a single deliberative body, the National Assembly, to consider reforms to regenerate Louis XVI's realm. Graced with the luster of the Royal Academy of Metz's recent prize, Grégoire emerged as the Assembly's foremost advocate of equal rights and citizenship for France's Jews.

Most of the threads of Cerf-Berr's effort to reshape French policy were woven together one last time on the eve of the Revolution. In the spring of 1788 Chrétien-Guillaume de Lamoignon de Malesherbes undertook a royal commission to investigate the prospect of extending civil rights to Jews. A year earlier Louis XVI had appointed him minister of state with a mandate to administer a decree that restored civil rights to France's Protestants. The decree's reference to "other subjects to whom the exercise of a religion other than the Catholic religion is permitted" immediately raised questions as to whether the measure applied equally to Jews. During the course of this new inquiry, Mirabeau forwarded a copy of his essay on Mendelssohn—as well as a copy of Bernoulli's translation of Dohm's work. Malesherbes also solicited advice from a wide variety of public and private figures, including Cerf-Berr. Their encounter was instructive though not particularly pleasant for Malesherbes, according to Pierre-Louis Rœderer, chairman of the Academy of Metz jury that awarded Grégoire a gold medal for his essay and who assisted Malesherbes. Cerf-Berr, drawing distinctions between the religious practices of Alsatian Jews and the Sephardim of Bordeaux, insisted that the latter's observances were lax, and he exhausted the minister's patience as he provided examples. The following day, Malesherbes told Rœderer: "The king told me he made me a Jew [in order to carry out this inquiry], and now Cerf-Berr wants to make me a Jansenist...," a refer-

XX   F<small>REE AND</small> E<small>QUAL</small>

ence to a puritanical strand in seventeenth-century French Catholic thought that had been denounced as heretical by the Church and suppressed by Louis XIV. Malesherbes tentatively concluded that restrictions on France's Jews should be eased to prepare them for full entry into French society. But he continued to have reservations about the extent to which they were prepared to accommodate their religious and cultural traditions in order to integrate.

Whether the inquiry might have led the king to issue a decree of Jewish emancipation and what its terms might have been are ultimately unknowable, since the French Revolution began before Malesherbes could formulate recommendations. The most that may be ventured with any certainty is that by 1789, a decade after Cerf-Berr had approached Mendelssohn for assistance in framing an appeal to ease the plight of Jews in Alsace, the question of emancipation had risen far higher on the agenda of issues being addressed by the nation's political elites.

Indeed, the matter was taken up by the National Assembly in fairly short order. Its first consideration occurred on 14 October 1789, and after several more sessions, on 28 January 1790 a decree recognizing the Sephardic "Portuguese" Jews of southwestern France as citizens was adopted. Incorporated in that decree was a provision that consideration of granting the same status to the Ashkenazi Jews of northeastern France—Cerf-Berr's people—was postponed for future deliberation. There is no record of Cerf-Berr's reaction, but he might have noted a rueful irony: the coreligionists whom he had disparaged for lax religious observance during his meeting with Malesherbes had been deemed fit for citizenship by the National Assembly precisely because of their relative lack of "particularity." A century of internal exile in France, during which they had initially presented themselves as "New Christians," had enabled the Sephardim to blend into France's culture and economy. When they openly resumed their practice of Judaism, they continued to dress as their non-Jewish neighbors and to conduct their affairs according to French civil law. By the time their citizenship was affirmed, they had gradually and voluntarily limited the scope of the semiautonomy granted in their *lettres patentes* to governance of their synagogues, religious schools and charitable institutions. The Sephardim of the southwest had, intentionally or not, chosen to accommodate, acculturate and integrate, and the majority in the National Assembly recognized them as "French," and therefore accommodated them as citizens.

A majority, but certainly not all, of the National Assembly's members voted to acknowledge the Jews of the Southwest as citizens. A determined minority led by Catholic ecclesiastical officials and Alsatian rabble-rousers continued to oppose similar status for the Jews of the northeast. From that point on, Badinter emphasizes, the political task for advocates of Jewish emancipation was to formulate a proposal that would win over a sufficient number of undecided members to vote in favor of citizenship for the Ashkenazim and would attain the Ashkenazim's leaders' consent to its provisions. The outlines of that proposal were articulated and presented to the National Assembly by comte Stanislas de Clermont-Tonnerre during its session on the evening of 22-23 December 1789, when members were deliberating the measure that would recognize citizenship for the Sephardim. A single sentence from Clermont-Tonnerre's speech—"We must refuse everything to the Jews as a nation and accord everything to Jews as individuals"—has often been cited by Hertzberg and many others as evidence of a fundamentally hostile attitude in France toward its religious and ethnic minorities. Badinter provides a concise summary of Clermont-Tonnerre's remarks; but its text deserves to be quoted more fully and examined in detail because it set forth the terms on which the process of Jewish emancipation was completed.

Dismissing allegations made by emancipation's opponents that Jewish religious traditions, such as dietary laws and disapproval of intermarriage, rendered Jews "unsociable" and therefore inadmissible as citizens, Clermont-Tonnerre replied:

> ...As to their lack of sociability, it is exaggerated. Does it matter? What principle do you draw from it? Is there a law that compels me to marry your daughter? Is there a law that compels me to eat hare [a nonkosher animal], and to eat it with you? To be sure, these religious eccentricities will fade; and should they survive the influence of philosophy [*philosophie*, in the French text, meaning rational and liberal attitudes], and the delight of finally being real citizens and sociable people, *they are not offenses with which the law may or ought to concern itself.*
>
> But some will say to me, *the Jews have their own judges and laws.* To that I will reply: it is your fault, and you should not allow it. We must deny everything to the Jews as a nation

and grant everything to Jews as individuals; *we must withdraw
recognition of their judges; they should have none but our
own; we must deny legal sanction to the so-called laws of their
self-governing Judaic structure; they should not be allowed to
constitute within the state either a political group or a social
order*; they must be citizens individually. [8]

Critics of French Enlightenment thought about Jews and Jewish
customs seize upon Clermont-Tonnerre's third sentence in the second
paragraph above as evidence that even the staunchest proponents of
Jewish emancipation were covertly in league with their anti-Semitic
adversaries to eradicate group solidarity and identity as part of a plan
to force Jews to assimilate and disappear as a distinct religious group.
That assertion is clearly not supported by a close reading of the text.
Clermont-Tonnerre expressly rejected the proposition that equality
demanded uniformity of belief, thought and behavior. Indeed, he
clearly defended the right of French Jews to retain their "religious
eccentricities" without interference, affirming that religious practices were a private matter beyond the scope of the state's interest or
intervention. Moreover, to construe Clermont-Tonnerre's use of the
term "*nation*" as a coded reference to an alien subculture that could
never be integrated into French society misinterprets and distorts the
term as it was understood in eighteenth-century France. "*Nation*," as
Clermont-Tonnerre employed the word, followed customary usage in
his era's legal and political discourse to describe subcultures within
France, consistent with its use for more than two centuries in the
lettres patentes granted to France's Jews.[9]

In agreeing with his opponents that Jews should no longer be
considered or treated as a *nation*, Clermont-Tonnerre explicitly fo-

---

8 Stanislas de Clermont-Tonnerre, *Opinion de M. le comte Stanislas de Clermont-
Tonnerre, député de Paris, Le 13 Décembre 1789* (Paris: Baudouin, 1798), 12-13. Emphasis
added.

9 The dictionary *Larousse de la langue française. Lexis* provides the following definition, which is cited as being in use *circa* 1270: "Grande communauté humaine
installée en général sur un même territoire ou dans des territoires dépendants et
qui se caractérise par des traditions historiques et culturelles communes, par des
intérêts économiques convergents et par une unité linguistique ou religieuse." [A
large human community settled, in general, on the same territory or dependent territories, and which is characterized by common historical and cultural traditions, by
convergent economic interests, and by linguistic or religious unity.] Paris: Librairie
Larousse, 1977.

cused on a single, "national" Jewish institution that symbolized France's Ashkenazi Jews' separation from the mainstream of French society: their rabbinic courts. He reminded opponents of emancipation that these courts were a legacy of the Ancien Régime's custom of granting exemptions from uniform application of rights and laws to various social groups. In doing so, he called the Assembly's attention to the fact that the result had been vast social inequalities that had undermined the kingdom's internal unity and economy, and had weakened its standing among nations. Louis XVI had convened the États Généraux, representing France's three recognized "*états*," or social orders (the Catholic clergy, the nobility and the commons), to raise new taxes. The orders' response had been the Tennis Court Oath to reconstitute themselves in a single body as the National Assembly and to renounce all special privileges granted to their respective orders. Henceforth France was to be one nation, not a collection of *nations*. All inhabitants who had previously been grouped in various orders as subjects of the king were now individual citizens endowed with equal rights and equal standing in a legal and political system that allowed no exceptions or exemptions based upon membership in a group.

By specifically citing the rabbinic courts as an example of "everything" he would refuse to France's Jews "as a *nation*," Clermont-Tonnerre was alerting France's Jews that they would no longer be allowed to maintain their own courts and a separate body of law if they wished to be acknowledged as free and equal citizens. Jewish autonomy, separate and apart within French civil society, was a legacy of the Ancien Régime. If Jews wanted to benefit from the promise held out in the Declaration of the Rights of Man and of the Citizen, they would have to integrate themselves into the new civil structure without reservation or pleas for special consideration based on Jewish "particularity."

Left by the Sephardim to pursue citizenship on their own, leaders of the Alsace and Lorraine communities mounted lobbying efforts. They continued to press members of the Assembly and broke new ground by opening ties with sympathetic representatives of the Paris Commune, which under the rising influence of the radical Jacobin Club was beginning to play a powerful role in the Assembly. But as the Revolution's pace increased, other political controversies crowded emancipation from the legislative agenda. Disputes over the sale of Church properties, proposals to reform Church governance by allowing laypeople to elect bishops and priests, and the royal family's attempt to flee to Germany created crises that permitted emancipation's opponents to delay consideration of the "German" Jews' status as citizens.

Despite Clermont-Tonnerre's clear statement, four months later Berr Isaac Berr, Cerf-Berr's counterpart in Lorraine as the recognized spokesman of the province's Jewish communities, remained unwilling to accept its terms. In April 1790 he addressed a public letter to the bishop of Nancy, who was a member of the National Assembly and a staunch opponent of emancipation, in which Berr proposed that the Jews of the East would renounce their rights to vote and hold elective office in return for the right to "remain a private community and to have amongst them, and to bear the costs of rabbis and leaders, as much for civil as for religious law." As Badinter explains, Berr's proposal would have had all Jews of the region relinquish recognition as full and equal citizens of France "in return for the right to maintain their communal structures and the judicial authority of their rabbis." But Berr apparently miscalculated his influence as a community leader. Later that month, his nephew, Jacob Berr, issued his own public letter, also addressed to the archbishop, in which he criticized his uncle's offer.

The quest to secure citizenship for France's Jews of the East dragged on for almost twenty-one months. When they finally won their cause in the Assembly, victory came unexpectedly and almost inadvertently. It was a moment at once dramatic for those who had so long sought emancipation and virtually anticlimactic for the deputies who voted it. On 3 September 1791 the Assembly completed debate on a formal constitution, which the king accepted eleven days later. Its work almost finished, the body continued to consider motions intended to tie up loose ends. At its session on 27 September, after adopting a decree forbidding citizens "from assuming in any way titles or privileges that have been abolished..., or to affix coats of arms to their coaches," Adrien Du Port, a moderate who had been elected as a representative of Paris's nobility, asked for the floor. He proposed that since the Assembly had recently defined criteria necessary for citizens to vote in elections, it was time to revoke the decree of 24 December 1789 which had postponed final determination of the Jews of the East's status. He moved that Jews become citizens with voting rights if they met the provisions set forth in the constitution. "I believe," Du Port stated, "that freedom of worship [guaranteed by the Declaration of the Rights of Man] no longer allows that any distinction may be made among citizens' political rights on the basis of their beliefs. And I believe equally that the Jews cannot be the only exception to enjoyment of these rights, when pagans, Turks, Muslims, even the Chinese—people of all sects, in a word—are admitted."

The Assembly's presiding officer, eager to conclude the session, cut short debate and called for a vote. It was adopted. In a last futile gesture of opposition, Jean-François Rewbell, an Alsatian deputy who was a vituperative and resourceful opponent of emancipation, objected that the Assembly had just passed a decree without having a written text upon which to vote. The presiding officer asked Du Port to provide a formal text. It stated: "The National Assembly, deeming that the necessary conditions to be French citizens...are fixed by the Constitution, and that all men who, satisfying the aforesaid conditions, take the civic oath and undertake to fulfill all duties that the Constitution imposes, are entitled to all advantages that it offers, revokes all postponements, reservations and exceptions inserted in preceding decrees relative to individual Jews who take the civic oath."

With these bland phrases, the campaign for emancipation ended. All of France's Jews were now recognized as citizens.

The following day, the Assembly voted an additional decree, declaring its intention that "the taking of the civic oath on the part of Jews be regarded as a definitive relinquishment of civil and political laws to which Jewish individuals think they are subject." This was the Revolution's last, Voltairean brickbat against "Talmudic obscurantism," aimed at dismantling autonomous rabbinic courts and supplanting the Talmud as the foundation for French Jews' conduct in French civil society. Berr Isaac Berr had resisted trading these distinctively Jewish institutions for full citizenship for his people. But when given the opportunity, the Jews of Alsace and Lorraine embraced citizenship and the Jewish communities of northeastern France embraced the Revolution's new dispensation.

IN *FREE AND EQUAL* ROBERT BADINTER MARSHALS MANY OF the same source materials as Arthur Hertzberg did in *The French Enlightenment and the Jews*, but reaches significantly different conclusions about the Revolution's intellectual environment and its political aims concerning emancipation. His assessments derive not from revisionist intent but from an alternate perspective about the essence of Jewish identity and the structures necessary to sustain it.

Hertzberg's view, alluded to above, deserves elaboration. Talmud and Torah (the Five Books of Moses, the first five of Hebrew Scripture), which traditional Judaism reveres as divinely revealed foundations of the faith, command a specific people to undertake a holy mission to live according to ethical and moral codes intended to produce a well-ordered civil society. In this perspective, Judaism is holistic: there is no separation of secular and religious spheres; no individual identity without reference to the larger body of Jews who share kinship, belief, history and circumstances; no religious identity without affiliation with and participation in a community of Jews. To be a Jew is to be part of a distinct culture that requires specific social institutions to embody, express and preserve its values.

The standard against which Hertzberg judges the Revolution is the degree to which, in extending civic equality to Jews, it also acknowledged that Judaism commands the particular way of life embodied in the Talmud's precepts and civil codes. His assessment is that the Revolution did not, given the Revolution's demand that the Jews of the East relinquish their "particularism." For the National Assembly's legislators, who were attempting to knit a unified society from the legacy of autonomous social *corporations* inherited from the Ancien Régime, the most salient symbol of the Eastern Jews' "particularity" was their system of autonomous civil institutions, exemplified in rabbinic courts whose jurisprudence was based not on French civil law but on the Talmud's codes. That the Assembly rejected a motion requiring Jews to relinquish the "civil and political laws to which Jewish individuals think they are subject"—on grounds that, since Jewish civil law is also Jewish religious law, the proposal in effect asked Jews to renounce their religion—does not alter Hertzberg's judgment that Jewish emancipation as conceived by the French Revolution constituted an assault on Jewish "particularity."

Robert Badinter's evaluation of Jewish emancipation derives from a different outlook known as Franco-Judaism, a perspective that took shape in the process of French Jews' accommodation to French society in the Revolution's aftermath. During the succeeding nineteenth and twentieth centuries, the vast majority of France's Jews looked upon their adaptation to French society as integration rather than assimilation (in the sense of forsaking their identities as Jews). Franco-Judaism accepted—even welcomed—modernity's divorce of the secular and religious dimensions into separate spheres, and defined its immediate mission as securing the physical and economic well-being of Jews within French society. The Revolution made Jewish emancipation possible by severing the link between religious belief and the state with respect to citizenship. The rights and protections of civil law delineated in the Declaration of the Rights of Man and of the Citizen were no longer granted only to those who professed the Catholic faith. Jews and Protestants—as well as "pagans, Turks, Muslims, even the Chinese," as Du Port noted—were now eligible to participate in civil society and avail themselves of its equal and impartial protections so long as they consented to abide by its codes. In turn, separation of religious belief and the state meant that the state would not intrude in the private sphere of religious belief. Within that sphere, Jews were free to create and maintain institutions they deemed necessary to preserve, practice and transmit to succeeding generations Judaism's moral and ethical prescriptions for a well-ordered society. And in a civil society dedicated to treating all of its citizens impartially and equally, autonomous parallel civil institutions were no longer required. Under these conditions it was deemed both possible and beneficial to integrate into civil society, forgoing outward signs of distinctive behavior while retaining membership in a distinctive people defined by a shared heritage of history and values.

Franco-Judaism's standard for assessing the French Revolution and its emancipationist project is whether it provided Jews a framework for security and maintaining Jewish identity. Badinter's answer is an affirming yes. To objections that France betrayed emancipation during the Dreyfus Affair and the Vichy regime, his response is that both were periods when segments of the French polity, still unreconciled to the outcome of the Revolution, exploited the Third Republic's political weaknesses to attack its institutions and secular republican values. In the first instance, the Republic rallied and prevailed, freeing Captain Alfred Dreyfus, acknowledging the army's role in wrongfully court-martialing and imprisoning him on a false charge of treason, and finally restoring him to its ranks. Moreover, the Affair provided impetus to the Republic's supporters to reinforce republican values. In 1906, after a fierce political and social battle, it severed the state's last link with religion by making the nation's primary and secondary education system public rather than a service provided by the Catholic Church. Similarly, Vichy represented a final assault on the Revolution and French republicanism, one that succeeded by virtue of German invasion and occupation. The regime's craven eagerness to outdo the Nazis in circumscribing and revoking Jews' equal protection under republican law, its complicity in gathering and deporting Jews to death camps, and its overall failure to protect France's national sovereignty ensured that antirepublican values were discredited and marginalized in the post-liberation period. France has had two republics in the half-century since Vichy, but the transition from the Fourth to the Fifth Republic was the outcome of demands for a more stable and effective national government, not an assault on the French Revolution and the Declaration of the Rights of Man's principle that religious belief has no bearing on its citizens' enjoyment of free and equal rights.

A NOTE ABOUT ROBERT BADINTER

Robert Badinter brings unique qualifications to illuminating the intellectual, social, legal and political crosscurrents that shaped the struggle for Jewish emancipation during the French Revolution. Born in Paris in 1928, his parents were Russian Jewish refugees from Kishinev (now called Chisinau, capital of the post-Soviet republic of Moldova). During World War II, his father was arrested by the Gestapo in Lyon and deported to the Sobibor extermination camp, where he died. Badinter, his mother and brother found refuge in a French village until the liberation of France. After the war he pursued his university and legal education at the Sorbonne and the University of Paris School of Law, as well as at Columbia University, where he earned a Masters degree in sociology in 1949.

Returning to France, Badinter was admitted to the Paris bar, where he gained prominence for his roster of celebrity clients (among them, Charlie Chaplin). A severe skiing accident in the early 1970s led him to reassess his professional goals and he turned his attention to defending capital punishment cases. Convinced that the death penalty was wrong, he launched a campaign to abolish it. His first book, *L'Éxécution*, published in 1973, recounted his unsuccessful defense of a convict who was later executed, and set forth his arguments for abolition.

Badinter's public and professional activities drew him into national politics. In June 1981 he was appointed minister of justice by newly-elected President François Mitterrand. Five months later, with considerable drama, Badinter stood before the National Assembly and introduced the bill that ended capital punishment in France. His account of the political and legislative process, *L'Abolition*, published in 2000, won France's prestigious Fémina literary prize.

During the next five years, his initiatives as justice minister decriminalized homosexuality and broadened the ability of citizen groups to initiate legal proceedings against persons accused of crimes against humanity and racially-motivated acts. In 1986 he was appointed president of France's Constitutional Court. When his term ended in 1995 he won election as a member of the French Senate, where he currently represents the constituency of Hauts-de-Seine in the Paris region.

Badinter remains active in international human rights and legal affairs. He is a frequent contributor to the daily newspaper *Le Monde* and the weekly newsmagazine *Le Nouvel Observateur* on these and other issues. Most recently, he was associated with former French President Valéry Giscard d'Estaing's commission to draft a constitution for the European Union. He also serves as a member of New York University School of Law's Global Law Faculty, as professor emeritus of law at the University of Paris-I, and as a member of the American Academy of Arts and Sciences.

Notwithstanding the demands of political life, Badinter has found time to write or edit ten books and a play. When *Free and Equal* appeared in its original French edition (published as *Libres et égaux... : L'émancipation des Juifs 1789-1791* by Fayard in 1989), it was unreservedly welcomed by François Furet, France's preeminent historian of the French Revolution, as a significant contribution to the history of France and of human rights. This was high praise, given that Badinter is an attorney rather than an academic historian. His other works include *Condorcet: Un intellectuel en politique* (coauthored with his wife Elisabeth Badinter), a 1988 biography of the marquis de Condorcet, a mathematician, scientist and educational reformer of the French Enlightenment who supported both the American and French Revolutions; *Un autre justice* (1989), a collection of essays by various experts on criminal justice systems; *La*

Prison républicaine (1992), an examination of France's penal system; *C.3.3.*, with a forward entitled *Oscar Wilde ou l'Injustice* (1995), a play about the Anglo-Irish author's trial for homosexuality; *Un antisémitisme ordinaire* (1997), a history of the exclusion of Jews from France's legal system under the collaborationist Vichy regime during World War II; *Une constitution européene* (2000), a constitution for the European Union; *Le plus grand bien* (2004), a study of the making of France's Code Civil of 1804; and *Contre la peine de mort* (2006), a collection of his articles and speeches against the death penalty.

— ADAM SIMMS

FOREWORD

CERTAIN BOOKS EMERGE FROM LONG-MATURING PLANS. OTHERS are the fruit of chance encounters. Nothing, frankly, predisposed me to undertake a history of Jewish emancipation during the French Revolution—until one day, as I was researching a biography of the marquis de Condorcet,[1] I came across the delegation of the Jews of Paris, led by attorney Jacques Godard, who came to ask the Commune of Paris in January 1790 to support their cause in the National Assembly. Here was concrete evidence of discussions, resistance and political conflict over whether or not the Revolution would grant French citizenship to Jews. I was going to pursue my research when my wife reminded me of the task at hand: a biography of Condorcet, not Jewish emancipation. So I returned to Condorcet, resolving to return one day to my Jews.

That task completed, I have kept my oath.

My first discovery was that the struggle to gain equal civil and political rights for Jews, so fraught with consequences in the history of the Jews of France and Europe, was a minor episode within the totality of events that constitute the French Revolution. During the thirty-one months when the Constituent Assembly was in session, from May 1789 to September 1791, fewer than forty hours of debate were devoted to the destiny of the Jews. Of the Assembly's 1,315 deputies, at most thirty or so took part in the discussion, and fewer than a dozen played real roles. The classic histories and historians of the French Revolution do not mention Jewish emancipation or they allude to it only briefly. It has never been a strong focus in Revolutionary studies.

Yet when closely analyzed, this episode is extraordinarily significant because if on the eve of the Revolution emancipation was almost at hand for the Jews of southwestern France, and particularly

---

1 Elisabeth Badinter and Robert Badinter, *Condorcet. Un intellectuel en politique.* (Paris: Fayard, 1988; Livre de poche, 1990).

for those of Bordeaux, it was nothing less than uncertain for the
others. There is little doubt that their status as an excluded people
could not continue following the king's edict of toleration issued in
1787 on behalf of non-Catholics. Amelioration of French Jews' situation was inevitable at the end of the Ancien Régime. But absolute
equality of rights with the Catholic subjects of His Most Christian
Majesty was beyond their reach, at least for the mass of Jews in the
eastern provinces of Alsace, Lorraine and the Trois-Évêchés, who
were looked upon by the region's inhabitants as alien by virtue of
their laws, customs and language, and who remained hostile toward
them. As the most eloquent of their spokesmen, Berr Isaac Berr,
wrote in 1789: "We would not extend our horizons to formulate demands for total liberty." Until those perceptions changed on the part
of both the French and France's Jews, political necessity commanded
that the Jews' incorporation into the body politic be deferred, or at
least that it be carried out gradually, to the degree that the Jews of
the East would or could be integrated into the mainstream of French
society. But this cautious course of action was irreconcilable with the
principles of the Declaration of the Rights of Man and of the Citizen,
proclaimed in August 1789 by members of the Constituent Assembly. To refuse Jews the right to be citizens as others, and on the same
bases as others, was to deny them the status of human beings like
others and to renounce the Revolution itself. Jewish emancipation—
the term universally adopted by historians to denote recognition by
various European nations during the late eighteenth and nineteenth
centuries that Jews were to be granted equal civil and political rights
as citizens of the nations in which they lived—appeared, in the end,
as a striking victory of French Revolutionary ideology over political
expediency, of the force of French Revolutionary principles over social and political inertia.

There are many today who look with suspicion upon the French
Revolution's decision to emancipate the Jews. These critics detect in
emancipation less a desire to grant rights that had always been refused to Jews throughout Europe than a scheme to solve the "Jewish
question" by making the Jews disappear as special subjects within
the Nation, by destroying their community institutions and their
own laws—in short, by destroying their Jewish identity. These critics see in Abbé Henri-Baptiste Grégoire less a tireless fighter for the
Rights of Man than a Catholic priest who entertained a plan for a

massive conversion of the Jews that would result in their complete assimilation into Christian society. They see in Clermont-Tonnerre's famous remark—"Everything must be denied to the Jews as a nation and everything granted to them as citizens"— less a declaration of liberation than a threat of cultural destruction.

I do not share these views. Jewish history in Europe, marked for the past two centuries by many anti-Semitic furors and by genocide, did not follow the fortunate course for which champions of emancipation had hoped. That it did not does not diminish the gratitude I bear these Revolutionary leaders as a human being and as a Jew.

It cannot be denied that many proponents of Jewish emancipation were unsympathetic, suspicious or hostile to the Jews' unshakable attachment to their laws and customs, and to their Jewishness. They equated this fierce attachment with forms of religious fanaticism, which they detested, and saw in it a restraint on the sovereignty of the people. Despite such negative reactions, however, they had the courage to attribute the flaws they criticized—an inordinate passion for money, the practice of usury, religious obscurantism—to the logical consequences of persecution by Christians and not to immutable characteristics inherent in the Jews' nature.

The revolutionaries' decision to include the Jews in their program to unify the nation—both socially and politically—was perfectly legitimate. One cannot posit, as the subject of historical study, mankind as an entity at once both universal and abstract, and still want to allow the Jews to remain "a nation within the nation," endowed with special legal privileges and exceptions which set them apart from their fellow citizens. When Clermont-Tonnerre lost patience with the Jews of the East's demands that they be allowed to retain their Jewish exceptionalism, it was in order to be better able to create a united and indivisible French nation. When Abbé Grégoire attacked Yiddish, he did so because he saw in it a foreign tongue, like Breton or Basque, which he deemed another obstacle to the Republic's cultural unification.

In this sense, supporters of Jewish emancipation, if friends of the Jews, also appear to be enemies of Jewishness—which is not to be confused with the Jewish religion. They were driven not by hostility to the Jewish people, but by faith in the future of a human society in which all men were free, equal and fraternal. This society, in order to emerge, first had to free itself from its antiquated demons, its cleavages and conflicts: religion against religion, community against community and, in this particular instance, Christian against Jew. Jewish emancipation was indeed intended to make Jews meld into Mankind—just as the provinces melted into the Nation and, in a still vaster perspective, the Nation into mankind.

Though bitterly disappointed by subsequent history, who can criticize the Revolution's generosity and brotherhood? To do so is to overlook and ignore the human dimension that drove advocates and supporters of Jewish emancipation: the humiliation, exclusion and misery which the vast majority of Jews in France experienced at the end of the Ancien Régime. There were Jews in Bordeaux, to be sure, who were prosperous and respected and, here and there, in this great kingdom, some untroubled islands of Jewish life. Some Jews were especially fortunate, such as Cerf-Berr, the powerful supplier of the royal armies in the eastern provinces, or Abraham Gradis, the "Jewish king" of Bordeaux. But their splendid successes could not make up for the mass of Jews, impoverished and despised, who populated the ghettoes or villages of the East, or who traveled with their wares on the roads of France.

It was for them, when all is said and done, that those who led the fight for Jewish emancipation kept up their struggle. Emancipation offered its advocates and supporters no political benefit. On the contrary it aroused against them the passions of traditional anti-Judaism: accusations that they were in the pay of the Jews, that they preferred "the deicide people" to Christ's Church. Nor did they expect political support from the Jews or even immediate gratitude. Simply, by proclaiming on 27 September 1791 that all Jews in France were full citizens, they took a truly revolutionary step by acting on their beliefs, making their ideals, embodied in the Declaration of the Rights of Man and of the Citizen, triumph over prejudice and political caution. In doing so they also opened a new era for all the Jews of Europe: nowhere else on the continent—in England or Holland, where they were well treated; in Austria, where Joseph II had taken significant initiatives on their behalf; or even in Prussia, where Berlin's Jewish Enlightenment shone brightly—were Jews acknowledged by law as citizens equal in rights to others, free at last from centuries of servitude and legal exclusion, and granted human dignity.

No one can criticize Jewish emancipation's advocates and supporters for not foreseeing that nationalism, to which the French Revolution gave birth, would give rise to the modern anti-Semitism that took the place of traditional anti-Judaism. Nothing would be more unfair than to view Abbé Grégoire through contemporary Jewish eyes or those of a Holocaust survivor or of a survivor's son. The Jews of France's Revolutionary era and their supporters who championed emancipation must be understood as people who acted within the historical context of their own days, and not any other. It is within the midst of revolutionary turmoil, when other, infinitely more pressing matters occupied their attention, that the complex political struggle for Jewish emancipation was fought. And if the Dreyfus Affair erupted a century later, and then fifty years after that the most terrible trial the Jews have ever known, it still remains that it is in France—and nowhere else in Europe—and during the French Revolution, not under the Ancien Régime—that Jews were decreed by a sovereign assembly to be "free and equal."

It does not seem to me unimportant to recall these facts two centuries later.

— Robert Badinter

CHAPTER I

AS THEY WERE . . .

O N 28 JANUARY 1789 ROYAL LETTERS ANNOUNCING CONVO-
cation of the États Généraux were read out in every commune of
France. "His Majesty," proclaimed the election notice, "desires that
even in the farthest and least-known corners of his realm, each should
be able to make known to him his wishes and complaints."

The impact was electrifying. For the first time in one hundred
and seventy years, the king had consulted the people, no matter how
humble, inviting them to reflect upon their circumstances and to
speak up. "The spirit of the Revolution that stirred the urban middle
class," wrote Tocqueville, "immediately raced via a thousand chan-
nels through this agrarian population . . . down to its roots." [1]

Whether isolated in cities or secluded in the remotest villages of
Alsace, France's Jews could not ignore the ferment. Throughout history they had more often encountered bitter setbacks than longed-for
advances. Hope had always been accompanied by anxiety. At this
moment, however, like all inhabitants of the realm, Jews, at least the
most clear-sighted or most enterprising among them, pondered the
experience of the "Jewish nation" in France. [2]

How many Jews were there? Fifty thousand, according to the
Jewish community of the era; [3] certainly not less than forty thou-

---

1 Alexis de Tocqueville, *L'Ancien Régime et la Révolution* (Paris: Gallimard,
1953), 2:125. [The États Généraux, or Estates General, was a representative body of
France's three "estates": the Clergy of the Roman Catholic Church, the Nobility,
and the commons (known as the Third Estate). Its function was to approve new
taxation proposed by the monarch. Prior to 1789 the États Généraux had last met in
1614.—*TRANSL.*]

2 The term "nation" was commonly used to designate communities or specific
populations. Thus Mirabeau spoke of "the Jewish nation" as he did of "the Provençal
nation." And Jews used this term to designate their communities.

3 Cf. "Réponse des Juifs de la province de Lorraine à l'Adresse présentée à
l'Assemblée nationale par la Commune de la ville de Strasbourg," 24 July 1789, p.
2, in *La Révolution française et l'émancipation des Juifs.* 8 vol. (Paris: Edhis [Éditions
d'Histoire Sociale], 1968). Vol. 5: *Adresses, Mémoires et Pétitions des Juifs, 1789–1794.*

LA MANCHE / ENGLISH CHANNEL

THE NETHERLANDS

GERMANY

Thionville·
Verdun·
·Metz
LORRAINE
·Nancy
Lunéville·

ALSACE

·Hagenau
·Strasbourg

·Colmar

Versailles· ·Paris

·Basle

SWITZERLAND

ATLANTIC OCEAN

ITALY

·Bordeaux

GUYENNE

COMTAT
VENAISSIN
·

Avignon·

PROVENCE

Bayonne

·Toulouse
Montpellier·
LANGUEDOC

·Marseille

MEDITERRANEAN SEA

SPAIN

FRANCE, 1789
Sites of major Jewish communities shown in italics

sand.[4] In a kingdom of twenty-five million inhabitants, one out of each five hundred subjects was a Jew—a small number compared to other European states, such as Austria or Poland.[5]

Moreover, they lived in only a few regions: in Bordeaux and Bayonne in southwestern France; and Alsace, Lorraine and the Trois-Évêchés (Three Bishoprics) of Metz, Toul and Verdun, in the east. Several hundred Jews resided in Paris. In certain provincial cities, such as Toulouse, Marseille and Montpellier, some families were tolerated. In Avignon and the Comtat Venaissin, which were under the sovereignty of the pope rather than the king, several thousand were crowded into ghettos. Such was the pattern of Jewish settlement in France on the eve of the Revolution. Considering the breadth and diversity of France's provinces, the kingdom seemed, save in the east, nearly devoid of Jews.

Confined in a few cities, or rather in a few urban districts, and scattered among several hundred villages, the "Jewish nation" was extremely diverse and anything but homogeneous. The result of a painful, often cruel history, the status of Jews varied according to region, city and feudal domain. Jews, in fact, did not constitute a single, separate "nation" within France. Rather, they lived in communities organized along a variety of systems of internal governance.[6] Equally

Cf. "Nouvelle Adresse des Juifs à l'Assemblée nationale," 24 December 1789, p. 3, in *Adresses, Mémoires…*, op. cit.

4   Cf. Robert Anchel: "There were 20,000 to 25,000 in Upper and Lower Alsace; 2,000 in Metz; 1,500 in the countryside around Metz; 4,000 in Lorraine; 2,300 in Bordeaux; 1,000 to 1,200 in Saint-Esprit, opposite Bayonne. Moreover, 2,500 Jews lived in Avignon and the Comtat Venaissin. In total there were about 40,000 Jews in France." In Robert Anchel, *Napoléon et les Juifs* (Paris: Presses Universitaires de France, 1928), 1–2. One should add the some five hundred Jews living in Paris, and those spread across France who were not members of organized Jewish communities.

5   Of a Jewish population estimated at two million in Europe, Poland contained approximately half, and 270,000 lived in the Austrian Empire.

6   This diversity was not novel in a kingdom that Turgot described in 1775 as a "society composed of different orders poorly united and a people whose members have only very few social bonds." Cf. "Mémoires sur les municipalités," Anne-Robert-Jacques Turgot, baron de Laune, *Œuvres de Turgot, et documents le concernant.* G. Schelle, ed. 5 vol. (Paris: F. Alcan, 1913-1923), 4:576. Cf. Patrick Girard, *La Révolution française et les Juifs* (Paris: R. Laffont, 1989), chap. 1. [Turgot (1727-1781) was an economist and statesman. As intendant, or royal tax collector, of Limoges from 1761 to 1774, he traveled widely and suggested economic reforms. Appointed comptroller-general in 1774, he proposed free commerce in grains and suppression of various taxes and privileges. He was forced to resign in May 1776 and was succeeded by Jacques Necker.—TRANSL.]

significant were distinctions France's Jews made among themselves, especially between the Sephardim of the Midi, France's southern region, and the Ashkenazim of the eastern provinces.

THE JEWS OF BORDEAUX

The Jewish community of Bordeaux, founded in the sixteenth century, was unquestionably the most prosperous and best integrated during the Ancien Régime. In 1492 King Ferdinand and Queen Isabella of Spain ordered all Jews, at least those who had not converted to Catholicism, expelled from their kingdom. Many went to Portugal, where King Manuel, rather than see them leave, forced them to undergo baptism. By the mid-sixteenth century there were no longer, officially, any Jews on the peninsula. However, many of the *conversos* practiced Judaism in secret. Known as Marranos, they were hunted by the Inquisition. Bordeaux seemed like a refuge. [7]

France's royal authorities viewed the arrival and settlement of these "new Christians," as the Marranos were called, in terms of wealth-creation. Thus Henry II issued *lettres patentes* in 1550, granting them complete liberty of travel, commerce, and acquisition and disposal of all goods, including real estate.[8] The Parlement of Paris registered these *lettres patentes* without any problem. The Parlement of Bordeaux proved to be more hesitant. However, on 17 March 1574, at the request "of the Portuguese merchants," it issued a decree prohibiting "all inhabitants, whatever their social station, from molesting the new Christians, or from forcing them to leave the city."[9]

---

7 In 1472 Louis XII, in order to develop maritime commerce, had granted to aliens who settled in Bordeaux the right to trade freely and exemption from the *droit d'aubaine* [right of godsend], which gave the state ownership of the property of an alien who died in France. [A *lettre patente* was a royal act granting an individual or group a right, status or privilege. Rights enumerated in the *lettres* were customarily granted for the duration of a sovereign's reign. When a new king ascended the throne holders of *lettres patentes* were obliged to petition for renewal of the *lettres* in order to continue to enjoy the rights previously granted. Cf. fn. 9, below.—*TRANSL.*]

8 Cf. Pierre Pluchon, *Nègres et Juifs au XVIIIᵉ siècle: Le racisme au siècle des Lumières* (Paris: Tallandier, 1984), 48–49.

9 Henry III, upon his accession to the throne in 1574, reaffirmed Henry II's *lettres patentes*, which were at last registered by the Parlement of Bordeaux on 19 April 1580. From that time until the Revolution, these letters were continuously renewed by all kings. [During the Ancien Régime, thirteen *parlements*, located in Paris and other major provincial centers, functioned as final courts of appeal, and wielded both administrative and judicial powers. A *parlement* could issue administrative rulings

Over the course of a century and a half the "new Christians" continued to conduct themselves in public as Marranos. They were baptized, married and buried according to Catholic rites but practiced Judaism in secret. Gradually, however, the truth came to light and by the end of the second half of the seventeenth century they were regarded as Jews. Growing religious intolerance during the reign of Louis XIV led, in 1684, on the eve of the revocation of the Edict of Nantes, to the expulsion of ninety-four of Bordeaux's poorest Jewish families.[10] In 1723, however, Louis XV confirmed the privileges of the "Portuguese merchants" with new *lettres patentes*. From then on, they were officially recognized as Jews. They stopped celebrating their marriages in church and baptizing their infants, and created a strong communal organization, Sedaca, in order to take care of indigent Jews and, later, to oversee religious observance. It became the community's regulatory body. Every Jew was obliged to contribute to Sedaca. Those who did not were excluded from the community. Community elders, chosen from among the wealthiest families, se-

---

which, if not overturned by the royal council, became part of local law. In turn, royal edicts had to be registered (i.e., approved) by the *parlements* in order to take effect in their jurisdictions, and this power was used at various times to protest and frustrate royal decrees.—TRANSL.] Letters of safe conduct, granted 11 November 1574 by Henry III, revealed the hostility of Bordeaux's merchants toward the "Portuguese": "Spiteful and envious of the aforementioned dealing [of the Portuguese], [Bordeaux merchants] endeavored several times to stop them, falsely and slanderously ascribing to them numerous crimes in order to provoke them to abandon the city and the country"; quoted in Théophile Malvezin, *Histoire des Juifs de Bordeaux* (Bordeaux: C. Lefebvre, 1875), 110–111. Cf. also Frances Malino, *Les Juifs sépharades de Bordeaux, assimilation et émancipation dans la France révolutionnaire et impérial*. Translated from English by Jean Cavignac, *Les Cahiers de l'I.A.E.S.* [Institut Aquitain d'Études Sociales], 5 (1984), chap. 1. [Originally published in English as *The Sephardic Jews of Bordeaux: Assimilation and Emancipation in Revolutionary and Napoleonic France* (University: University of Alabama Press, 1978).—TRANSL.]

10 On 21 February 1722 a decree of the King's Council ordered compilation of a detailed inventory of goods owned by Jews settled in Bordeaux and Auch, in order that the goods might be seized and delivered to the king. The intendant of Bordeaux, M. de Coursin, defended the "Portuguese merchants" by emphasizing that their activity was indispensable to the city's prosperity. Cf. Bernhard Blumenkranz, ed., *Histoire des Juifs en France* (Toulouse: Privat, 1972), 233. [The Edict of Nantes, issued in April 1598 by Henry IV, granted freedom of religious conscience to France's Calvinist Protestants, known as Huguenots, and reinstated the civil rights of which they had been deprived during France's "wars of religion." In October 1685 Louis XIV revoked the edict and commanded that Protestant schools be closed and Huguenot houses of worship be razed. During the next twenty years an estimated two hundred thousand to half a million French Protestants sought refuge by emigrating to North America and elsewhere in Europe.—TRANSL.]

lected the organization's administrator, whose title was syndic, and appointed the rabbi.[11]

With its strong structure, Bordeaux's Jewish community prospered throughout the eighteenth century. It numbered 500 people in 1713; 1,598, according to the census of 1751,[12] and 2,300 in 1788.[13] Certain Jewish families played an important role in the city's maritime trade.[14] The Gradis family was in charge of provisioning Quebec during the Seven Years' War. Upon his death, the family's leader, Abraham Gradis, left a considerable fortune, estimated (solely on the basis of his personal estate) at ten million livres. He enjoyed the trust of government ministers,[15] and princes of the blood attended his funeral. Other Jewish merchants in Bordeaux who established close contact with their Sephardic counterparts in Amsterdam and London, the commercial centers of Europe, amassed considerable fortunes. (These included the Raba family, owner of the "Chantilly Bordelais";[16] Antoine Francia, a banker and maritime insurer; and Joseph and Jacob Lopes-Diaz, who were stockbrokers).[17]

11　Cf. Blumenkranz, *Histoire des Juifs…*, 235. Cf. Malino, 23–24. [A syndic was the representative of a parish or a corporation, and defended the interests of the community in judicial matters.—TRANSL.]

12　Cf. Jean Cavignac, *Dictionnaire du judaïsme bordelais aux XVIIIᵉ et XIXᵉ siècles: biographies, généalogies, professions, institutions* (Bordeaux: Archives départementales de la Gironde, 1987), 4. The census of 1808 enumerated 2,063 Jews.

13　According to a letter written by David Gradis, 8 April 1788, in Malvezin, 246.

14　Cf. letter of Pudefer, secretary to Boucher, intendant of Guyenne, in 1734: "Five or six of these families are engaged in the arms and commodities trade with America; several others, in banking. Their trade is very considerable." In Malino, 47. In 1771 Bordeaux accounted for nearly forty percent of France's foreign trade. On the Gradis family, "one of the most celebrated, if not the most celebrated, Israelite families of Bordeaux," cf. Jean Cavignac, *Dictionnaire…*, 52–57.

15　Cf. letter of the duc de Choiseul, 13 April 1762: "I am going to entrust you, my dear Gradis, with an expedition that means a great deal to me." In Jean de Maupassant, *Les Armateurs bordelais au XVIIIᵉ siècle. Abraham Gradis et l'approvisionnement des colonies (1756-1763)* (Bordeaux: G. Gounouilhou, 1909), 37. [The North American theater of the Seven Years' War is known in the United States as the French and Indian War (1754-1763).—TRANSL.]

16　Blumenkranz, *Histoire…*, 249.

17　Cf. Cavignac. Regarding the impact of the capitation (head tax) in Bordeaux during 1744, twenty-five percent of the Jews paid more than one hundred livres of tax, whereas among Christians, sixteen percent paid more than fifty livres. As for the *taille*, a direct tax on movable wealth and land, the Jewish community paid the greatest tax among the guilds or communities taxed. Cf. Malino, 35, 36. However, distribution of wealth within the community was highly unequal. Of 330 heads of Jewish families, only 158 were subject to the capitation.

Jacob Rodriguez Pereire, their representative in Paris, was well connected in powerful circles. Proud of their success, the wealthy Jews of Bordeaux—notably Pereire, Louis Francia, and David Gradis—contributed splendidly to the intellectual life of the city.[18]

The "Portuguese Jewish nation of Bordeaux"[19] made it a point of honor not to be confused with any other "Jewish nation." Its sensibilities and behavior were, in the eyes of other Jews, downright aristocratic. Nothing is more revealing of its attitudes than the pamphlet Isaac de Pinto, a "Portuguese" Jew who lived in Holland, composed at Pereire's request as a response to Voltaire's ferocious attacks against the Jews. According to Pinto, "a Portuguese Jew from Bordeaux and a German Jew from Metz seem to be two entirely different beings."[20] His description of the Jews of Bordeaux is revealing: "They do not wear beards, and do not affect any distinctive costume or dress; in this respect the well-off among them dress with studied elegance, refinement and magnificence compared with the other nations of Europe, from whom they differ only in their form of worship."[21] Emphasizing the desire of the "Portuguese" Jews to keep the Ashkenazim at a distance, Pinto added: "Their disagreement with their other brothers is of such a degree that if a Portuguese Jew, in Holland and in England, married a German Jew, he would immediately lose his standing in the Jewish community..., he would be cut off entirely from the body of the nation."[22] Moreover, the elders who exercised power in Bordeaux's Jewish community had no hesitation about having the royal authorities expel from the city "German" Jews who wished to settle there, as well as poor Jews from Avignon.[23]

---

18 Cf. Malino, 54. Pereire, a teacher of deaf-mutes and a major collector of books and engravings, was admitted to the Academy of Arts of Bordeaux in 1774, only six years after its creation. Cf. Pierre Barrière, *L'Académie de Bordeaux, centre de culture internationale au XVIIIᵉ siècle, 1712-1792* (Bordeaux: Bière, 1951).

19 This was the term commonly used. Cf. "Lettre adressée à l'abbé Grégoire par les députés de la nation juive portugaise de Bordeaux, 14 août 1789," in *La Révolution française et l'émancipation des Juifs.* Vol. 5: *Adresses, Mémoires ....*

20 Isaac Pinto, *Réflexions critiques sur le premier chapitre du VIIᵉ tome des œuvres de Monsieur de Voltaire, au sujet des Juifs,* cited by Pluchon, 61.

21 Ibid., 61.

22 Ibid.

23 Expulsion of Jewish vagabonds from Bordeaux in 1730; of Jews from Avignon and "Teutonic" Jews in 1734; of thirty-five "Teutonic and Italian" families in 1744; of 152 Jews, of whom only six were "Portuguese," in 1761, by the duc de Richelieu at the request of the "syndics of the nation." In Blumenkranz, *Histoire...,* 245.

These acts reflected the fact that they bore the financial burden of providing relief to the Jewish community's poor.

Their pride and affluence went hand in hand with their drive to expand their commercial activities. Prohibited by the Code Noir of 1685 from settling in the Antilles, they gained a foothold there despite resistance and obstacles.[24] In 1776 the "Portuguese" asked Louis XVI to extend explicitly to the colonies the privileges they had been granted in Bordeaux since the reign of Henry II. In 1782 maréchal de Castries, minister of the navy, finally authorized the registration in Santo Domingo of *lettres patentes* granted to the "Portuguese" in 1776. The "Portuguese" continued to encounter restrictions: even those who acquired the right to conduct business were barred from becoming members of Bordeaux's chamber of commerce and were excluded from guilds and municipal office.[25] But on the eve of the Revolution, the Portuguese Jewish nation of Bordeaux shone with incomparable splendor among all the Jewish communities of France. Its members were justifiably proud of their accomplishments and status—a pride which they expressed in the disdain they displayed toward their counterparts elsewhere in the kingdom.

THE JEWS OF BAYONNE

The other "Portuguese Jewish nation" was based farther south. In January 1597 the Parlement of Bordeaux decreed that those "Portuguese" unable to prove they had lived in the city for ten years would be forced to leave.[26] The newcomers left, settling in Peyrehorade, Bidace, Labastide-Clairance and, especially, Bayonne. Jealous of competition that the new group introduced, Bayonne's guilds obtained, through the mayor's and the aldermen's intervention with the king, the expulsion of the "new Christians." The refugees settled in

24 In particular, the Gradis family obtained on 24 August 1779 *lettres patentes* authorizing it to engage in commerce and own land in all French colonies. Cf. Henry Léon, *Histoire des Juifs de Bayonne* (Paris: A. Durlacher, 1893; reprint Marseille: Laffitte Reprints, 1976), 153. Cf. also Pluchon, 111. [The Code Noir was a royal decree regulating relationships between slaveholders and slaves in France's overseas colonial possessions.—*TRANSL.*]

25 Malino, 44.

26 This decree of the Parlement of Bordeaux was in point of fact instigated by the elders of the Jewish community who feared that the influx of new "Portuguese" would add to their expenses. Cf. Léon, 19.

Bourg-Saint-Esprit, on the right bank of the Adour river, near Bayonne, where they went each day to conduct their business.

Their number grew rapidly. Toward the middle of the eighteenth
century, there were about thirty-five hundred Portuguese in Bourg-
Saint-Esprit.[27] They created a communal organization, Hebera,
modeled on Sedaca in Bordeaux. Added to its expenses were heavy
taxes:[28] on the eve of the Revolution the community owed more than
twelve thousand livres.[29]

The local authorities, however, repeatedly opposed any expan-
sion of the Jews' economic activity. Between 1692 and 1761 five
edicts were adopted against them. In 1762 the aldermen sought to
exclude them from Bayonne's prosperous chocolate trade, in which
they specialized. The Jews protested and submitted a complaint to
the King's Council in 1763, requesting that they be granted "the right
and enjoyment to engage in retail commerce in Bayonne as they do in
Bordeaux."[30] Their attorney stated: "They are subjects of the crown,
they are French, they are as much citizens of Bayonne as the inhabitants of the suburbs of Chartrons are citizens of Bordeaux."[31] Their
adversaries pleaded that if the Jews were permitted to extend their
commercial activities to Bayonne, soon "we would see synagogues
alongside our churches, and our children perverted by the example
and association with the Jews, whose depravity is reported to be at
its peak..."[32] The royal authorities did not intervene to alter the
conditions of Bourg-Saint-Esprit's Jews.

On the eve of the Revolution their situation appeared to be less
promising than that of Bordeaux's "Portuguese" Jews. There were
probably some affluent families among them, such as the Nounèses,
the Castros and the Mendès Frances.[33] But they hardly compared

---

27 Abbé Jean-Joseph Expilly, *Dictionnaire géographique, historique et politique des
Gaules et de la France* (Paris: 1762-1770), 1:301; cf. Blumenkranz, *Histoire...*, 249.

28 According to Henry Léon, "the Jews at this time comprised one twenty-
eighth of the population [of Bayonne and its environs]; and relative to the total public
taxes, they paid one third." Op. cit., 151.

29 Expilly, vol. 1.

30 Philippe Sagnac, "Les Juifs et la Révolution française (1789-1791)," *RHMC*
[Revue d'Histoire moderne et contemporaine], 1 (1889): 8; cf. Léon, 69ff.

31 Sagnac, op. cit.

32 Cf. Léon, 161, 166–167, where the author provides a table, drawn up in 1794,
of the principle fortunes of the commune of Bourg-Saint-Esprit, renamed "the commune of Jean-Jacques Rousseau" during the Terror.

33 Blumenkranz, *Histoire...*, 249.

to their fellow Jews on the banks of the Gironde. Moreover, the community declined in number: in 1785 there were no more than twenty-five hundred inhabitants in Bourg-Saint-Esprit, and no more than several Jewish families in Peyrehorade and Labastide-Clairance.

THE POPE'S JEWS

In the wake of persecutions under King Philip IV, who reigned from 1285 to 1314, numbers of Jews living in the south of France took refuge in the pope's trans-Alpine possessions of Avignon and the Comtat Venaissin. In 1589 Pius V decreed that Jews were to be expelled from all pontifical domains except Rome and Ancona—an order only partially carried out.[34] Jews who managed to remain in Avignon, Carpentras, Cavaillon and L'Isle were herded into certain sections of the city called *carrières*, from which they could leave only during daytime. They were crowded together in houses which they could enlarge only by adding stories.

Passing through Avignon in 1747 Charles de Brosses, presiding magistrate of the Parlement of Dijon, described "the small and poorly constructed Jewish quarter, and the Jews, poor as is their way, though, to be sure, it is definitely not their fault."[35] Such constrictions prevented Jews of other cities from gaining admittance to the *carrières*. Similarly, the hospitality Jews traditionally accorded Jewish travelers was strictly regulated.[36] As a result the Jewish population remained stable throughout the eighteenth century.[37]

---

34 Similarly, a new papal bull, ordering expulsions, issued in 1593 by Pope Gregory XIV, had little effect. Cf. Blumenkranz, *Histoire...*, 194.

35 In Pluchon, 75.

36 Thus on 18 September 1773 a group of seventy "German" Jews were forcibly ejected from the L'Isle *carrière*, and identical measures were taken in Avignon. Cf. Blumenkranz, *Histoire...*, 195. [In contemporary French, *une carrière* is a "quarry" or "sandpit." However, Esther Benbassa suggests that the term was borrowed from the Provençal *carriero*, meaning "street." Esther Benbassa, *Histoire des Juifs de France*, reéd. (Paris: Seuil "Points-Histoire," 1997), 76.—TRANSL.]

37 Avignon and the Comtat Venaissin only became part of France at the conclusion of the Constituent Assembly, on 14 September 1791, following violent episodes. The Jewish community numbered 279 individuals in 1746, 385 in 1759, and 350 in 1789; in Carpentras it numbered 750 Jews in 1743, a thousand in 1780, but only 705 in 1789. The same year there were about 200 Jews in Cavaillon, and 350 lived in the "*carrière* of L'Isle-sur-Sorgue." Cf. H. J. de Dranoux, in Blumenkranz, *Histoire...*, 191. According to a census of 1791, cited by Robert Anchel, there were 340 Jews in

These Jews were subject to pontifical authorities who, under pressure from local municipalities, saw no harm in imposing strict and humiliating rules. Jews were obliged to wear yellow hats or a distinctive badge on their clothing. They were prohibited from working on Sunday outside their *carrières*, and from employing Christian servants. In 1781 the Holy Office tightened these restrictions yet again. No Jew was permitted to sleep outside the *carrières* without written authorization, and a Christian gatekeeper stood watch at ghetto entrances. The Jews' activities were strictly regulated. They were prohibited from engaging in commercial transactions dealing with new merchandise, foodstuffs and horses; forbidden to possess either lands or houses, other than their residences; and money lending at interest, in which they were permitted to engage, was governed by minutely detailed rules.[38]

By degrees, however, the Jews of Avignon and the Comtat Venaissin extended the scope of their economic activity. Several even acquired considerable wealth, possessing valuable properties and gilded clothing, and provided their children with educations appropriate to the expectations of the era.[39] Despite the existence of several large fortunes, the majority, however, remained very poor. In 1782 one third of the Jews of Carpentras were considered indigent. Crushed by taxes and expenditures to care for their poor, the communities had to resort to borrowing funds.[40] Tightly organized and administered by a council of *baylons*, who kept watch over religious observance and instruction, the community's central organizations provided aid to the poor and collected taxes imposed on members of

---

Avignon; op. cit., 2, note 3. According to René Moulinas, the Jewish population of the pontifical territories would not reach three thousand persons on the eve of the Revolution; René Moulinas, "Les Juifs d'Avignon et du comtat Venaissin," in Girard, *La Révolution française...*, 147.

38 Cf. Dranoux, in Blumenkranz, *Histoire...*, 197.

39 Cf. Expilly, 2:105–106.

40 The community of L'Isle-sur-Sorgue was in bankruptcy since 1778; the Carpentras *carrière* was eight hundred thousand livres in debt in 1786. Paradoxically, these borrowings countered all threats of expulsion, as Christian creditors opposed the departure of their debtors. During the reign of Louis XVI Jews became brokers, silk merchants and jewelers in Alès, Uzès, Pont-Saint-Esprit and Beaucaire. In 1789 about fifty Jews from Carpentras settled in Montpellier. There were some forty Jewish families in Nîmes. In 1779 and 1780 several Jewish families regained permission to reside in Marseille. In 1789 there were thirty-six Jews from Carpentras in Aix, and nine in Arles; cf., Blumenkranz, *Histoire...*, 211–212.

the community.[41]

Weary of restrictions and taxes that overwhelmed them, many Jews of the Comtat left the papal territories and settled throughout Languedoc and Provence, despite a ban imposed by the Parlement of Aix, which decreed that Jews who settled there would be flogged. At the end of the eighteenth century this migration accelerated. And despite official hostility some measure of social integration developed. In 1779, in Carpentras, some Christians attended the synagogue during marriages and naming ceremonies. Some Jews were admitted to Masonic lodges. In 1784 they were admitted to a number of coffee houses. And in 1786 a certificate from the vicar of Avignon, signed by many aristocrats and notables of the city, attested that "it has never come to our attention that the Jews had given cause for any complaint whatever in that which concerns religion, manners or commerce."[42]

THE JEWS OF ALSACE

Far from the Sephardic "Portuguese" and Avignonnais Jews— in the provinces of Alsace and Lorraine and in the Trois-Évêchés of Metz, Toul and Verdun—lived the mass of "Germans," France's Ashkenazic Jews. This was Judaism's "heart of darkness" during the Ancien Régime: an archipelago of Jewish communities, some long-established (as in Metz), others composed of recent immigrants from Germany or Central Europe, and all subjected to an age-old policy of exclusion and humiliation. Segregated from a hostile and scornful Christian world, the "German" Jews led an impoverished existence, brightened only by enduring faith, strict ritual observance and warm family life.

In 1789 Alsace was home to the largest concentration of Jews in all of France's provinces.[43] In contrast with the Sephardim of the

---

41 Cf. Patrick Girard, *Pour le meilleur and pour le pire. Vingt siècles d'histoire juive en France* (Paris: Bibliophane, 1986), 205–206.

42 Dranoux, in Blumenkranz, *Histoire...*, 209.

43 Under the Treaty of Westphalia of 1648, which handed control of the province to France, at most 2,000 Jews were settled there. A century later, in 1755, there were 13,600, in a total population of 450,000 inhabitants. The census of 1795 mentions 3,913 families, comprising 19,077 individuals. Undoubtedly, there were still others: close to 22,000 in a province of 624,000 inhabitants. Thus the Jewish communities of Alsace represented half the Jews of the kingdom, and more than three percent of the province's population. Cf. Blumenkranz, *Histoire...*, 166; and Maurice Liber,

Southwest, these "German" Jews were not city dwellers, but scattered among 187 rural communes. Indeed, since the medieval era, cities had responded with hostility to any influx of Jews because merchant guilds feared their competition. On the other hand the nobles of Lower Alsace gladly welcomed their presence in return for payment of a special "reception" fee, which provided significant revenues. In Upper Alsace Jews paid the king a "protection" tax of ten and a half florins a year.[44]

From the time that Louis XIV assumed sovereignty over the territory, royal authorities ensured that restrictions adopted by previous rulers were maintained. Jews remained forbidden to dwell in Strasbourg and could enter only during daylight hours after they paid a "body toll" of three livres; this was known as "the cloven-hoof fee," which equated Jews with impure [non-kosher] animals. Moreover, they had to be escorted by the *Gelert*, a municipal employee to whom they paid four sous.[45] At sunset Jews were reminded to leave the city by the blare of an "odious horn, whose mournful sound spread every evening at nightfall from high in the cathedral, and brought terror to the souls of all those who were not regular visitors."[46] Louis XVI abolished the toll in 1784,[47] but Strasbourg's horn still echoed in 1790.

Jews throughout Alsace were hemmed in by a web of prohibitions. They were excluded from guilds, which controlled production and distribution of applied industrial arts and crafts. They could not purchase real estate, cultivate land, employ agricultural workers or enjoy the benefits of common lands. They were thrown back

---

"Les Juifs et la convocation des États Généraux," *Revue des études juives*, 63 (1912), 185–186.

44 Cf. R. Marx, "La régénération économique des Juifs d'Alsace à l'époque révolutionnaire et napoléonienne," in Bernhard Blumenkranz and Albert Soboul, eds., *Les Juifs et la Révolution française. Problèmes et aspirations* (Toulouse: Privat, 1972), 106.

45 Blumenkranz, *Histoire...*, 152.

46 "Rapport lu à l'Assemblée de la Société des Amis de la Constitution, Le 27 février mil sept cent quatre-vingt-dix, sur la question de l'état civil des Juifs d'Alsace," p. 26, in *La Révolution française et l'émancipation des Juifs*. Vol. 8: *Lettres, Mémoires et Publications diverses, 1789-1806*. The burden weighing upon the Jews was considerable and the benefit to the city was considerable, since 20,610 entries into the city were recorded in 1781; cf. Blumenkranz, *Histoire...*, ibid.

47 "Édit du Roi portant exemption des droits de péage corporel sur les Juifs," 17 January 1784, in David Feuerwerker, *L'émancipation des Juifs de France de l'Ancien Régime à la fin du Second Empire* (Paris: Albin Michel, 1976), 34.

upon jobs in mining, peddling, trading in old clothes and second-hand goods. Some of the more enterprising among them traded in livestock and horses.[48] Still others engaged in usury, lending money on a large scale in the countryside, most often to poor farmers who pawned their possessions in order to secure loans. In a province in which credit institutions were nonexistent, and in an era when religious teachings prohibited Christians from lending money at interest, the Jews were impelled by force of circumstances to engage in usury to pay the taxes that overburdened them,[49] and to ensure the survival of their families and the most impoverished among their fellow Jews. Such commerce in money, however, also condemned them to the hostility, and sometimes the hatred, of the population around them.

In 1778, in this tense climate, the "affair of the forged receipts" erupted. On the advice of swindlers, some farmers, in order to free themselves of debts they were unable to meet, forged receipts stating that their debts had been paid. The affair aroused intense emotion. After a painstaking preliminary examination,[50] the Supreme Council of Colmar passed severe sentences on the forgers. But the farmers who had resorted to the forged receipts gained long delays in repaying Jewish moneylenders. The *bailli* of Lanser, François-Antoine-Joseph Hell, who was suspected of originating the scheme, declared that "the forged receipts were a crime necessary to save farmers from the Jews' rapacity."[51]

---

48 Cf. Blumenkranz, *Histoire...*, 174–175. Cf. Marx, 106.

49 "What can a Jew do who settles among us? I assume he has a thousand écus, and I suppose he is well-off; he will be very happy if the lord of the manor only asks him for one hundred francs for the welcome tax. He must pay this lord thirty-six livres for the habitation tax to the king, in addition to the protection tax in the former domain, the head tax, the *vingtième* [a tax of one-twentieth of one's income— TRANSL.], upkeep of the main roads and other taxes; to the community, as much as two livres and ten sous that he pays at times[,] twenty sous as a head tax ..." In "Rapport lu à l'Assemblée des Amis de la Constitution de Strasbourg, le 27 février 1790, sur la question de l'état civil des Juifs d'Alsace," p. 19, in *La Révolution française et l'émancipation des Juifs*. Vol. 8: *Lettres, Mémoires....*

50 An inquiry made in 1780 by a king's counsel to the Supreme Council of Alsace stated that the farmers of eighty-eight villages in Sundgau owed the Jews 335,000 livres. The greater part was composed of debts of less than one hundred livres. But these debts proved to be heavy for these frequently poor farmers. Cf. Sagnac, 17; Blumenkranz, *Histoire...*, 116.

51 F.-J. Hell, *Observations d'un Alsacien sur l'affaire présente des Juifs d'Alsace* (Frankfurt: n.p., 1779). Hell had orchestrated the entire affair of the forged receipts in order to inflict damage on the Jews. Cf. Zosa Szajkowski, *Jews and the French Revolutions of 1789, 1830 and 1848* (New York: Ktav, 1970), 202ff. On 10 June 1780 Hell was sen-

Segregated from Christian society, the Jews also set themselves apart through their dress and customs.[52] They reacted to exclusion by clinging to their traditions. Men dressed in black frock coats and wore long beards and side locks; women wore wigs. They ate only kosher food and spoke Judeo-Alsatian, a unique form of Yiddish, written with an alphabet based on Hebrew characters that rendered their documents unintelligible to non-Jews. The great majority led a wretched existence. "The Jewish nation, generally speaking, lives extremely badly," wrote the *bailli* of Molsheim. "A great number of them make do during the day with a morsel of bread or some apples, pears and other fruits that are in season."[53] It is estimated that ten percent of Jews survived on the charity of fellow Jews.

Nevertheless, some exceptionally wealthy individuals of extraordinary talent emerged from this ocean of misery. One was Cerf-Berr,[54] who would play an important role in the struggle for Jewish emancipation. Born in 1726 in the Saar region near Lorraine, Cerf-Berr was the son of a well-to-do merchant. In 1756, at the beginning of the Seven Years' War, the duc de Choiseul entrusted him with provisioning several regiments. Clever, obstinate and efficient, Cerf-Berr earned the minister's confidence and soon became an important supplier to the royal armies. In 1771 he used his influence in the royal court to obtain the right to stay in Strasbourg, where he purchased a large mansion

tenced to a brief exile. Upon returning to Alsace he was given a martyr's welcome. Elected to Alsace's provincial assembly in 1787, he proposed various anti-Jewish laws. As a deputy in the États Généraux, he fought emancipation of the Jews. A conservative monarchist, he was guillotined in 1794. [A *bailli* was an officer of a royal court, called a *bailliage*, who rendered justice in the name of the king or a local noble. The British equivalents were "bailiff" and "bailiwick," respectively.—*Transl.*]

52 Cf. the important role of the rabbis in the communities of the East, not only in terms of their religious functions, but their temporal powers as well. The Jews were, as a matter of fact, dependent upon their own laws in matters of their civil status and their relationships with other Jews. The rabbis were consequently empowered by the king to act as judges of the first instance [lower court justices], and to function as notaries, who drew up writs and inventory lists.

53 Cf. G. Weill, "Un texte de Montesquieu sur le judaïsme," *Revue des études juives*, 49 (1904): 178.

54 Cf. Roger Levylier, *Notes et documents concernant la famille Cerf-Berr, recueillis par un de ses membres* (Paris: Plon, 1902–1906), 3 vol. [Naftali (Herz) Cerf-Berr died in 1794. See Paula E. Hyman, *The Emancipation of the Jews of Alsace: Acculturation and Assimilation in the Nineteenth Century* (New Haven and London: Yale University Press, 1991), 13, for attribution of Cerf-Berr's first name; and Esther Benbassa, *Histoire des Juifs de France*, réed. (Paris: Seuil "Points-Histoire," 1997), 110, for the year of his death.—*Transl.*]

with the assistance of a front man, M. de La Touche. In 1775 Louis XV granted Cerf-Berr letters of naturalization. Secure in his new status, Cerf-Berr added two properties to his mansion to accommodate his large family and a household staff of thirty-six domestic servants. The Magistrat of Strasbourg, the city's executive council, was furious, and initiated legal proceedings against Cerf-Berr for having violated the ban that barred all Jews from residing in the city. The action was still before the courts on the eve of the Revolution.

Cerf-Berr's grain and fodder business extended throughout eastern France and south into Burgundy. In addition to his sons and sons-in-law, he employed some sixty people. In 1786 he bought the *seigneurie* of Toublaine, near Nancy, with its feudal rights.[55] Very devout, he took a close interest in the Jewish community's affairs, and became its syndic-general. Throughout Louis XVI's reign he fought to improve the condition of Jews in Alsace, going so far as to assume payment of the body toll imposed on Jews when they entered Strasbourg. In this he prefigured the great Jewish notables of the nineteenth century who placed their wealth at the community's service—men for whom money and faith, ambition and tradition, fierce competition and generosity were closely entwined.

Confronting the anti-Jewish fever that spread through Alsace during the affair of the forged receipts, Cerf-Berr, "the official-in-charge of the Jewish nation of Alsace," deemed it absolutely necessary to bring the question of the Jews' condition directly to the king. He commissioned a long memorandum setting forth the fiscal oppression, social humiliation and economic exclusion of his fellow Jews.[56] Cerf-Berr proposed three principal reforms: freedom of commerce; the right to free settlement, except for foreigners; and official recognition of the Jewish community's institutions. The government requested the opinion of provincial officials. A special commission was convened, and two important decisions emerged from its deliberations. The first, intended as a humanitarian measure, was the

---

55 Cf. Moses Ginsburger, "Les familles Lehmann et Cerf-Berr," *Revue des études juives*, 59 (1910): 106–130. Cf. Moses Ginsburger, *Cerf-Berr et son époque. Conférence faite à Strasbourg le 17 janvier 1906* (Guebwiller: J. Dreyfus, 1908); Levylier, 13. [A *seigneurie* consisted of the manor house, farm buildings and lands owned by peasants under feudal obligations to a noble.—*TRANSL.*]

56 "Mémoire sur l'état des Juifs en Alsace," in the appendix to C. W. Dohm, *De la réforme politique des Juifs*. Preface by Dominique Borel. (Paris: Stock, 1984), 113–138.

decree of 17 January 1784, which exempted Jews from the body toll, especially upon entry at Strasbourg; the second decision, of a political nature, was to issue *lettres patentes* on 10 July 1784, which determined the conditions under which Alsace's Jews lived until the end of the Ancien Régime.

According to the terms of the royal declaration, these *lettres patentes* were intended to reconcile "the interest of the Jews of our province of Alsace with those of our subjects."[57] In fact, they were issued with one concern in mind: to end growing tensions in Alsace over usury practiced by Jews. The special commission had envisaged two principal means to accomplish this: providing the Jews with other ways to earn livelihoods, and limiting their number in the province. Therefore the royal order lifted economic restrictions which weighed heavily upon the Jews. Henceforth they were able to lease land, vineyards and forests—but on the condition that they worked these themselves, without the aid of agricultural laborers, and without the ability to become owners. They were also permitted to establish factories, work mines, engage in wholesale and retail trade, and become bankers. These measures demonstrate the constant concern of the royal intendants to harness competition provided by the Jews' entry into the marketplace as a way to stimulate economic activity in the provinces. At the same time, however, the authorities took rigorous steps against usury: all loans had to be negotiated in the presence of two witnesses, and documents regarding the terms of these loans could not be written in Hebrew.[58] In order to prevent growth of the Jewish population in the province, Jews without a fixed domicile or who had not paid "protection" fees had to leave the kingdom. Finally, Jews had to obtain royal authorization to marry, based on approval provided by the intendant.

The *lettres patentes* satisfied neither the Jews nor their enemies. The Jewish communities sent a memorandum to the King's Council protesting the cruel restrictions and unjust conditions imposed on them but not on other Jewish communities in the kingdom, notably those of Metz, Nancy and, especially, Bordeaux.[59] Cerf-Berr continued in vain to intervene and reiterate his protests. The minister of justice, Miromesnil, remained indifferent. Nor did the Jews' enemies

---

57 Robert Anchel, *Les Juifs de France* (Paris: J.-B. Janin, 1945), 215.

58 Cf. Weill, 157.

59 Ibid., 159.

yield. A royal commissioner in Strasbourg wrote in August 1786, "the city's magistracy views, as does all of the middle class, the legal entry of Jews as a plague destroying commerce, industry and good order."[60] The Provincial Assembly, meeting in 1787, expressed its wish that the *lettres patentes* be reviewed. The Intermediary Commission, which took over the assembly's functions in 1788, and which included a number of the Jews' adversaries—especially François Hell, Étienne-François-Joseph Schwendt and Jean-François Rewbell[61]—proposed a law to tighten the restrictions imposed in 1784 by adding a strict limitation on marriages, a strict numerical quota and a total ban on money lending. It was in this atmosphere of intense anti-Jewish sentiment in Alsace that both Alsatians and Jews looked toward elections to the États Généraux and drafted their petitions of grievances to present to the king and the nation's representatives.

THE JEWS OF THE TROIS-ÉVÊCHÉS

In the Trois-Évêchés—the cities of Metz, Toul and Verdun—most Jews were city dwellers, living crowded together in cramped ghettos. The Jewish community of Metz was the most important in the kingdom. Its history was shaped by the city's military character. When French troops occupied Metz in 1552, Jews had been forbidden to live there. Maintaining a garrison fort entailed serious problems of supply and payroll, and several Jews were authorized to come into the city to assist the army in providing these services. In 1567 the military governor granted four families the right to settle in Metz under certain conditions: they had to live in outlying residences, pay an annual fee, and lend money only at a rate of interest fixed by royal authority. The Jewish community of Metz was born. Two centuries later its representatives wrote to the National Assembly: "This community was formed by members native to this city. They were born subjects of the king; they are the descendants of four families settled in the city for centuries."[62]

---

60 Levylier, 1:5–39.

61 Cf. Anchel, *Les Juifs...*, 226–231. [Intermediary commissions were administrative bodies designated to act between plenary sessions of provincial assemblies. On Jean-François Rewbell (sometimes rendered "Reubell"), see chap. 4, fn. 30, below.—TRANSL.]

62 "Mémoire particulier pour la communauté des Juifs établis à Metz, rédigé par Isaac Ber-Bing, l'un des membres de cette communauté," in *Archives parlementaires de*

The community developed very quickly. The special status that the Jews enjoyed in a city long placed under military administration, where the commercial possibilities seemed favorable, led to an influx of Jews. "To chase the Jews to the frontiers," wrote Lieutenant General Tallard in 1694, "would completely destroy trade in this region."[63] Despite protests by local guilds and decrees of the parlement, the Jewish community continued to grow: from twelve hundred people in 1666 to 480 households consisting of more than three thousand people in 1718, in a city of some ten thousand inhabitants at the start of the century. A number of small communities settled, with the agreement of royal authorities, on the flat countryside surrounding Metz.

At that time the community of Metz seemed a paragon for other Jewish communities in the kingdom: "The Jews enjoyed in Metz privileges and prerogatives they found in no other city in the kingdom. They had free exercise of religion. They had their own court, their own customs governing their agreements and the principal proceedings of civil life [i.e., births, marriages and deaths] ... "[64] Elected syndics, chosen from among an oligarchy comprised of military suppliers or bankers, ran the community. Three rabbis conducted worship services and provided religious instruction. The grand rabbi of Metz enjoyed considerable prestige. He was elected to his post and his election was submitted for the king's approval. Moreover, the community was entitled to participate as a group in all ceremonies marking births, marriages and deaths in the royal family.[65]

In return for these "privileges," however, Metz's Jewish community was burdened by taxes and fees. In 1715 the royal regent created a "protection" fee which the community paid to the regent's two close friends, the duc of Brancas and the comtesse de Fontanes. In 1718 this "Brancas tax" was set at twenty thousand livres annu-

---

1787 à 1860. Première série (de 1787 à 1799). Recueil complet des débats législatifs et politiques des Chambres françaises. Jules Mavidal and Émile Laurent, eds. 32 vol. (Paris: P. Dupont, 1862-1888), 9:446.

63   Cf. Anchel, Les Juifs..., 179; and Gilbert Cahen, in Blumenkranz, Histoire..., 83.

64   Statement of the General Council of the commune of Metz in 1791, cited by Henri Tribout de Morembert, "Les Juifs de Metz et de Lorraine, 1791–1795," in Blumenkranz and Soboul, eds., Les Juifs..., 90.

65   During the reign of Louis XVI, his brother, the comte de Provence, was welcomed in the synagogue and blessed by Grand Rabbi of Metz Léon Assen. Cf. Blumenkranz, Histoire..., 85.

ally, payable in a lump sum. Other taxes weighed on the Jews: "They
pay 450 livres to the General Hospital, to which they are never admitted. They pay 200 livres annually to the parish vicar, 500 livres
for lodging soldiers, and 200 livres to the *bailliage*..."[66] Added to
these were customary gifts to the military governor, local officers,
magistrates and other officials. After having paid these tributes, the
community had to provide for both its own upkeep and assistance
to its poor. Its annual expenditures reached the enormous sum of
150,000 livres on the eve of the Revolution, an increase from 53,000
at the beginning of the century, and its total indebtedness amounted
to 400,000 livres in 1789.[67]

The community's syndics resorted to levying a graduated tax on
community members, proportional to their wealth, and they imposed
taxes on sales, inheritances and dowries. Despite these measures the
community was unable to meet its obligations. To avoid new burdens it shut its doors to newcomers. Toward 1767 new members were
admitted only upon approval of the syndics and royal authorities,
and after payment of a prohibitive entry fee of eighteen thousand
livres.[68] By 1788 the Jewish population shrank to between 410 and
420 households (approximately three thousand people), with another fifteen hundred Jews residing in the royal administrative district
surrounding Metz.[69]

Severe prohibitions always weighed heavily on the Jews of Metz.
Guilds refused to admit them. They were forbidden to work in craft
industries, and could own neither land nor real estate outside the
Jewish quarter.[70] Nevertheless, several made fortunes provisioning
the army, concluding deals in important commodity markets during
times of war or scarcity by utilizing a network of Jewish business

66 Isaac Berr Bing, "Mémoire particulier...," *Archives parlementaires...*, 9:446.

67 A. Cahen, "Les Juifs de Metz, budget de la communauté," *Mémoires de la Société d'archéologie lorraine*, 3d ser., 3 (1875): 144–149.

68 G. Cahen, in Blumenkranz, *Histoire...*, 86.

69 Cf. Liber, op. cit., *Revue des études juives*, 63 (1902), 195.

70 Cf. E. Harsomy: "The Jewish quarter was located to the north of the city and
limited on the right bank of the Moselle river by the entrenchment of Guise. This
neighborhood consisted of only two streets (the rue des Juifs and the quai des Juifs)
and narrow alleyways, unwholesome, humid, crowded in with old, dilapidated,
overpopulated houses, and of two old synagogues." E. Harsomy, "Metz pendant
la Révolution," *Mémoires de l'Académie nationale de Metz, années 139–140*. 5th ser., 59
(1957–1959): 42. Cf. Roger Clément, *La Condition des Juifs de Metz sous l'Ancien Régime*
(Paris: Jouve, 1903).

representatives abroad.[71] Sumptuary laws kept a tight rein on the conspicuous display in which the wealthiest families indulged during weddings and circumcisions. A law adopted in 1779 obligated all heads of families to wear a black coat and a turned-down collar which, combined with the religious custom that required men to maintain beards, readily identified them as Jews. Sumptuary laws, however, applied to only a small portion of the community. The majority of Metz's Jews lived in wretched poverty. Isaiah Berr Bing described "these pallid faces, these itinerant second-hand clothes dealers..., burdened with all sorts of rags upon which they daily base the hope of bread, accompanied by so many insults and so much scorn that the horror of famine alone can make them decide to seek it... They return to hole up in the evening in their gloomy homes, like tombs, which they share with their families."[72]

Isaiah Berr Bing was not the only observer to note the misery afflicting so many of Metz's Jews. These lines, written in 1787, were echoed in the topic of an essay competition sponsored that year by the Royal Academy of Metz: "Is there a way to make the Jews more useful and happier in France?"

THE JEWS OF LORRAINE

Jews migrated to the duchy of Lorraine from Alsace and Metz. During Lorraine's occupation by French troops, from 1633 to 1661 and then from 1670 to 1683, the royal governor authorized several Jewish families to reside in Nancy and Bar-le-Duc. In the face of protests from the towns, he was obliged to revoke this permission.[73] In 1697, when France evacuated the duchy, duc Léopold, pressed by fiscal needs and a desire to encourage commerce in his states, authorized several Jews to reside there.

One of these, Samuel Lévy, son of a banker and syndic of Metz, was able to settle in Lunéville. His rise was stunning. He served as

---

71 They constituted, as one intendant said, "a sort of republic and neutral nation among states." Anchel, *Les Juifs...*, 169.

72 "Lettre du S' I. B. B. [Sieur Isaïe Berr-Bing], Juif de Metz, à l'auteur anonyme d'un écrit intitulé: 'Le Cri du citoyen contre les Juifs,' " p. 51, in *La Révolution française et l'émancipation des Juifs*. Vol. 8: *Lettres, Mémoires....*

73 Cf. Blumenkranz, *Histoire...*, 84; Christian Pfister, *Histoire de Nancy*. 3 vol. (Paris: Berger-Levrault, 1908), 3:310–328.

both the duke's banker and as purveyor to the court.[74] In 1715, despite opposition by the duke's treasury officials, Levy was named receiver-general of taxes. In September 1717 he hosted a sumptuous reception during the Jewish high holy days at his mansion in Nancy, "with grand illuminations that blazed for miles around, and whose guests, with their usual shrieks and songs, were heard throughout the neighboring area..."[75] The Court of Nancy judged such gatherings "illicit, scandalous and reckless," and forbade all Jews to conduct themselves in such fashion under pain of a ten thousand-livre fine.[76] Unfortunately the extent of Lévy's loans, especially to duc Léopold and the emperor, and the failure of a Frankfurt bank, hastened his bankruptcy. Léopold imprisoned both Lévy and his wife, an act which freed the duke from an embarrassing creditor. Lévy was expelled from Lorraine in 1721.[77]

Lévy's fall led to harsh measures against the province's Jews. An edict in August 1720 reinstated previous measures against usury.[78] On 12 April 1721 Léopold ordered the expulsion of all Jews who had settled in the duchy after 1680. Only seventy-three households, dispersed among eighty towns, were authorized to remain, of which only four were in Nancy.[79] In 1726 Jews were compelled to reassemble in ghettos.

Economic self-interest soon led to the decree's reversal. In 1733 Léopold's widow, the regent Élisabeth-Charlotte, raised to 180 the number of Jewish families permitted to live in the duchy, on condition that they pay an aggregate tax of ten thousand livres annually. The accession of Stanislas, who had demonstrated goodwill toward the Jews in Poland, marked the beginning of a prosperous period for Jews in Lorraine. In 1728 restrictions imposed on their business activities were lifted, and all male descendents who lived with a household were added to the register of the 180 families granted offi-

74 Cf. Blumenkranz, *Histoire...*, 87.

75 Decree of the Court of Nancy, 17 September 1717. *Ordonnances de Lorraine*, 2:133–134.

76 Ibid.

77 Cf. Ginsburger, "Samuel Lévy, rabbin et financier," *Revue des études juives* 65 (1913): 274–300; ibid., 66 (1913): 111–133, 263–284.

78 All Jews had to be escorted by a Christian "man of probity," designated by the mayor or provost, who witnessed all transactions conducted by Jews and countersigned their legal documents.

79 Blumenkranz, *Histoire...*, 89.

cial residence. Special permissions were also granted to some wealthy merchants, such as the syndic Isaac Berr, who served as purveyor to the court.[80]

These arrangements were maintained after Stanislas's death and Lorraine's union with France, and by 1789 Lorraine was home to nearly five hundred Jewish families, comprising some four thousand people. Forty-five families lived in Lunéville, although most were not authorized to reside there.[81] Ninety-seven households settled in Nancy, of which fifty lacked authorization. The Jews were well-established there, possessed small shops outside the ghetto, and engaged in selling silks and fabrics in street stalls. Others introduced the spice and silver trades to Nancy, provided supplies to the military or created manufacturing workshops.[82] Certain wealthy families were also noted for their "studied elegance in furniture and clothing, even taste for acquiring all the enjoyments and good things of life."[83]

Some well-to-do notables, such as the Goudchaux family, the Berrs or the Halphens, were members of an oligarchy that held power in Lorraine's Jewish community, whose structure was similar to its counterpart in Metz. Thanks to the notables' contributions, Nancy's Jewish community was financially stable. Success among a few, however, could not hide the poverty of others, many of whom relied upon charity.[84] Speaking Yiddish and eking out bare existences, they shared the destitution of the mass of Jews of eastern France and were prey to the deeply rooted anti-Jewish sentiments of the populace. In 1761 three Jews accused of sorcery were hanged and two others sent to the galleys. A feeble-minded Jew suffered the same penalty for stealing the consecrated host from a church.[85] And in 1788, during a grain shortage, Cerf-Berr, accused of starving the people, found his warehouses in Nancy attacked by rioters.[86]

---

80 Ibid., 91.

81 Tribout de Morembert, 102.

82 Blumenkranz, *Histoire...*, 113.

83 Claude-Antoine Thiéry, *Dissertation sur cette question: Est-il des moyens de rendre les Juifs plus heureux et plus utiles en France?*, p. 64, in *La Révolution française et l'émancipation des Juifs*: Vol. 1.

84 Jacques Godechot, "Les professions des Juifs nancéiens au XVIIIe siècle," *Revue juive de Lorraine* 2 (1926): 136–138.

85 Pfister, 3:328.

86 Ibid.

THE JEWS OF PARIS

Paris's Jewish population was very small: about five hundred people in 1789.[87] Their situation, too, was the product of historical caprice. Jews had been officially forbidden to reside in Paris without special authorization since 1394, following an edict ordering their expulsion from the country. Under Louis XIV several "Portuguese new Christian" families settled there to conduct business, taking advantage of the ambiguity of their status. They were tolerated.

The regime relaxed its restrictions during the eighteenth century. "German" Jews, mostly from Metz, made their way to Paris.[88] Little by little, the Jews of the capital organized their community. Placed under police surveillance they had to obtain a passport stamped by the lieutenant of police and live in designated neighborhoods: the "Germans," who were more numerous, in Saint-Denis and Saint-Martin; the "Portuguese," who were better integrated, in Saint-Germain-des-Prés.[89]

Jacob Rodriguez Pereire headed the "Portuguese" community and played an active role representing the interests of the city's Sephardic Jews. He arranged publication of a collection of the *lettres patentes* which, from Henry II to Louis XV, guaranteed their rights. He clashed with the mercantile guilds, which in 1767 demanded all Jews be expelled. In 1776 he obtained Louis XVI's renewal of the *lettres patentes*. In 1780 he acquired land for the first Jewish cemetery in Paris, in La Villette,[90] now part of the city's northeastern nineteenth arrondissement. All "Portuguese" who sought permission to reside in the capital had to accompany him to the lieutenant general of police and present a certificate issued by the syndic of their original place of residence. Pereire was thus recognized by his fellow Jews and the authorities as the de facto representative of the "Portuguese Jewish nation" in Paris.

Less satisfactory was the situation of the "Germans." There were none among them like the Bordelais Jewish gentlemen of fash-

---

87 Cf. Léon Kahn, *Histoire de la communauté israélite à Paris. Les Juifs de Paris au XVIIIe siècle, d'après les archives de la Lieutenance générale de police à la Bastille* (Paris: A. Durlacher, 1894); *Les Juifs de Paris pendant la Révolution* (Paris: P. Ollendorff, 1899), chap. 1.

88 Paul Hildenfinger, *Documents sur les Juifs à Paris au XVIIIe siècle. Actes d'inhumation et scellés* (Paris: E. Champion, 1913), 150.

89 Blumenkranz, *Histoire...*, 251.

90 Hildenfinger, 150.

ion who haunted stylish cafés, swords dangling at their sides.[91] Many were peddlers, second-hand clothes dealers, horse traders or pawn-brokers. Some succeeded in setting themselves up as gold- or silver-smiths and jewelers. However, when the king personally granted several of them the status of master merchants as notion-dealers and jewelers, Paris's guilds reacted by having guards seize their goods. And in 1777 the King's Council again prohibited Jews from engaging in such commerce in Paris.[92]

Nevertheless, several Jewish military suppliers or bankers attained wealth and influence. Liefman Calmer obtained letters of naturalization and went on to acquire a barony which conferred upon him, without having to convert to Catholicism, the office of *vidame* of the cathedral of Amiens;[93] and the powerful Cerf-Berr, whose extensive business activities often brought him to Paris, close to the seat of the royal government in Versailles, acquired Montrouge cemetery for the "German" Jews in 1789.[94]

Though small groups of enterprising men existed among the Jews of Paris, where they established synagogues[95] and supported rabbis, they did not create an organized community, as had the oli-garchs of Metz and Bordeaux. Rather, their diversity of national and cultural origins and social status mirrored in miniature the "Jewish nation" of France: a motley mosaic of groups whose circumstances varied widely, and whose members were bound by restrictions from which they were trying to break free.

THE DYNAMISM OF THE JEWS

Economic development, the impact of the Enlightenment and increasing contact with the Christian world all fostered a desire among those Jews who were the most enterprising and enmeshed in the life of their era to escape from the constraints and humiliations

---

91 Kahn, in Blumenkranz, *Histoire...*, 53.

92 Decree of the King's Council, 7 February 1777; cf. Sagnac, 23.

93 Blumenkranz, *Histoire...*, 250. [A *vidame* represented the bishop in tempo-ral matters and commanded his troops. The title and function dates to the Middle Ages.—TRANSL.]

94 Hildenfinger, 23.

95 Sephardic Jews worshiped at sites located on the rue Saint-André-des-Arts. Ashkenazim gathered at the hôtel du Chariot d'Or, on rue Turbigo. Cf. Roger Beng, "Synagogues à Paris," in *Vieilles maisons françaises*, no. 988, no. 124: 80.

they had encountered. The "Portuguese" merchants of Bordeaux, the great maritime city whose commerce relied heavily on France's colonial trade, bitterly resented provisions in the Code Noir of 1685 that prohibited Jews from settling in the Antilles. Defying the code, a number of the members of Bordeaux's Jewish merchant families settled in Martinique and, especially, Saint-Domingue, where they acquired plantations and owned black slaves.[96] Similarly, prosperous traders among the Jews who earned their livelihoods roaming the roads and fairs of the Comtat Venaissin decided that they would no longer put up with having to wear yellow hats in Avignon or being locked up at night in the *carrières*, and they left the pontifical territories for the south of France.[97] In Alsace Cerf-Berr, armed with his wealth and connections, willingly defied social restrictions and Strasbourg's municipal authorities by settling his family and large staff of servants in the very heart of the city.[98] Similarly, in Paris, where in principle Jews were forbidden to reside, the fact that certain of them flaunted their presence in public places and were willing to confront the lieutenant of police's agents[99] bore witness to their refusal to submit to the old rules.

Jews thus became enmeshed in ferment and dissent against the established order during the waning years of the Ancien Régime. Challenges to traditional authority even emerged within the heart of France's Jewish communities.[100] On the eve of the Revolution France's "Jewish nation," surprisingly diverse and far from monolithic or static, was astir with impatience and, among its most energetic elements, longing for a radical transformation of its plight. Change, however, depended less on its own efforts and aspirations than upon the Christian society in which they lived.

---

96   Cf. Pluchon, pt. 2, chap. 2, "Les Juifs de Saint-Domingue."

97   Cf. Blumenkranz, *Histoire...*, 210–211.

98   Cf. Levylier, 15, 16.

99   Kahn, in Blumenkranz, *Histoire...*, 53.

100 Cf. Girard, *La Révolution...*, 47ff.

"THE MOST LOATHSOME PEOPLE ON EARTH." — VOLTAIRE

A century of the Enlightenment's challenges to conventional ideas did not free France from traditional anti-Judaism.[101] In 1689 Mme de Sévigné wrote to her daughter: "This hatred that people have for them [the Jews] is extraordinary."[102] A hundred years later Malesherbes, addressing the king, noted pensively: "A very strong hatred against the Jewish nation still exists in Christian hearts..."[103]

Of the numerous expressions of this hostility toward Jews, some of the sharpest and most notable appear in Voltaire's writings. Despite the fact that throughout his long life he liked to think of himself as the leader in the struggle for tolerance, Voltaire's antipathy for "the most loathsome people on earth"[104] never waned. In 1745 he declared in his *Dictionnaire philosophique*, "You will find in them only an ignorant and barbarous people who have long combined the most sordid greed for money with the most detestable superstition" (though, he added, "Nonetheless, it is not necessary to burn them...").[105] In 1773 he wrote to the chevalier de Lisle: "These foreskinless ones of Israel... are nothing less than the greatest rogues who ever tarnished the face of the earth";[106] and to Isaac Pinto, he responded with scornful irony: "I will say to you with the same frankness that a good many people can put up with neither your laws nor your books nor your superstitions. They say that your nation has done at all times much harm to itself and to mankind. If you are a *philosophe*, as you appear to be, you will think as these gentlemen do, but you will not admit it..."[107]

Montesquieu, the famed Bordeaux magistrate who knew firsthand of the contributions that the "Portuguese Jewish nation" made to his city's prosperity, was more forthright in urging a policy of

---

101　Cf. notably Léon Poliakov, *Histoire de l'antisémitisme*. Vol. 3: *De Voltaire à Wagner* (Paris: Calmann-Lévy, 1968), 38-45 and 88-173. Also, Yves Chevalier, *L'Antisémitisme: Le Juif comme bouc émissaire*. Preface by F. Bourricaud. (Paris: Éditions de Cerf, 1988), 269.

102　Letter of 26 June 1689 to Mme de Grignan, in *Madame de Sévigné. Correspondance*. R. Duchêne, ed. (Paris: Gallimard "Bibliothèque de la Pléiade," 1957), 3:456.

103　Pierre Grosclaude, *Malesherbes, témoin et interprète de son temps* (Paris: Fischbacher, 1961), 405.

104　Voltaire, *Dictionnaire philosophique*, "Anthropophages," in *Œuvres de Voltaire*. Adrien-Jean-Quentin Beuchot, ed. 72 vol. (Paris: Werdet et Lequien fils, 1829), 26:402.

105　Ibid., "Juifs," 30:462-3.

106　Letter of 15 December 1773, *Œuvres de Voltaire*, 68:393-4. Cf. Poliakov, 107.

107　Letter of 21 July 1762. Cf. Pluchon, 298.

tolerance toward the Jews. Even so, his arguments were grounded in a mercantilist exchange of economic benefits. In his *Très humble remonstrance aux inquisiteurs d'Espagne et de Portugal* [Very Humble Petition to the Inquisitors of Spain and Portugal],[108] Montesquieu denounced fanaticism which, in the name of Christ, burned Jews at the stake; but he stopped short of granting Jews rights equal to those of Christians. Reflecting on ways "to restore the kingdom's affluence and finances," he proposed that "all taxes levied solely on the Jews" be abolished, and that the loss be recaptured by "sell[ing] extensive privileges to them for a princely sum payable over three years, equal to a value of one million in revenue..."[109] He further suggested that a Jewish city be created within the kingdom, "on the Spanish frontier, in a place good for commerce, like Saint-Jean-de-Luz or Ciboure. They [the Jews] would go there en masse and end up bringing all their wealth into the realm."[110]

Considerations of economic benefit underpinned much of eighteenth-century discussion of tolerance toward Jews. "The Jews," the great *Encyclopédie* revealed, "are today tolerated in France, Germany, Poland, Holland, England, Rome and Venice, in exchange for tribute which they pay to princes."[111] In his article entitled "Jews," the chevalier de Jaucourt noted: "Holland and England, animated by the noblest principles,... have granted them all possible kindnesses under the constant protection of their governments," whereas "France harmed itself in driving them out." The Encyclopedists saw advantages in letting the Jews pursue commerce in order to build a modern state, rejected excesses of fanaticism and denounced intolerance, including that of Jews themselves. Still, their calls for tolerance did not extend to calls to grant liberty, much less equality, to Jews.

Rousseau's ideas were more complex. On one hand, he fell back upon ancient Christian imagery when he described the Jews of antiquity as "the most vile people who may have existed in those

---

108   Montesquieu, *De l'esprit des lois* (Paris: Garnier-Flammarion, 1979), bk. 25, chap. 12: "You live in an age when natural light is brighter than ever, in which *philosophie* has enlightened spirits... Therefore, if you do not abandon your old prejudices, which, if you do not watch out for them, are your passions, you will have to admit that you are all depraved."

109   Cf. Poliakov, 100.

110   Ibid.

111   Article, "Judaïsme"; cf. Poliakov, 131.

days";[112] but he also denounced harsh restrictions imposed upon the Jews: "They experience misfortunes at our hands. The tyranny that we exercise toward them renders them fearful; they know how little injustice and cruelty trouble Christian charity."[113] More interesting, Rousseau paid homage to the Jews of the diaspora as a people who, though "scattered, dispersed over the face of the earth, enslaved, persecuted, scorned by all nations, [have] nevertheless preserved their characteristics, their laws, their customs, their patriotic love of their first social relationship, when all bonds appear broken... Athens, Sparta, Rome have perished and have left no children on earth; Zion defeated has not lost its [children]."[114] At a time when *philosophes* were inclined to consider the Jews' attachment to their religious practices an expression of prejudice and ignorance,[115] this was rare praise.

At best the *philosophes* preached tolerance; at worst, their thoughts and statements remained permeated with traditional anti-Judaism.

ANTI-JUDAISM

Anti-Judaism fed from two sources: one was religious, the other economic.

The Church's centuries-old anathema that the Jews were a "deicide people" bred persistent hostility and scorn in France toward a group whose faith and practices, and sometimes its use of a foreign language, seemed alien.[116] Exclusion and rejection were constant. Even in Bordeaux, where the "Portuguese" were apparently well-integrated, the common folk detested the Jews, and horrifying legends, most notably allegations about child abductions,[117] were widespread.

---

112 Poliakov, 121.

113 Jean-Jacques Rousseau, *Émile*, bk. 4, in *Œuvres complètes*. Bernard Gagnebin and Marcel Raymond, eds. (Paris: Gallimard "Bibliothèque de la Pléiade," 1969), 4:64.

114 Unpublished ms., in the library of Neuchâtel. Cf. Poliakov, 123.

115 Cf., notably on the anti-Judaism of d'Holbach, Poliakov, 138–141. Similarly, in 1786 the writer Louis-Sébastien Mercier published a science-fiction novel, *L'an 2440, rêve s'il en fut jamais*, in which he described the proliferation of the Jews, their machinations to dominate Europe, and the measures necessary to combat them, in terms which prefigure modern anti-Semitism; cf. Poliakov, 165–166.

116 Chevalier, 268ff.

117 Cf. Paul Butel and Jean-Pierre Poussou, *La Vie quotidienne à Bordeaux aux XVIIIᵉ siècle* (Paris: Hachette, 1980).

In January 1755 students armed with clubs rioted against the "Portuguese" and smashed the windows of their houses.[118] In Avignon the requirement that Jews wear yellow hats made them targets for repeated assaults.[119]

Hostility was even more pronounced in the eastern provinces. The filth of the Jews' overcrowded ghettoes bred contempt and revulsion. Rather than questioning the causes of this misery, observers attributed such conditions to the Jews themselves, from whose presence they fled. "It is not healthy in the midst of these Jews," wrote a traveler who refused to attend a wedding in Metz's synagogue. In Strasbourg the Society of Friends of the Constitution deplored, in 1790, the "outrageous tales against the Jews told to children every day, which...sow in their hearts seeds of hatred, which become widespread through education, take root and become indestructible...The prejudices with which the people of Strasbourg are steeped, this blind hatred against the Jews, is due in great measure to their origin...in the absurd stories they have been told, and which tradition lovingly preserves."[120] Booklets for children, consisting of both catechisms and secular works that were widely disseminated in the countryside by peddlers, always depicted the Jews in the darkest terms: "ingrates, unbelievers and cruel."

Economic fears heightened passions stirred by such images. Shopkeepers and artisans viewed the Jews as real or potential competitors to be reduced or eliminated. Merchants and guilds struggled throughout the eighteenth century against Jews' persistent efforts to relax the restrictions which bound them. "The Jews will soon take over France's commerce," the merchants of Gien exclaimed in 1732.[121] "We entreat you to stop the advances of this nation, which will inevitably disrupt all commerce,"[122] proclaimed Montpellier's trade representatives in 1734. "This Jewish nation seems to grovel, the better to rise and en-

---

118 Pluchon, 60.

119 François Marlin, *Voyages en France et pays circonvoisins depuis 1775 jusqu'en 1807.* 4 vol. (Paris: Guillaume, 1817), 1:48. [Title as given in card catalogue of the Bibliothèque nationale de France: *Voyages d'un Français, depuis 1775 jusqu'en 1807.—TRANSL.*]

120 "Rapport lu à l'Assemblée de la Société des Amis de la Constitution, le 27 février 1790, sur la question de l'état des Juifs d'Alsace," pp. 26–27, in *La Révolution française et l'émancipation des Juifs.* Vol. 8: *Lettres, Mémoires....*

121 Poliakov, 39.

122 Ibid.

rich itself,"[123] Toulouse's chamber of commerce declared in 1744. The merchants of Aurillac denounced "the Jews [who] make a practice of deceiving people through shady deals,"[124] and appealed to the royal intendant with a request that Jewish merchants be expelled. In 1765 the attorney for merchants and traders in Paris petitioned against the admission of Jews: "One can compare the Jews to wasps who are introduced into hives only in order to kill the bees, open their stomachs and extract honey from their entrails."[125]

Such talk was common currency in the guilds, where mercantilism joined with anti-Judaism to confine Jews within the constricted range of activities to which they were relegated. Legal proceedings grew and parlements maintained vigilant watch over bans imposed on Jews. When Jewish merchants from Bordeaux tried to settle in La Rochelle, their attempts to engage in commerce led to actions against them;[126] when the "Portuguese" visited Nevers three or four times on business, attempts were made to forbade them to go there.[127] The same prohibition was decreed against all settlement of Jews in the province.[128] The Parlement of Aix forbid the Jews of the Comtat Venaissin to try their luck in Provence, under penalty of being flogged.[129] In Bayonne a "chocolate war" broke out between the city's guilds and the Jews of Bourg-Saint-Esprit.[130] In Paris merchant groups fought the king's award and won their case before the King's Council after Louis XVI conferred upon some Jews the status of master jeweler.[131]

In the eastern provinces usury fed hatred of Jews among the populace. It reached a fever pitch in 1777 when, during the affair of the forged receipts, "men decorated with false insignia of public office openly proclaimed that the time had arrived to exterminate the Jews. They incited the populace and declared that the great massacre would take place on 30 September, the day when the Jews would

---

123 Blumenkranz, *Histoire...*, 268.
124 Pluchon, 80.
125 Poliakov, 4
126 Parlement of Paris, decree of 22 August 1729, in Sagnac, 7.
127 Decree of the King's Council, 13 April 1740.
128 Sagnac, 9.
129 Ibid.
130 Cf. p. 9, above.
131 Decree of the King's Council, 7 February 1777.

be gathered in synagogue for twenty-four hours of prayer."[132] The army's intervention thwarted this plan for a St. Bartholomew massacre of Jews; but such a call for collective murder during the reign of Louis XVI indicates the intensity of anti-Jewish emotion that raged in Lower Alsace.

Confronted with such public hostility,[133] parlements were attentive to the numerous prohibitions that burdened the Jews.[134] The Parlement of Paris, despite letters from the king, refused to ratify the decree of 17 January 1784, which abolished the body toll collected from them, declaring that "this decree was infinitely dangerous in its consequences because it would involve acknowledging publicly that the Jews have a right to dwell in the kingdom."[135] As of June 1788 the Parlements of Bordeaux and Toulouse had still not ratified it.

Similarly the Parlement of Metz only agreed to a decree of 28 November 1787, which granted civil rights to non-Catholics, "on condition, insofar as it concerns the Jews within its jurisdiction, that it will do nothing to set new precedents, and that the decrees, declarations and regulations passed by this parlement will continue to be executed with regard to the Jews."[136] Whether the parlement viewed this stipulation as a detail or a significant addition, the Jews of Metz remained excluded from the benefits of the edict of tolerance. The Parlement of Toulouse was even more aggressive. In its protests to the king on 1 April 1788 it declared: "To establish in positive and general law that the fiercest enemies of the Christian faith, such as the Jews, pagans, Mohammedans, shall not at all be excluded from holding

---

132 "Lettre d'un Alsacien sur les Juifs d'Alsace à M. Rewbell, député de cette province à l'Assemblée nationale," pp. 15–16, in *La Révolution française et l'émancipation des Juifs*. Vol. 8: *Lettres, Mémoires....*

133 In the *Dictionnaire universel françois et latin*, commonly called the "dictionary of Trévoux," 1771–1772, one finds under the entry for "Jew": "One says familiarly 'I would much prefer to be in the hands of the Jews' to speak of people who are hardhearted. In speaking of a merchant whose prices are too high or who lends money at usurious rates, one says 'He's a Jew, a real, out-and-out Jew.' One says the same of all those who show a great greediness for money..." *Dictionnaire universel françois et latin, vulgairement appelé Dictionnaire de Trévoux*. 6th ed. 8 vols. (Paris: La Compagnie des Libraires Associés, 1771), 5:302.

134 Cf. H. Linguet, attorney and publicist, commenting on a decree assented to by the Parlement of Paris, 21 July 1777: "Habits, religion, policies, reason, or perhaps at least an instinct justified by many reasons, require us to attach to the name of 'Jew' as much scorn as dislike." Cited by Poliakov, 42.

135 Archives départementales de la Moselle, B. 100, man. fos., 276–280.

136 Cf. Feuerwerker, *L'émancipation...*, 44.

municipal office..., is to demonstrate a tendency which we should not at all expect from Your Majesty..."[137]

On the other hand, the royal administration's attitude toward the Jews was totally pragmatic. This was especially true among its intendants, who were well informed about the kingdom's economic realities. Responding to complaints registered by merchants in Toulouse, the intendant noted: "Their best option, which they would do well to exercise, is to stock their stores with the same quality of goods that the Jews provide in theirs, and to be content with a smaller profit if they do not do so"; to the merchants of Béziers: "If they complain of the economic harm that the Jews cause them, it is their own fault. They need not skin the public and seek to make such large profits"; to the merchants of Montpellier: "It is the difference of the little profit to which the Jews are reduced, and the excessive high prices that the merchants charge for their cloth, which has established the public's attitude..."[138] Similarly, the intendant of Languedoc responded to the anger in the horse-dealers' guild when the Jews of Avignon imported cows and horses from Poitou: "The Jews sold their livestock at suitable prices, proportionate to prices people of the countryside could afford..."[139]

Nonetheless, La Galaizière, the intendant in Alsace, who was familiar with local hostility toward the Jews, opposed Cerf-Berr's request that Jews be allowed freedom of commerce and settlement.[140] La Galazière resolved to fight growth of the Jewish population in the province and he suggested that Jews who had recently immigrated be expelled en masse. Taking advantage of a provision in the *lettres patentes* issued in July 1784, he saw to it that the king did not provide formal approval of any Jewish marriages unless the couple obtained the intendant's recommendation. Despite protests that ensued, the royal administration enforced the provision with relative severity between 1784 and 1789. Though Jews already settled in Alsace obtained permission to marry without difficulty, permission was systematically denied to recent immigrants. Moreover, an order expelling all unregistered Jews from Alsace was drawn up on 13 December 1788

---

137   Ibid., 158.

138   Poliakov, 39.

139   N. Roubin, "La vie commerciale des Juifs comtadins en Languedoc au XVIIIe siècle," *Revue des études juives* 34-36 (1896–1897): 98.

140   Blumenkranz, *Histoire...*, 156, 158.

and only the onset of the Revolution prevented its execution. Such measures adopted on the very eve of the Revolution demonstrate that, with respect to the future of the Jews in France, the government of Louis XVI had not yet decided on a consistent or coherent policy.[141]

---

141 Cf. R. Anchel, "Les lettres patentes du 10 juillet 1784," *Revue des études juives* (1932): 133–134.

CHAPTER 2

DAWN

T HE FIRST FAINT GLIMMERINGS OF CHANGE APPEARED IN THE EAST. Since the sixteenth century, each of the three hundred-odd states of the Germanic Holy Roman Empire had individually decided the fate of its Jews. Pressed for money or wishing to promote commerce, princes or cities granted Jews the right to reside and do business in return for payment of high taxes. Playing off rivalries and conflicts among these many principalities, Jews integrated themselves deeply in economic life. In Leipzig at the end of the eighteenth century, a quarter of the merchants involved in the city's great fairs were Jews; and in Frankfurt, Germany's financial center, more than three thousand Jews lived crowded together in its ghetto. "The closeness, the filth, the commotion, the accent of a dialect displeasing to the ear—all this produced a strongly unpleasant impression," wrote Goethe, evoking his memories of adolescence.[1]

Certain Jews, however, escaped from this widespread poverty. "Court Jews," skillful financiers able to satisfy the needs of princes, played an important role in these small states, at times undertaking political missions. They lived outside the ghettos and amassed fortunes and honors, arousing jealousy and hatred among some Christians. When Alexandre David, banker to the duke of Brunswick, died, his remains were transported to the cemetery in the duke's hearse, which was accompanied by all the court's members. Others, like Süss, were hanged.[2]

---

1 Cf. Léon Poliakov, *Histoire de l'antisémitisme*. Vol. 3: *De Voltaire à Wagner* (Paris: Calmann-Lévy, 1968), 31, n. 4.

2 Ibid., 34. [Joseph ben Issacher Suesskind (1698/9–1738), known to history as "Jud Süss"—"the Jew Süss"—was a financial advisor and "court Jew" to the duke of Wuerttemberg, in Germany. His economic reforms, lavish lifestyle and accusations of licentiousness levied against him led to his arrest and trial on charges of embezzlement following the duke's death. He was found guilty in what is generally

When it came to dealing with Jews, Frederick William I gave his son, Frederick the Great, a simple piece of advice: "If you need money, tax all the Jews twenty or thirty thousand thalers a year every three or four years, over and above the protection money they pay you. You should press them, for they betrayed Jesus Christ, and you should never trust them because the most honest Jew is a swindler and a cad—you may be sure of it."[3] Frederick the Great protected Jews, to the degree that they were useful to the Prussian economy, against popular hostility and the jealousy of merchants. Poor Jews who sought asylum in Prussia, however, were expelled without mercy. During his reign Berlin's Jewish community prospered financially,[4] and thanks to wars and Prussia's development certain of its members made considerable fortunes.[5] They constituted a Jewish elite, at once wealthy and anxious to take their place in society. Naturally cosmopolitan, they welcomed the Enlightenment and renounced traditional Judaism. This Jewish expression of the Enlightenment, the *Haskalah*, was heresy in the eyes of central Europe's Orthodox Jews; among them "Berlinism" became a synonym for modernism, assimilation and, therefore, repudiation.

Thus Berlin, with its climate of tolerance and contempt, rather than Paris, first provided an arena where Enlightenment intellectuals grappled with ameliorating the Jews' conditions and with admitting them into the mainstream of European society. The playwright Gotthold Lessing's social drama, *The Jews*, whose virtuous hero is a Jew, was first performed in 1749. But more than anyone else, it was the philosopher Moses Mendelssohn, whose thought and fame extended throughout Enlightenment Europe, who decisively influenced enlightened minds. "A man cast by nature into the heart of a degraded horde, born without any sort of advantages..., was raised to the rank of the greatest writers of the century born in Germa-

---

considered to have been a judicial murder, and hanged. A film, *Jud Süss*, produced during World War II by the Nazi-controlled Continental Studios and distributed throughout occupied Europe, is a classic anti-Semitic version of Suesskind's alleged crimes.—*TRANSL.*]

3 In Poliakov, 30. [Frederick William I reigned from 1713 to 1740; his son, Frederick II ("the Great") reigned from 1740 to 1786.—*TRANSL.*]

4 In 1743, the community numbered 1,850 members. In 1777 it consisted of 4,245 individuals, five percent of the capital's population. Paris at that time had six hundred thousand inhabitants, including five hundred Jews, less than one per one thousand inhabitants.

5 According to Mirabeau, the only millionaires in Berlin in 1780 were Jews.

ny"⁶ was Mirabeau's description of Mendelssohn, a frail hunchback and son of a poor schoolmaster. Mendelssohn had arrived in Berlin in 1742, and worked in a silk shop to earn his living. Thanks to Israël Moyse, a scholarly Jew and Berlin schoolteacher, and Abraham Kisch, a doctor from Prague, he learned the rudiments of science and philosophy. In 1748 he struck up a friendship with Salomon Gumpertz, a young Jewish mathematician and philosopher, who introduced him to Berlin's youthful intellectual circle. They found Mendelssohn a self-taught genius and genuinely fascinating. Among that circle was Lessing,⁷ who would much later model the hero of his play, *Nathan the Wise*, on him. Mendelssohn's fame spread throughout Enlightenment Europe following publication of his philosophical work, *Phaedon*. His modest and virtuous life, his tolerant mind and the brilliance of his thought cast him as the embodiment of the eighteenth-century *philosophe*. Mirabeau, citing "the ascendancy of a reason so profound and a conduct so pure," wrote: "The Germans awarded him the title of 'a modern Plato.' "⁸

As an advocate of religious tolerance, Mendelssohn was led, almost by force of circumstances, to support the cause of the Jews publicly. It was Lessing who involved him. Responding to Johann David Michaelis, a Protestant theologian and fierce champion of traditional anti-Judaism who denied that a Jew could ever be able to attain the truth, Lessing published a moving letter Mendelssohn had written in defense of his fellow Jews: "Let them continue to oppress us…, let them expose us to the ridicule and scorn of the whole world; but let them not seek to challenge our virtue, the sole consolation of ill-fated souls."⁹ Among the virtues Mendelssohn evoked were those of family, horror of violence, love of justice and passion for knowledge, which had sustained Jews during centuries of persecution.

The debate began. In 1763 Pastor Johann Caspar Lavater

6 Mirabeau, *Sur Moses Mendelssohn, sur la réforme politique des Juifs*, p. 2, in vol. 1 of *La Révolution française et l'émancipation des Juifs*. 8 vol. (Paris: Edhis [Éditions d'Histoire Sociale], 1968). [Moses Mendelssohn was born in 1729 and died in 1786.—TRANSL.]

7 "Lessing, at once a scholar, a poet and philosopher, and remarkable in all these endeavors, appeared to have been one of the greatest polymaths of this century," Mirabeau, 14. [*Phaedon* was published in 1767. On Mirabeau, see fn. 56, below.—TRANSL.]

8 Mirabeau, 2, 3. *Phaedon* went through seventeen German editions and was translated into ten foreign languages. Cf. Poliakov, 187.

9 Poliakov, 186. [Johann David Michaelis (1717–1791).—TRANSL.]

It is not by polemics, but by the exercise of virtue that I wish to be able to refute the scornful opinion that people have of the Jews.

— MOSES MENDELSSOHN

challenged Mendelssohn to refute Christianity or to convert.
Mendelssohn refused Lavater's alternative—or trap—and asserted
his wish "to speak only in his writings of the truths common to all
religions."[10] At the same time he articulated his demanding moral
code: "It is not by polemics, but by the exercise of virtue that I wish to
be able to refute the scornful opinion that people have of the Jews."[11]
Thrusts and parries followed, engaging and energizing supporters
of the *Aufklärung*. A French translation of the exchange appeared
in 1771. From then on enlightened Europe considered Mendelssohn
the champion—better, the embodiment—of the potential "regeneration" of the Jews.

Moses Mendelssohn would influence the fate of France's Jews in
a number of curious, roundabout ways. Cerf-Berr, the wealthy overall official-in-charge of the "Jewish nation" in the eastern provinces,
knew of Mendelssohn's reputation and his efforts on behalf of fellow
Jews. As anti-Jewish passions flared in 1779 during Alsace's "affair
of the forged receipts," Cerf-Berr sought Mendelssohn's assistance in
responding to a harsh pamphlet written by François-Joseph Hell.[12]
With an eye toward informing the German philosopher about the
situation, Cerf-Berr sent him his *Mémoire sur l'état des Juifs en Alsace* [Memorandum on the Status of the Jews in Alsace], intended for
Louis XVI's Council of State, in which he entreated the sovereign to
consider and remedy the wretched condition of Alsace's Jews.[13]

Mendelssohn thought that rather than open a philosophical or
religious debate, it would be much better at that moment to pose the
problem in political terms, and that it would be better were a Chris-

10 Ibid., 187. [Johann Caspar Lavater (1741–1801).—*TRANSL.*]

11 Moses Mendelssohn, *Lettres juives du célèbre Mendelssohn, philosophe de Berlin avec
les remarques et les réponses de M. le Docteur Kölble et autres savans hommes* (Frankfurt and
The Hague: n.p., 1771).

12 F.-J. Hell, "Observations d'un Alsacien sur l'affaire présente des Juifs d'Alsace"
(Frankfurt: n.p., 1779); cf. Dominique Bourel, preface to Christian Wilhelm Dohm,
De la réforme politique des Juifs (Paris: Stock, 1984), 14.

13 Cerf-Berr especially requested the right of Jews to settle freely in all provinces,
and to engage in all forms of commerce, as well as the right to maintain their communal organization and the judicial authority granted to their rabbis. In exchange,
Cerf-Berr, who was very well-informed of the king's financial difficulties through
his position as a military supplier, offered "with respectful recognition, to the King
and nobles who have the right to it, the tribute that the sovereign would deign to
set in a stable and invariable form." He probably hoped by this means to win for the
Jews a favorable status that could not have been won by mere appeal to reason and
tolerance. Cf. "Mémoire sur l'état des Juifs en Alsace," cited in Dohm, 138ff.

tian to speak on behalf of the Jews. Since the populace complained of the Jews' economic activities, the time had come to look at ways to transform their circumstances so that they could become more useful to the societies in which they lived. With these premises in mind Mendelssohn approached Christian Wilhelm Dohm, a young, high-level Prussian official, a well-known jurist of public law and a professor of public finance in Berlin. Dohm wanted to demonstrate that, historically, "the state of oppression in which they [the Jews] live...is but a remnant of adverse prejudices that are contrary to [public] policy and humanity, to which the darkest ages gave birth and which are unworthy of us to permit to continue."[14]

Well informed thanks to Cerf-Berr, Dohm drew up a thorough assessment of the Jews' situation in Europe. He emphasized the benefit England and Holland had gained from admitting Sephardic Jews expelled from Spain and Portugal.[15] Dohm contrasted the condition in France of "a number of Portuguese, who enjoy considerable privileges in Bordeaux and Bayonne," with that of Jews in the eastern provinces, where "this nation...continues to be confined and oppressed."[16] In Italy Jews were treated with "more gentleness and sound policy."[17] Dohm acknowledged that in Poland, where Europe's largest Jewish population lived, there were bitter complaints against them; but he attributed the situation to Poland's social structure, "where one finds only nobles or serfs, so that all commercial activity has been completely left to the Jews."[18] Jews were not admitted to Norway and Sweden. Russia had expelled them in 1742. Even in Germany Jews were forbidden to enter some provinces. Reaching the end of this distressing panorama, Dohm concluded: "These policies...are unworthy of the Enlightenment which characterizes our century, and we should have ceased to follow them long ago."[19]

Reason and justice, wrote Dohm, dictated that the Jews "be

---

14 Dohm, 28. [Dohm was born in 1751 and died in 1820.—*TRANSL.*]

15 "It is in this republic [Holland] and in England that Jews truly enjoy human and civic rights and that they appear to be very useful members of the state," in Dohm, 60. In 1753 the British Parliament had granted the right of residence to Jews settled in England. But in the face of riots provoked by this measure, it was repealed the following year.

16 Dohm, 60.

17 Ibid., 61.

18 Ibid.

19 Ibid., 99.

completely furnished with the same rights that citizens enjoy."[20]
All of the criticisms directed at them—lust for money, the practice
of usury—were results of crushing, restrictive laws.[21] He therefore
advocated that Jews be given "complete freedom to work and earn
their livelihoods," hoping that they might become artisans or dedicate
themselves to agriculture. His belief that manual labor would lead the
way to the Jews' physical and moral "regeneration" prefigured the essay contest sponsored in 1787 by the Academy of Metz, which posed
the question of how to "make the Jews happier and more useful"
in France. But Dohm had no intention of restricting Jews to manual
labor. He wanted schools and universities to admit them so that they
might practice the arts and medicine, and he intended to tear down
the ghettos' walls.[22] Free to live where they saw fit and to pursue all
activities, Jews would also be able to practice their religion freely.

There was only one restriction that Dohm believed useful to
maintain, at least for the time being: access to public office, "the
honor of serving the State."[23] This special limitation no doubt reflected a lingering prejudice on the part of Frederick's high-ranking
official. Still, Dohm emphasized that this disability should remain
in force only for as long as it took the Jews to absorb the education
and principles necessary to carry out the functions of these offices;
and he refuted contentions that Jews were incapable of serving their
country because sabbath observance prevented them from fulfilling
military obligations.

As an invitation to Christians to show tolerance and humanity,
Dohm's work was a strong, well-argued plea in favor of a radical
political reform to improve the Jews' conditions and status. Frederick the Great remained unmoved by his official's eloquent appeals;
but Cerf-Berr had made no mistake in commissioning it. The Alsatian immediately arranged a French translation, undertaken by

---

20 Ibid., 77.

21 "The moral depravity and policy of the Jews," he wrote, "follow principally
from the fact that they have been driven to engage exclusively in commerce." Ibid.,
78.

22 Dohm denounced "these 'Jewries' [ces juiveries], in France and elsewhere,
which lead to the disadvantage . . . of involving the Jews in expanding their houses
upward in the most disproportionate fashion, of living crowded one on top of the
other, from which follows a continual slovenliness and stench, illnesses, disorderli-
ness and risks of frequent fires." Ibid., 78.

23 Ibid., 83.

Jean Bernoulli, a mathematician, member of the Berlin Academy of Sciences and a friend of Mendelssohn's. On 22 March 1782 Mendelssohn wrote to Dohm: "Monsieur Cerf-Berr is very pleased with the French version and wrote to me from Paris, where he is presently, that its style was very appreciated and that one could hardly believe that a German had made the translation."[24] Unfortunately, in April 1782, when copies reached France, most of them were seized and destroyed by the royal censor because the publisher had failed to obtain permission to issue the work. Only a handful survived. Abbé Henri Grégoire and Chrétien Malesherbes, who several years later would become key figures in efforts to improve conditions for France's Jews, had copies of this tract in favor of emancipation.

Dohm's work, however, received an enthusiastic reception in Berlin salons where the spirit of the *Aufklärung* reigned. Its success led the Protestant theologian Johann David Michaelis, "the most formidable enemy of the Jews, an ingenious savant well-versed in the Law of Moses,"[25] to respond.[26] He framed his argument by contrasting emancipation's aims with what he asserted were insurmountably innate characteristics of the Jews, which arose from their unquestioning devotion to Jewish religious laws. These laws isolated them from other nations by commanding rites and special obligations designed to prevent social interaction with Christians. The Jews had always lived as foreigners in all nations, observing their own sabbath, eating only kosher food, speaking their own language, living in expectation of the Messiah and their return to Palestine. Worse still, according to Michaelis, their religion dictated hatred of non-Jews and they would always be Christians' enemies. The Jews' small physical stature and their frail health, along with their religion's prohibition against engaging in combat during their sabbath, rendered them unfit for military service.

Emancipation, Michaelis contended, would be nothing more than an illusion—worse, an injustice to Christians—because the rights of citizens would be granted to people who would be unable to fulfill the duties of citizens. Moreover, their prolific birthrate, owing

---

24 In Bourel, preface to Dohm, 12. [Jean Bernoulli was born in 1744 and died in 1807.]—*Transl.*]

25 Mirabeau, 110.

26 Johann David Michaelis, *Orientalische und exegetische Bibliotek* (Frankfurt: Johann Gottlieb Garbe, 1782).

to early marriages, and their extreme cunning would quickly enable them to displace Christians everywhere because Christians would be unable to resist their competition. What would a state gain from such emancipation, other than to see a "perverse and detestable" race dishonestly prosper within its borders? He sought to prove this assertion by referring to a detailed analysis of several centuries of German criminal records which, he contended, proved that Jewish criminals were twenty-five times more numerous than their Christian counterparts.[27] How many generations would be required, he asked, to bring about improvement in a people so corrupt. Rather than emancipating the Jews, Michaelis declared, it was necessary to maintain, and even intensify, their exclusion, to ban them from all public office and even to refuse access to the sciences and education. At the very most, the Jews might be permitted to work uncultivated land and be compelled to pay special taxes in return for the tolerance they were shown. Modern anti-Semitism, grounded in the notion that all Jews bear the same innate, unchanging and negative characteristics, found its first ideologue in this Protestant theologian.[28]

Michaelis's attack was so harsh and his intellectual standing so great that Mendelssohn reversed course and decided to enter the debate. The result was *Jerusalem, or On Religious Power and Judaism*, in which he refuted Michaelis's propositions and asserted his idea of a religiously neutral state, open to citizens of all faiths. The flaws for which the Jews were criticized, Mendelssohn asserted, were rooted in neither their religion nor their nature, but were the result of unfair and harsh conditions to which they found themselves subjected for centuries by Christians. He demanded recognition of the Jews' civil and political rights. But at the same time he declared that equality could only be realized in a state dedicated to complete religious neutrality, where all of the churches' roles in civil and judicial matters would be eliminated. Mendelssohn was consistent: this requirement would apply to the Jews as well and he therefore called for abolition of the rabbinic courts' civil jurisdiction. Reason prevailed over Jewish tradition.

---

27 Cf. Mirabeau, 112. In his refutation of Michaelis, Mendelssohn, after having made his own study of the criminal records, noted that twenty-five times more thieves and receivers of stolen goods were to be found among German second-hand dealers than among Jewish second-hand dealers. Cf. Mirabeau, 125.

28 Cf. Poliakov, 194–195.

Jerusalem outlined the fundamentals of a doctrine of Jewish emancipation and integration that inspired a new generation of Enlightenment *philosophes*. Mendelssohn denounced, on one hand, the crimes of Christian intolerance and intolerance fed by Jewish obscurantism. On the other hand he proposed that Jews, in return for obtaining the same dignity as Christians, relinquish all uniqueness other than religious affiliation. Mendelssohn's proposal set forth a vision that would shape the future for all of Europe's Jews.

THE AUSTRIAN EXAMPLE

At about the same time that Dohm's work was published and being read and discussed in Berlin's salons, Austria's emperor, Joseph II, the most active of the era's "enlightened despots," announced two bold measures intended to change conditions under which Jews within his empire lived. Vienna had started thinking about the Berlin *Aufklärung*. His edicts of 19 October 1781 and 2 January 1782[29] were especially significant because they affected 260,000 people, dispersed over the vast expanse of his hereditary states. The emperor-*philosophe*'s political intentions were obvious: to integrate the Jews into the empire's economic life by giving them access to all sectors of activity. Agriculture was opened to them, though only as tenant farmers. Joseph, a committed physiocrat, viewed land as the primary source of wealth, and ownership of real estate as the basis of citizenship, and in this respect Jews remained segregated.

At the same time, Joseph II took a number of significant steps to hasten the Jews' integration through a program of cultural adaptation. Not only would Jews have access to all schools and universities in the empire, but alongside Jewish religious academies would be established "a school where, without any prejudice to their worship or faith, their youth will be educated according to the principles of the normal school."[30] His purpose was to break down the intellectual ghetto in

---

29 Cf. Dohm, 108–111. Cf. David Feuerwerker, *L'émancipation des Juifs en France de l'Ancien Régime à la fin du Second Empire* (Paris: Albin Michel, 1976), 166.

30 Young Jews would be sent to "central" Christian schools, where they were to be trained to become teachers of their coreligionists. Exams would be supervised by the director of the Christian schools, who would have the power to inspect the Jewish schools. Teaching materials used in these schools would be the same as in other schools, with the exception of religious subjects. In short, Joseph II created secular and compulsory elementary schools for Jews. Cf. Dohm, 198.

which Judaism had been shut away and protected throughout the centuries. To hasten the process of integration Jews were prohibited, after a two-year delay, to use a language other than the official languages of the empire when they drafted any legal or commercial document. These cultural measures were balanced by humanitarian provisions that abolished body tolls and rescinded laws requiring Jews to wear distinctive insignia on their clothing. But in order not to offend local anti-Jewish prejudices, Joseph II retained quotas that limited the Jewish population in each province or city; and he banned Jews from serving in public office or the army. They had to serve Austrian prosperity; the time had not yet come for them to share power or honors.

Despite its limitations and reservations the edict of 1782 seemed to the Jews of Europe, and especially to Jews in eastern France, the most daring and favorable proposals on their behalf ever implemented on the continent. Jean Bernoulli, the translator of Dohm's book, appended the edict's text to the 1782 French edition of the work.[31] In 1788 the Jews of Bordeaux cited the edict as an example to Louis XVI. Cerf-Berr would make use of it in his arguments on behalf of the Jews of the East. Thus advocates of Jewish emancipation in France found powerful cultural and political support in the evolution of ideas in Germany and in the laws of Austria.

THE METZ COMPETITION

In Enlightenment Europe, where ideas circulated among a small group of people, the debate soon reached France. Groundwork had already been laid there in 1775 when Pierre-Louis de Lacretelle,[32] the attorney for two Jewish merchants who brought suit against a guild in Thionville, Lorraine, declared to the court: "They [the Jews] have virtues as well as vices. Who will tell us that it is up to us to uproot or to cultivate one or the other? Let us open our towns to them. Let them spread out across our countryside … Let them learn to be

31 "This new law," he wrote, "gives the Jews a series of rights and privileges after having lost, so to speak, the custom of being treated as human beings and citizens. I think the imperial edict, which promises the Jews so beautiful an age, could not be placed in a more suitable place than at the end of this work." In Dohm, 107.

32 Pierre-Louis de Lacretelle (1751–1824) was an attorney and writer, and was associated with the Encyclopedists. A deputy in the Legislative Assembly and a founder of the Club des Feuillants, he later supported Bonaparte and was a deputy in the Corps législatif.

honorable, let them become truly French."[33] The Jewish merchants lost their suit; but their case aroused interest, if not popular support, thanks to this courtroom speech, which was printed and widely circulated.

In the autumn of 1782 the Prussian baron Anacharsis Cloots[34] engaged in a historical-theological controversy about the condition of the Jews with Court de Gibelin, spokesman of Paris's Protestants.[35] Like Dohm, Cloots emphasized the economic benefits France derived from the Jews' presence.

It is not surprising, therefore, that the Royal Society of Sciences and Arts of Metz (the Metz Academy) at its meeting of 25 August 1785 decided to sponsor an essay contest in 1787 on the topic, "Is there a way to make the Jews happier and more useful in France?" The winner's prize was to be "a gold medal worth 400 livres."[36]

The question posed was revealing because it implicitly recognized that the Jews' circumstances satisfied neither humanitarian demands nor the kingdom's interests. Each of the jury's five members held high municipal office;[37] they and the city's leaders were well acquainted with how events had shaped the Jewish community, and that knowledge prompted them as enlightened civic leaders to seek appropriate measures to remedy an appalling situation. Dohm had framed the issue in exactly that perspective, and discussion in Berlin's salons seemed to be finding an echo in France.

On 11 February 1786 the newspaper *Mercure de France* greeted the announcement of the competition with a favorable notice.[38] Nine

---

33 Pierre-Louis de Lacretelle, *Plaidoyers* (Brussels: n.p., 1775), 15–17.

34 Anacharsis Cloots (1755–1794) was a wealthy Prussian who settled in Paris in 1789. Calling himself "orator of the human race," he served as a deputy to the Convention. He was guillotined with the Hébertists on 25 March 1794.

35 Cf. [Anacharsis Cloots], *Lettre sur les Juifs à un ecclésiastique de mes amis, lue dans la séance publique du Musée de Paris, le 21 novembre 1782, par M. le B. d. C. D. V. D. G.* (Berlin: n.p., 1783). Cf. Poliakov, 166.

36 Cf. Feuerwerker, *L'émancipation...*, 61.

37 The five-person jury was composed of two councillors to the Parlement of Metz: Pierre-Louis Rœderer, who played a key role in this literary event, and baron Henri-Jacques de Poutet; a parliamentary attorney, Jean-François-Nicolas Blouet; a military officer, Jean-Gérard de Lacuée, comte de Cessac, and a treasury official, Jean Le Payen.

38 "A new question, interesting, worthy of the wisest *philosophie* and of true eloquence...No academy has yet dedicated its prize to so noble a disquisition." In Feuerwerker, *L'émancipation...*, 62.

essays, two of which were inspired by traditional anti-Judaism,[39] were submitted to the academy. The jury was divided in deciding about awarding a prize. On 25 August 1787 Pierre-Louis Rœderer,[40] in his report on the essays presented, cited two of the entries as promising: one by Claude-Antoine Thiéry,[41] an attorney in Nancy, and the other by Abbé Henri-Baptiste Grégoire, a secular priest in Embermesnil, near Lunéville. These works, Rœderer declared, demonstrated "a sound and sometimes sublime *philosophie* [rational and liberal attitudes]," but he did not judge them to be up to the academy's expectations. Accepting his conclusions, the Royal Society decided to award the prize after a new competition and set August 1788 as its new deadline. The three finalists chosen in 1787 resubmitted their essays, and three other entrants submitted works, among them a "Polish" Jew, Zalkind Hourwitz, who was the secretary-interpreter of Oriental languages of the Royal Library of Paris.[42] The jury hesitated and then awarded prizes to Hourwitz, Thiéry and Grégoire.

The new chairman of the competition, Jean Le Payen, a senior treasury official, emphasized that "the three essays [are] based on the same premises, supported by the same facts, and virtually the same

---

39 Maillecourt, the public prosecutor of the Parlement of Metz, suggested "transporting them en masse to the desert of la Guyane"; the Benedictine clergyman Dom Chais, "to confine them strictly to agriculture." Cf. Rita Hermon-Belot, preface to Henri-Baptiste Grégoire, *Essai sur la régénération physique, morale et politique des Juifs* (Paris: Flammarion, 1988), 11.

40 Pierre-Louis Rœderer (1754–1835) was advisor to the Parlement of Metz and an academician, deputy to the États Généraux and a moderate *patriote*, who was elected general-syndic (public prosecutor) of Paris in 1791. [*Patriote* was a designation given in 1789 to partisans of "new ideas," in contrast to *les aristocrates*; it was used during the Revolution as a synonym for "revolutionary." *Larousse de la langue française. Lexis.* (Paris: Librairie Larousse, 1977).—TRANSL.] On 10 August 1792 he encouraged the king to take refuge in the Assembly. Named a member of the Institute in June 1796, he threw in his lot with Bonaparte and was one of the actors of 18 Brumaire. Appointed to the Council of State, he ended his career in the Chamber of Peers under the July Monarchy.

41 Claude-Antoine Thiéry, *Dissertation sur cette question: Est-il des moyens de rendre les Juifs plus heureux et plus utiles en France?* in vol. 2 of *La Révolution française et l'émancipation des Juifs.* 8 vol. (Paris: Edhis [Éditions d'Histoire Sociale], 1968). Berr Isaac Berr, of Nancy, probably contributed to Thiéry's essay, preferring not to enter the competition under his own name. [Regarding Berr, see chap. 3, fn. 31, for additional biographical information.—TRANSL.]

42 Zalkind Hourwitz, *Apologie des Juifs en réponse à la question: Est-il des moyens de rendre les Juifs plus heureux et plus utiles in France?* in vol. 4 of *La Révolution française et l'émancipation des Juifs.* 8 vol. (Paris: Edhis [Éditions d'Histoire Sociale], 1968). [Zalkind Hourwitz was born in 1752 and died in 1812.—TRANSL.]

means [of analysis]." He added: "All the papers we have received, or nearly all, emphasize that our prejudices against the Jews are the primary cause of their degradation..."[43] Thiéry's treatise was published in November 1788; Grégoire's essay, *Sur la régénération physique, morale et politique des Juifs* [On the Physical, Moral and Political Regeneration of the Jews], in January 1789;[44] and Hourwitz's, in March. All received favorable, if guarded, receptions in the press.[45] The timing, however, was unfortunate, since political discussion was dominated by the king's decision to convoke the États Généraux. Still, the Metz competition influenced the course of Jewish emancipation by fueling growing interest within enlightened circles regarding the Jews' status. It led one man in particular, Abbé Grégoire, to take a leading role in favor of their emancipation. Elected to the États Généraux, he became the most zealous and best informed advocate of their cause.

ABBÉ GRÉGOIRE

Henri-Baptiste Grégoire was almost forty years old. His tall stature, regular features and warm nature won friends easily. Of modest origin—his father was an impoverished tailor—he had grown up in the countryside not far from Lunéville and discovered the wretched poverty of the Jews in his province. His first essay on the topic, published in 1779, "on the means to restore the Jewish people and lead them to happiness everywhere," was evidence of his long-standing concern about their suffering and of his desire to alleviate their situation. After becoming curé of Embermesnil, he made friends with the region's Jewish notables, notably with Isaiah Berr Bing, of Metz, a man of learning and conviction who deeply felt the injustices imposed on Jews, and who provided Grégoire with a wealth of information about Jewish laws, history and customs.[46] In 1785, when a synagogue was opened in Lunéville, Grégoire delivered a sermon

43 In Feuerwerker, *L'émancipation...*, 119.

44 Cf. Grégoire, *Essai...* (Paris: Stock, 1988), with a preface by Robert Badinter.

45 Cf. D. Feuerwerker, *L'émancipation...*, 135–138. An English translation of Grégoire's essay appeared in London in 1789.

46 Cf. P. Latrice, "L'Abbé Grégoire, Ami de tous les hommes," and "La régénération des Juifs," in *Mélanges de science religieuse*, 36, 3 (September 1979): 149, published by Facultés catholiques, Lille. [Grégoire was born in 1750 and died in 1831. As a secular priest, he held ecclesiastical office, but one from which he derived no

in one of the city's churches expressing his feelings of brotherhood toward Jews. A follower of Enlightenment currents, he knew of Mendelssohn's reputation and literary works and had read Dohm's book. His knowledge of Judaism and Jewish history was considerable for a Catholic priest of his era. Most of all, his broad spirit was deeply moved by the predicament of these men and women, children of the same God to whom Jesus had prayed. He considered it an insult to the Gospel and to justice that they were outcasts in a country in which they had lived for centuries, confined in ghettos of stone and contempt. Grégoire emerged to support, with more passion and constancy than any other public figure, the Jews' cause, just as he would defend, with Condorcet, Brissot, Mirabeau and La Fayette, the cause of blacks in his capacity as a member of both the Society of Friends of Blacks and as a deputy to the Constituent Assembly and the Convention.

Of the three essays awarded the Academy of Metz's prize, Grégoire's was the only one to have real influence on a portion of public opinion. His political career generated keen interest in his writing, and his essay was a noteworthy event for that era: an appeal on the Jews' behalf written by a Catholic priest. The other two prize winners were a Jewish scholar, Zalkind Hourwitz, and Claude-Antoine Thiéry, a liberal attorney. It was hardly extraordinary that a Jew would support his fellow Jews, or that an attorney defended victims of injustice as part of his professional calling. But a curé who openly and boldly sided with the Jews surprised and moved public opinion. In the temporal world the Catholic Church had branded Jews a deicide people, stiff-necked and obstinate in their refusal to acknowledge Jesus' divine nature. Anti-Judaism in Europe had its source in Catholic tradition, even if economic motives had superseded religious anathemas.

Nonetheless Grégoire was sometimes harsh when writing about the people whose cause he championed. He was outspoken in refuting accusations of ritual crimes, which had been attributed to Jews for centuries: slaughtering Christian children at the time of Jewish holidays, or poisoning wells and causing great epidemics. But he also described Jews as being "pale-faced, hook-nosed, pointy-chinned, with strongly pronounced constrictor muscles around the mouth... Nearly

revenue generated by an endowment. Isaiah Berr Bing was born in 1758 and died in 1805.—TRANSL.]

Rosselin édit. Quai Voltaire, 21.

Lith Auguste Bry, 154, r. du Bac.

Grégoire.

+ Grégoire

The Jews are members of this universal family which must establish brotherhood among all peoples.
— ABBÉ HENRI-BAPTISTE GRÉGOIRE

all have sparse beards... Most seem old at an early age... They always exude a foul odor..."⁴⁷ Similarly, he denounced their usury in
Alsace: "One weeps with pity, one shudders with indignation at the
sight of the evils the Jews cause in this province."⁴⁸ Nor was Thiéry
much kinder: "They present themselves to us with a brow covered
with disgrace and a soul often blemished by vice."⁴⁹

Yet both were certain about the causes of such distasteful circumstances and activities. "It is we who must be accused of these
crimes for which the Jews are so justly blamed... It is we who force
them into it," Thiéry wrote.⁵⁰ Grégoire agreed: "Their usury follows
immediately and necessarily from the oppression that makes them
moan. The height of inconsistency is to criticize them for crimes after
forcing them to commit them... "⁵¹ He emphasized the Jews' family
virtues, the respect they showed their parents, the love they bore for
their children. The cause was clear to Grégoire: the failings of the
Jews were the poisoned fruits of exclusionary laws and hatred that
Christians had heaped on them during their dispersion.⁵² If these odious laws were abolished, these barriers demolished, the evil would
disappear with its cause.

Grégoire expected emancipation to lead to assimilation. He
scorned the Talmud, which he described as a "vast reservoir..., vir-

47 Grégoire, *Essai...* [Badinter edition], 57–58.
48 Ibid., 84. Grégoire was sometimes carried away by his own highly declama-
tory rhetoric: "Residents of Sundgau, answer if you still have the strength: Is not the
condition to which several Jews have reduced you a frightening picture? They have
left you only your arms, emaciated through pain and hunger; and if you still remain
in rags and tatters to bear witness to your misery and to soak them in your tears, it is
because the Jewish usurer has scorned to wrest them from you."
49 Cf. Poliakov, 170. Lopes Dubec, a delegate who represented Bordeaux's Jews
in discussions with Malesherbes in 1788, and later before the National Assembly
in 1790, wrote on 15 September 1789, regarding the Metz competition's laureates:
"They have presented so hideous a portrait of the vices with which they [the Jews]
are charged that it seems more likely to increase than diminish the prejudices that
hold sway against them [the Jews], above all for the bulk of readers who are permitted
to easily escape the causes which exonerate them for not seeing the things they condemn...", in Zosa Szajkowski, "La délégation des Juifs de Bordeaux à la commission
Malesherbes en 1788 et à l'Assemblée nationale de 1790," *Zion*, 18 (1951): 33ff.
50 Poliakov, 170.
51 Grégoire, *Essai...* [Badinter edition], 56.
52 "Let us speak only with horror of St. Bartholomew [the massacre of French
Calvinist Protestants on 24 August 1572 during France's "wars of religion."—
TRANSL.]. But the Jews were victims of two hundred times as many acts just as tragic,
and who were the murderers?" Grégoire, *Essai...* [Badinter edition], 33ff.

tually a cesspool in which are gathered the fevered confusions of the human mind."[53] He wanted Yiddish to disappear, along with all provincial dialects. He would open the doors of colleges and universities to Jews. He advocated mixed marriages and conversion to Catholicism—through gentle persuasion—of large numbers of Jews.[54] Even as he supported religious freedom, Grégoire's wish remained that the Jews would gradually melt into the French community by joining its dominant religion. Still, while he awaited fulfillment of this distant hope, natural for a Catholic priest, Grégoire concluded his essay with a passionate appeal to Christians, in favor of the Jews: "Authors of their vices, may you become authors of their virtues, discharging your debt and that of your ancestors...The Jews are members of this universal family which must establish brotherhood among all peoples."[55] As early as 1788 the abbé spoke the republican language of 1793.

MIRABEAU AND THE JEWS

While the Academy of Metz's essay competition was underway, Honoré-Gabriel Riqueti, comte de Mirabeau, decided to have his say about the matter. Mirabeau had been in Berlin during 1785, had participated in salons where Christian partisans of the *Aufklärung* and Jewish supporters of the *Haskalah* gathered, and had made friends with Dohm. He was attracted to Dohm's thinking, and even more to Mendelssohn's. By temperament and experience Mirabeau was sensitive to injustice. He also calculated how much political interest could be generated by the issue of improving the Jews' conditions, and the benefits he could derive from aligning himself with those in the Enlightenment camp who were the Jews' champions. In 1787, when he returned from Berlin, Mirabeau published *Sur Moses Mendelssohn et sur la réforme politique des Juifs* [On Moses Mendelssohn and on Political Reform of the Jews], a slapdash essay that essentially re-

53 Ibid., 74. Cf. Rita Hermon-Belot, preface to Grégoire, *Essai...*, 25. Cf. Montesquieu: "Among this crowd of rabbis who wrote, not one had a little sparkle of genius," cited by G. Weill, "Un texte de Montesquieu sur le judaïsme," *Revue des études juives* 49 (1904): 154.

54 "Complete religious liberty granted to the Jews will be a great advance step in order to reform them and, I dare say, to convert them. For truth is only persuasive in so far as it is sweet." Grégoire, *Essai...*, [Badinter edition], 132.

55 Ibid., 175.

stated Dohm's and Mendelssohn's themes. "Do you want the Jews," wrote Mirabeau, "to become better people and useful citizens? Then banish from society all discrimination that degrades them; open up to them all means of subsistence and acquisition. Instead of forbidding them to engage in agriculture, the professions and mechanical arts, encourage them to devote themselves to these activities ... Place Jewish schools on the same footing as Christian schools in everything that does not concern religion. If, in a word, they are put and supported in possession of all the rights of citizens, before long this equitable arrangement will place them among those who are the most useful members of the State..."[56]

Mirabeau recognized the Jews' right to freedom of worship and declared that they ought to be allowed to "live and be judged according to their own laws."[57] On that latter point he differed with Mendelssohn and supported Jewish demands for communal autonomy that would allow Jews to preserve their special laws and religious jurisdictions. His advocacy of both emancipation and autonomy may have been a result of too rapid an analysis of the issues or political realism, of opportunism or reflection. Whatever the case, he noted in a letter to Mme de Saillant on 8 June 1787: "Remember that Mendelssohn's preface was solely intended to address a German audience and circumstances"[58]—which suggests that Mirabeau may have thought that France and French society could accommodate both Jewish civil equality and Jewish autonomy.

Mirabeau's essay was useful because it introduced German Enlightenment ideas about Jewish emancipation to a French audience, especially after the French translation of Dohm's work had been seized and destroyed. It was significant that on the eve of the Revolution a publicist of Mirabeau's stature and ability supported the theory of emancipation by affirming that "The Jews, considered as human beings and as citizens, have been corrupted so long as they have been

56 Mirabeau, 89. [In his youth Honoré-Gabriel Riqueti, comte de Mirabeau (1749-1791) had been incarcerated, at his father's request, in the Château d'If, where Alexandre Dumas *père*'s fictional hero, the comte de Monte-Cristo, was wrongfully imprisoned. Perhaps this explains why Mirabeau *fils* was "sensitive to injustice."—TRANSL.]

57 Ibid.

58 Cf. F. Dreyfus, "Comment les Juifs sont devenus citoyens français," *Revue politique et parlementaire* 25 (July-September 1900): 57.

MIRABEAU.

An infallible way to make [the Jews] better is to make them happier.
       — HONORÉ-GABRIEL RIQUETI, COMTE DE MIRABEAU

refused the rights to be both,"⁵⁹ and that "An infallible way to make them better is to make them happier."⁶⁰ In his own way and fashion Mirabeau, too, had responded to the essay question posed by the Royal Academy of Metz.

THE MALESHERBES COMMISSION

There is a logic of liberty, a dynamic to toleration. A century after the revocation of the Edict of Nantes, when Louis XIV deprived French Protestants of their rights, the monarchy could no longer continue to do so. Public opinion, hostile or indifferent to the Jews, looked upon the situation of France's "reformed" Christians as a distasteful relic of an era when fanaticism and intolerance had triumphed. Benevolent by nature, Louis XVI leaned toward ending the exclusion from civil society decreed by his grandfather. Chrétien-Guillaume de Lamoignon de Malesherbes published two memoranda in 1785 and 1786, in which he proposed principles for radical transforming French Protestants' status by acknowledging their civil rights.

Brought into the government in 1787 as minister of state, Malesherbes set about implementing the reform for which he had laid the foundations. An "edict concerning all those who do not profess the Catholic religion," issued on 28 November 1787, restored the civil rights of Protestants. Their marriages, births and deaths could be recorded by local magistrates; their families were, from then on, legitimate.⁶¹ The spirit of toleration and liberty had won a great victory. But did the edict also apply to the Jews? Since its title referred to non-Catholics without qualification, it seemed impossible to exclude Jews from its provisions. In addition, Article 37 stated: "Moreover, we do not intend, by this edict, to deviate from concessions made...to Lutherans settled in Alsace, or to other subjects to whom the exercise of a religion other than the Catholic religion is permitted in some provinces or cities of our realm..."⁶²

59 Mirabeau, 57.
60 Ibid., 81.
61 Chrétien-Guillaume de Lamoignon de Malesherbes, *Mémoire sur le mariage des protestans en 1785* (n.p., n.d.); Malesherbes, *Second mémoire sur le mariage des protestans en 1786* (London: n.p., 1787). Cf. Feuerwerker, *L'émancipation....*, 145–155. [Malesherbes (born 1721) defended Louis XVI during his trial. He was guillotined in 1794.—TRANSL.]
62 In Feuerwerker, *L'émancipation...*, 155–156.

The Parlement of Paris registered the edict without reservations on 18 January 1788. Most other provincial parlements, as well as Colmar's Supreme Council, followed suit. But the Parlement of Metz, center of the largest Jewish community in France, registered it only "on the condition that, insofar as concerns the Jews within its jurisdiction, nothing will change."[63] The Parlement of Toulouse made strong protests to Louis XVI. The edict did not settle the Jews' status.

In the spring of 1788, confronted with continuing anti-Jewish agitation in Alsace, the king entrusted Malesherbes with the task of drafting proposals to address the civil rights of France's Jews.[64] Malesherbes seemed to be the proper person to undertake this mission, given his spirit of tolerance, his work on the statute concerning Protestants, and his interest in the Jews' history. Mirabeau had sent him, along with his 1787 essay, Bernoulli's French translation of Dohm's work, and Malesherbes corresponded with Abbé Grégoire on the topic.[65] His library contained more than seventy volumes of works about the Jews,[66] and he had served as private secretary to Pierre-Louis de Lacretelle, the attorney who in 1775 had pleaded brilliantly on behalf of the lawsuit brought by Thionville's Jewish merchants. Finally, Malesherbes turned for assistance to Pierre-Louis Rœderer, advisor to the Parlement of Metz and chairman of the Royal Academy of Metz's essay competition of 1787; Guy-Jean-Baptiste Target, the famous legal expert who had defended France's Protestants; and Dupré de Saint-Maur, the former intendant of Guyenne, who was friendly with leaders of Bordeaux's Jewish community.

Malesherbes revealed the fundamental outline of his thoughts

---

63 Ibid., 157.

64 This mission was commonly expressed by the remark, probably apocryphal, attributed by Rœderer to Louis XVI: "Malesherbes, you made yourself a Protestant; now I'm making you a Jew—take charge of them." Cf. Le Journal de Paris, 5 nivôse an IV; and Patrick Girard, La Révolution française..., 214. In a more verifiable fashion, Rœderer wrote to his father on 18 April 1788: "M. de Malesherbes was charged by the king to improve the condition of the Jews. M. de Malesherbes engaged me to work with him on ways to ameliorate the lot of this nation. I spent five hours in a row with him on Monday. We have decided on a program and several bases of work...," P[ierre]-L[ouis] Rœderer, Œuvres. 8 vol. (Paris: Firmin Didot Frères, 1853-59), 7:636.

65 Grégoire, Mémoires de Grégoire, ancien évêque de Blois, député de l'Assemblée Constituente et à la Convention nationale, sénateur, membre de l'Institut. 2 vol. (Paris: Ambroise Dupont, 1837), 1:301.

66 Feuerwerker, L'émancipation..., 159.

about the Jews when in 1788 he wrote an advisory opinion addressed
to the King's Council regarding a question that had arisen when
wealthy Jews purchased seigneurial estates:[67] did Jews, by virtue of
purchasing these properties, acquire the right to participate in provincial assemblies? He began by noting that the position of Jews in
the kingdom "is in many respects different from that of other non-
Catholics"—namely, Protestants. Then he observed that "a strong
hatred exists within the hearts of most Christians against all of the
Jewish nation, hatred based on the memory of their ancestors' crime
[the charge of deicide], and strengthened by the fact that Jews everywhere devote themselves to the kinds of trade that Christians regard
as causing their ruin."[68] Declaring this hostility to be deplorable,
Malesherbes then shifted his focus to what he viewed as a crucial
policy issue:

> This nation has always remained a foreign nation in the
> midst of all nations: an *imperium in imperio*. And I believe it is
> their policy to remain apart from all citizens of the countries in
> which they live, despite the daily disagreements it creates among
> people. They have become, moreover, a power independent of
> all others on earth and, in some instances, perhaps dangerous
> to those among whom they live, by virtue of the close relations
> among all Jews in the world.[69]

And he concluded: "I have not yet plumbed far enough into
the depths of this matter to dare to say whether a nation thus constituted can become useful or whether it can only be a danger."[70]
For Malesherbes, the Jews in France were a group that, by virtue
of its special laws, constituted a state within a state—*imperium in
imperio*—linked to other Jewish "nations" dispersed throughout the

---

67 "Avis de M. de Malesherbes," Archives nationales, Fonds Tocqueville, documents 41–42. [Regarding Guy-Jean-Baptiste Target, see chap. 7, fn. 75.—*Transl.*]

68 Ibid.

69 Ibid., 3 (underlined in the manuscript). Previously, in his *Second mémoire sur le
mariage des protestans en 1786*, Malesherbes had written: "If, during the period of the
Edict of Nantes, Protestants in France were an *imperium in imperio*, the Jews are an
imperium in imperio throughout the entire world." And he added: "It is not within the
sovereign's power to destroy in a short time this loathing for the Jewish nation, which
is no doubt carried too far." In Malino, op. cit., 89.

70 "Avis...," 3.

world. A man of the Enlightenment, tolerant and a lover a liberty, he was also, like his friend Turgot, a senior servant of the state, and it was from this political perspective that he approached his royal assignment.

Leaders of Bordeaux's "Portuguese" Jewish community were the first to be advised of Malesherbes's deliberations, probably through Dupré de Saint-Maur's correspondence with Moïse Gradis. [71] On 22 March 1788 Gradis drew Dupré's attention to the special circumstances of the "Portuguese"; on 8 April he emphasized the deep differences separating "Portuguese" from "German" Jews. The Bordeaux Jews, increasingly concerned about the direction of Malesherbes's thinking, deemed it necessary to arrange a meeting with the minister in order to plead their cause in person. On 3 April they deliberated among themselves and decided to dispatch Lopes Dubec [72] and Abraham Furtado the elder [73] to Paris as their representatives. Their goal was specific: to obtain through quiet negotiation the rights granted to non-Catholics in the edict of tolerance and—above all—to preserve the special status of Bordeaux's Jewish community.

After consulting with Mardochée Lopès Fonseca, a representative of Bayonne's Jewish community, the Bordeaux delegates arrived in Paris on 15 April and were given an official welcome by Dupré de Saint-Maur, who arranged for them to meet with Malesherbes. On

---

71   Cf. Feuerwerker, *L'émancipation...*, 159–161.

72   Salomon Lopes Dubec (1743–1835) came from a family of "Portuguese" shipowners that settled in Bordeaux during the seventeenth century, and was a wealthy merchant.

73   Abraham Furtado (1756–1817), known as Furtado l'aîné [Furtado the elder], was a merchant and one of the outstanding figures in Bordeaux's Jewish community. He was elected as one of the ninety electors of the *sénéchaussée* [an administrative and judicial district of a royal agent in southern France during the Ancien Régime — TRANSL.] of Guyenne in 1789, and was a *patriote*. In 1781 he founded, with Vergniaud and Gensonné, the Society of Friends of the Constitution in Bordeaux. A Girondist, he was elected to the General Council of the Bordeaux Commune. He survived the Terror in hiding. In 1797 he was named administrator of the municipality of Bordeaux. A member of the electoral college during the Empire, he presided over the "Great Sanhedrin" [an assembly of Jewish notables convened in October 1806 by Napoléon—TRANSL.]. He opposed the decrees of 17 March 1808 concerning the status of the Jews. During the Hundred Days, he refused to serve as assistant mayor. Decorated by Louis XVIII, he was named, after the Second Restoration, deputy mayor of Bordeaux. Cf. Jean Cavignac, *Dictionnaire du judaïsme bordelais aux XVIIIᵉ et XIXᵉ siècles: biographies, généalogies, professions, institutions.* (Bordeaux: Archives départementales de la Gironde, 1987), 46–48.

the basis of a long conversation, the Bordelais were able to gauge the minister of state's goal: a single law that granted civil status to all the Jews of the realm. Jews were to be integrated into guilds according to their occupations, and they would be able to form associations, but only for religious purposes. The way in which Jewish communities had traditionally been organized and governed, by syndics and rabbis, amounted to a "nation" within the nation, and had to disappear. Moreover, if Jews wished to have the same status as other royal subjects, France's Jews could no longer demand to be treated differently on the basis of whether they were "Portuguese" or "German." Malesherbes's objective was clear: the time had come to integrate the Jews. But the state would not sanction an *imperium in imperio* and would not accommodate anything different about the Jews, other than their religious faith.

Malesherbes expressed his thinking plainly in one of the questions he handed to the "Portuguese" representatives:[74] "Could it not be wished that they might seek to blend themselves with the other inhabitants of the kingdom, maintaining only those differences which they deem so essential to their religion such as would be impossible to do without?"[75]

The "Portuguese" responded sharply. They pointed out to Dupré de Saint-Maur that "to wish to jumble together and unite the different *corporations* [social groups] into a single entity would be to create an incoherent and grotesque collection of people fundamentally different in their customs, languages, occupations and prejudices, not to mention a mass of other nuances which separate them."[76] They agreed that a single law ought to define the status of all Jews.

---

74 *Mémoire remis par les députés juifs de Bordeaux à Monsieur de Malesherbes, ministre d'État.* Introduction and notes by Jean Cavignac. (Bordeaux: Archives départementales de la Gironde, 1988).

75 Malino, 83.

76 Malino, 78–79. On 8 May 1788 the syndics of Bordeaux's Jewish community wrote to their delegates: "You know too well the incompatibility of customs, habits and ways of life of other Jews with ours to not to make it known, as you should... You can show that they alter [religious dogma] with many ridiculous ceremonies and rabbinic ideas, and they are in some ways so much enslaved to all sorts of superstitions or boycotts that these have reduced them further in our eyes to the point that we never permit alliances with them through marriage." In Théophile Malvezin, *Histoire des Juifs de Bordeaux* (Bordeaux: C. Lefebvre, 1875), 253. "Lettre du 22 mai 1788 de Lopes Dubec et Furtado l'aîné aux syndics de la communauté de Bordeaux," in Zosa Szajkowski, "La délégation...," *Zion* 18 (1951): 29.

Their fundamental goal was to ensure their survival as distinct, organized communities so that the "Jewish nations" of southwestern France could remain vital and autonomous.

The Jews of Alsace and Lorraine were also quick to respond. Cerf-Berr, syndic of Alsace's Jews, and Berr Isaac Berr, syndic of Lorraine's, commissioned memoranda for Malesherbes. For Berr in Lorraine, as for Cerf-Berr in Alsace or Furtado and Lopes Dubec in Bordeaux, "regeneration" of the Jews was a matter of preserving their communities' institutions, which they controlled. Berr Isaac Berr's attitude toward the poor was similar to that of the wealthy "Portuguese." He was haunted by the idleness of Jewish beggars and planned to establish "houses of correction and discipline for . . . idle Jews." Moreover, he wrote, "In ten years, no Jew will be able to marry who has not previously acquired some sort of business, art or craft, as a plowman or professor of theology, or other learning for which he can prove his qualifications."[77] Therefore he advocated an education program inspired by Joseph II's edict of 1781. Extolling the virtues of integration through education, he hoped that public schools everywhere would be opened to Jews, and charity-supported workshops would teach children of the poor "all the crafts and mechanical arts society needs."[78] He loathed beggars and dreaded unauthorized immigrants who became burdens on the community— that is to say, its notables. These great notables wanted to improve the conditions and status of the Jews; but they also wished to preserve institutions that guaranteed both the maintenance of Judaism and their personal power over their communities.

Malesherbes also consulted Jacob Lazare and Trenel, the representatives of Paris's Jews, for their views.[79] When, at the end of April, Malesherbes, along with Dupré de Saint-Maur, met in person with the "Portuguese" delegates, the minister of state presented them with a thirteen-point questionnaire intended to elicit infor-

77 Ibid.

78 Berr Isaac Berr, *Réflexions sur l'enregistrement de l'édit des non-catholiques au Parlement de Metz, 10 mars 1788, et projet pour rendre les Juifs plus utiles et plus heureux en France.* Archives nationales, 154, AP 2, 135. Cf. M. Lemalet, "L'émancipation des Juifs de Lorraine à travers l'œuvre de Berr Isaac Berr," in Daniel Tollet, ed., *Politique et religion dans le judaïsme moderne: des communautés à l'émancipation. Actes de colloque tenu en Sorbonne les 18–19 novembre 1986.* (Paris: Presses de l'université Paris-Sorbonne, 1987), 68.

79 Cf. Feuerwerker, *L'émancipation…*, 161–162.

mation and perspectives about the conditions of Jews throughout Europe and in France. On 17 June 1788 Furtado and Lopes Dubec (assisted by a Jewish attorney and historian from Bordeaux, Louis Francia de Beaufleury, who resided in Paris) replied with a heavily documented and strongly argued memorandum in which they attempted to clarify their point of view.[80] On the eve of the Revolution, France's "Portuguese" Jews asserted their uniqueness, noting in particular their custom (in contrast to that of the "Germans") of integrating themselves with other inhabitants everywhere in Europe ("a Portuguese Jew is English in England and French in France, but a German Jew is everywhere German in his customs, which he rarely discards.")[81] Further, they stated that each social group should be allowed to maintain its own structures ("the law to be adopted ought not to forbid to each *corporation* or congregation its special system of governance..."), and they asked that no Jew be able to settle in a city in France without a favorable vote by a community meeting, so that the community could protect itself against an influx of impoverished Jews or "Germans."[82] On the question of the Jews' civil status, Furtado and Dubec wished it to be as similar as possible to the status Christians enjoyed: freedom to engage in all occupations, the right of all Jews to own land and houses, and admission to secondary schools

---

80 The memorandum consisted of 106 pages, divided into three chapters: 1. History of the Jews of Europe; 2. History of the settlement of Jews in Europe; 3. Views of the syndics of the Jewish nation regarding the type of constitution that the Jews particularly wish to have in France. Cf. *Mémoire remis....* Cf. Malino, 80–89.

81 *Mémoire présenté par M.M. Lopes Dubec père et Furtado l'aîné*, 17–18, in Malino, 80–81. The response of the "Portuguese" to Malesherbes's question concerning usury is revealing: "Their [the 'German' Jews'] opinions and customs are very different from those of the Portuguese Jews, and any plan to bring them together is impossible." Cf., Cavignac, op. cit. An anecdote told by Rœderer illustrates the very different behavior of the Bordelais Gradis and the Alsatian Cerf-Berr: "Gradis lived the life of a man of the world. Cerf-Berr, a rigid observer of the most meticulous observances dictated by Mosaic law, abstained from prohibited foods, did not eat with any Christian, took care not to engage in the least work on the sabbath ... One day when Malesherbes attempted to argue against Cerf-Berr's position on this subject [dining with Christians], Cerf-Berr undertook to prove to Malesherbes that the Bordeaux Jews' standards were lax, and held forth on Mosaic doctrine with stern enthusiasm. He irritated Malesherbes extremely, as one can believe. The next day I went to see him; he recounted this meeting and ended with these words: 'The king told me he made me a Jew, and now Cerf-Berr wants to make me a Jansenist: I no longer know whom to listen to.' " In Roger Levylier, *Notes et documents concernant la famille Cerf-Berr, recueillis par un de ses membres*. 3 vol. (Paris: Plon, 1902–1906), 1:28–29.

82 Cf. Malino, 86–88.

and universities, chambers of commerce and municipal offices.

The memorandum submitted by the "German" Jews has not survived; but their requests were probably not much different in 1788 from those set forth by Cerf-Berr in his *Mémoire sur l'état des Juifs en Alsace*,[83] addressed to the Royal Council of State, and which Dohm had reproduced as an addendum to his book: economic freedom, equality of taxation, and preservation of the Jewish communities' internal structures and rabbinic jurisdiction.[84] In sum, the Jews desired emancipation, but rejected integration. In doing so, they opposed Malesherbes's plans to improve their lot and pave the way to civil equality, as well as to make the kingdom's "Jewish nations" vanish.

During the summer of 1788, as the monarchy's political and financial crisis again worsened, Malesherbes's attention was absorbed with editing his *Mémoire sur l'état présent de la Nation* [Memorandum on the Current State of the Nation]. The Royal Council of State informed Furtado and Lopes Dubec that consideration of the Jews' status had been deferred. On 3 July the two representatives started back to Bordeaux. On 5 July the king announced his decision to convene the États Généraux. From then on, the fate of the Jews would be played out on another stage.

---

83 Cf. Dohm, 113–138.

84 Cf. along the same lines, the memorandum of an anonymous Jew from the eastern provinces, found in Rœderer's private papers, quoted in Feuerwerker, *L'émancipation...*, 187–189.

CHAPTER 3

ELECTIONS TO THE ÉTATS GÉNÉRAUX

THE ELECTORAL ASSEMBLIES AND THE JEWS

THE CONVOCATION OF THE ÉTATS GÉNÉRAUX AND THE KING'S IN-
vitation to all of his subjects to participate in drafting *cahiers de
doléances* [registers of grievances], posed a new question: Would the
Jews be able to participate in the assemblies that elected representatives to the États Généraux? According to the "General Rule" of 24
January 1789, signed by Pierre-Charles-Laurent de Villedeuil, gener-
al-secretary of the King's Household, "all inhabitants . . . born French
or naturalized, twenty-five years or older, domiciled and included in
the tax rolls"[1] were recognized as qualified to be electors. No mention was made of religion.

But were the Jews settled in France French?

The texts regulating their status in various localities throughout
the kingdom were complex, but the answer appeared to be clear: the
kingdom's Jews were *regnicoles*—in other words, subjects of the king.
They had been banished in perpetuity by Charles VI in 1394, whose
edict had been renewed in 1615 by a royal proclamation, and since
then they had never officially and collectively had the right to reside
in France. But each Jewish community had its own unique, specific
status. The "Portuguese" Jews of southern France could refer to their
lettres patentes, which they possessed since 1550 and which had been
renewed by all successive French sovereigns.[2] The Jewish communities in Alsace, Lorraine and the Trois-Évêchés had become subjects
of the king when those territories were incorporated into France. In
his courtroom speech of 1775 on behalf of the Jewish merchants of
Thionville, Lacretelle asserted: "There, where we have offered them

---

1 On the regulation, cf. Armand Brette, *Recueil de documents relatifs à la convocation
des États généraux de 1789*. 4 vol. (Paris: Imprimerie nationale, 1894-1915), 1:76–77.

2 *Lettres patentes du Roi, confirmatives des privilèges dont les Juifs portugais jouissent depuis
1550, données à Versailles au mois de juin 1776* (Paris: Imprimerie Destoupe, 1781).

asylum, they are residents, they are subjects of the king. They live under our laws, protected by them. They pledge fidelity to the government. They pay taxes to it. They have none of the characteristics that have marked the foreigners among us."[3] True, the Jewish population in the eastern provinces had grown through steady immigration; but the newcomers had clustered in existing communities and had been duly authorized to stay by the local nobility in return for payment of taxes. The *lettres patentes* of July 1784, which governed the status of Alsace's Jews, explicitly distinguished them from foreigners, who were slated for expulsion. When in January 1784 Louis XVI abolished the body tax affecting Jews, he justified his action by stating that he refused to continue imposing a tax which humiliated "any of his subjects." Legally, therefore, the Jews of the East were no more "German" than those of the Southwest were "Portuguese"; such terms denoted origins, not nationalities. France's Jews were *regnicoles*, but burdened with a special status that rendered them subjects with restricted rights and limited basic legal qualifications. These circumstances led to debate about whether their status as French nationals necessarily entitled them to elect representatives to the États Généraux.

The Jews supported a favorable interpretation, which generated various degrees of resistance that were clearly related to how well they were integrated into the everyday lives of local populations.

Jews in the Southwest overcame resistance and participated in the elections, although not without encountering difficulties. On 28 February 1789 the governor of Bordeaux and the city's mayor informed Versailles that "the other *corporations* are registering the greatest of opposition to admitting the Jews, and wish to have withdrawn the invitation previously sent to the *corporation* of Portuguese Jews."[4] They noted, however, that Bordeaux's Jews had "letters of naturalization which appear to entitle them to participate in the convocation."[5] The dispute was submitted to the archbishop, Champion de Cicé,[6] and to the governor for a decision. The verdict appears to

---

3   Cited by Lignac, "Les Juifs et la convocation des États Généraux," *Revue des études juives*, 64 (1912): 247.

4   In Maurice Liber, "Les Juifs et la convocation des États Généraux," *Revue des études juives* 63-66 (1912-1913): 252.

5   Ibid.

6   Jérôme-Marie Champion de Cicé (1735–1810), archbishop of Bordeaux, was a member of the Assembly of Notables in 1787, a deputy representing the Clergy in the États Généraux, and minister of justice from 3 August 1789 until 20 November

have been favorable, for the "Portuguese" were invited to take part in the electoral assemblies. David Gradis, among the wealthiest of the city's Jews, failed to become a deputy by only four votes;[7] but among the electors chosen to name deputies were four Jews.[8] Had Gradis won, his election as a representative of one of the largest cities of the kingdom would have been emancipation incarnate: living proof that the Jews were French, royal subjects and citizens of the nation, like all other subjects. Even without the success of the four Jewish electors, the Jews of Bordeaux would have been able to welcome the elections' results. On 18 April 1789 one of their notables wrote to Dupré de Saint-Maur, a member of the Malesherbes Commission: "That which crowned our satisfaction, Monsieur, is Article Twenty-five of the regulation for convocation of the États Généraux, which makes us an essential part of the State."[9] The citizenship of the "Portuguese" of Bordeaux was thus acknowledged even before the opening of the États Généraux.

The Jews of Bourg-Saint-Esprit, in the region of Bayonne, also succeeded in pressing their claims despite sharp opposition to their participation in electoral assemblies. The fact that they accounted for nearly a third of the local populace may have been a decisive factor in their favor. When local authorities in the *sénéchaussée* of Tartas refused to admit them to the assemblies, they lodged a complaint with the king's representative, baron de Laluge, who in turn wrote on 14 March to the minister of justice, Barentin:[10] "My opinion, Your Grace, is that the Jews' complaint is justified. Article Twenty-five of the regulations does not appear to me to leave any doubt in this regard; they enjoy civil existence in the kingdom, and they exercise all the rights of citizens... Finally, they pay taxes like any other citizen.

1790. He refused to take the oath to support the Civil Constitution of the Clergy and emigrated in 1791. He returned to France in 1802, was named archbishop of Aix, and made a count of the Empire.

7   Cf. Liber, 249, and David Feuerwerker, *L'émancipation des Juifs en France de l'Ancien Régime à la fin du Second Empire* (Paris: Albin Michel, 1976), 243.

8   They were Furtado the elder, Lopes Dubec (both members of the delegation sent the previous year to meet with Malesherbes), Azevedo and David Gradis.

9   Théophile Malvezin, *Histoire des Juifs de Bordeaux* (Bordeaux: C. Lefebvre, 1875), 247.

10   Charles-Louis-François-de-Paul Barentin (1738–1819) was president of the Tax Court, a member of the Assembly of Notables, and minister of justice until 16 July 1789. He emigrated during the Revolution, but returned during the reign of Louis XVIII, who named him honorary chancellor.

Thus they have an interest in the matter and are justified in wishing to be invited..."[11]

The minister of justice received a delegation of "Portuguese" from Bayonne, "as properly as possible,"[12] and agreed with their complaint—with one reservation. It was, he said, pointless for the invitation to be announced publicly in the synagogue, since it had already been announced in the church, and that should be sufficient. To prevent any incidents, given "the strong, natural antipathy that exists between this nation and Christians, and the latter against it,"[13] the Jews were permitted to hold their own assembly and to appoint their own representatives. Four members "of the Jewish nation of Bourg-Saint-Esprit" were thus named by their fellow Jews to participate as electors to choose *députés de bailliage* for the États Généraux.[14] On 22 April 1789 the assembly of the Third Estate of the *sénéchaussée* of Tartas, chaired by baron de Batz, the *grand sénéchal*, reduced this number to two: David Silveyra, representative of the "Portuguese" Jews in Paris, who was well-known in the capital's political circles, and Lopes Fonseca, who during the previous year had represented the Jews of Bourg-Saint-Esprit in discussions with Malesherbes.[15]

Since the Jews of Avignon and the Comtat Venaissin were under the authority of the pope, not the king, and since the other Jews of southern France were not part of legally sanctioned communities, they were ineligible to participate in the electoral assemblies. Nonetheless, when the États Généraux convened at Versailles on 5 May 1789, the "Portuguese Jewish nations" appeared to have won their objective from the royal government: their members were received at Versailles as subjects who possessed rights equal to those of His Majesty's Christian subjects.

The "German" Jews of the eastern provinces confronted extremely different circumstances. In certain *bailliages*, notably in Lower Alsace, local inhabitants nursed open hostility toward Jews; admitting them to electoral assemblies in the parishes and market towns appeared unthinkable. When the Jewish communities let pass

---

11 In Liber, 25.

12 Brette, 4:289.

13 In Liber, 258.

14 Cf. Gérard Nahon, ed., *Les Nations juives portugaises du Sud-Ouest de la France (1684–1791)* (Paris: Fundaçao Calouste Gulbenkian, 1981), 253.

15 Cf. Feuerwerker, *L'émancipation...*, 246.

the opportunity to name representatives to the assemblies, Abbé Grégoire wrote on 23 February 1789 to his friend Isaiah Berr Bing, of Metz: "Tell me, my dear fellow, on the eve of the États Généraux, ought not you meet with other members of your nation to demand the rights and benefits of citizens? More than ever, this is the moment."[16]

Royal authorities, however, feared that Jews' participation in the elections would lead to trouble. On 6 March at Étain, near Verdun, Lieutenant Rollin asked Minister of War de Puységur,[17] who had authority over the province: "We have seven or eight Jews born in France—elderly, resident here, and paying taxes. Have they the right to attend the assemblies by virtue of Article Twenty-five? It seems not, because at their times of birth the laws tolerated them only as foreigners..."[18] Legally, the lieutenant's analysis was wrong; but politically, the minister of war had no doubt as to the answer: "I think as you do that the Jews ought neither to be asked to attend nor, consequently, be admitted to the assemblies."[19]

Royal officials were even more straightforward about barring Alsace's Jews from participating in elections. On 5 March Lacante, the lieutenant general of the *bailliage* of Haguenau, asked Jacques Necker, royal director-general of finances, "whether Jews settled in the cities, villages and districts of Alsace..., who through *lettres patentes* enjoy a legal existence there and who contribute taxes to the province, should contribute to the deliberations as ordinary citizens or on the basis of their own corporate bodies."[20] Formulated in this fashion, the question appeared to acknowledge implicitly their status as electors. Nevertheless Necker's response was unequivocally negative: "The Jews may share in none of these advantages."[21] His decision had considerable political consequence and highlighted a

---

16 In Liber, 265.

17 Louis-Pierre de Chastenet, comte de Puységur (1727–1807) was a lieutenant general who served as minister of war from 30 November 1788 to 12 July 1789. He defended the Tuileries palace against the Fédérés on 10 August 1789. An émigré during the Revolution, he returned to Paris under Bonaparte.

18 In Feuerwerker, *L'émancipation...*, 247.

19 In Edmond Seligmann, *La Justice en France pendant la Révolution* (Paris: Plon-Nourrit, 1901), 160–161.

20 In Liber, 264. [Ironically, Louis XVI declined to appoint Necker, a Protestant of Swiss origin, as a royal minister because custom barred non-Catholics from assuming such posts. Regarding Jacques Necker, see fn. 23, below.—TRANSL.]

21 Ibid.

fundamental difference between the "Portuguese" Jews of the Southwest and the "German" Jews of the East. The "Portuguese" were
considered citizens because they were already more or less integrated
with the Christian population; the "Germans" were refused their
civic rights because they were rejected by the provinces' inhabitants.
From the royal government's perspective, citizenship was linked
to the degree to which Jews were socially accepted in their larger
communities. Whereas advocates of Jewish rights argued that emancipation was a prerequisite for the Jews' "regeneration," government
ministers demanded that "regeneration" must precede recognition of
equal rights.

Cerf-Berr responded to such opposition immediately and forcefully. After winning support from the syndics of Lorraine and the
Trois-Évêchés, he sent the ministry a *Mémoire pour la nation juive
regnicole établie dans les généralités de Metz, d'Alsace et de Lorraine* [Memorandum on behalf of the royal subjects of the Jewish
nation resident in the districts of Metz, Alsace and Lorraine].[22] In it he
noted that the primary objective of the États Généraux was to obtain
the consent of the king's subjects to new taxes. Since the Jews of the
East were composed of communities that derived their legal status
from their sovereign and paid taxes to him, they were therefore subjects of the king, like all others. However, rather than press for direct
participation in the eastern provinces' electoral assemblies, Cerf-Berr
proposed a compromise solution "in order to endeavor to reconcile all
proprieties and not at all to offend against prejudices": the Jews would
not participate in electoral assemblies with Christians, but would directly elect one or more of their own deputies to represent them in the
États Généraux. It was a politically adroit proposal: Cerf-Berr and
other leaders of the provinces' Jewish communities were assured of
being elected. Accustomed to major business dealings and having en-
trée to Versailles, Cerf-Berr was confident of his capacity to make his
fellow Jews' voice heard and to obtain recognition of their rights.

The memorandum and his proposal were ignored. As the date
of the États Généraux's opening session neared, Cerf-Berr intervened
directly with the all-powerful Necker.[23] Sentiment against the Jews
was rising, as evidenced in numerous *cahiers de doléances* submitted

---

22 Feuerwerker, *L'émancipation...*, 249–250.

23 Jacques Necker (1732–1804) was a Geneva banker who served as director-
general of finances from 1777–1781. Recalled to office on 25 August 1788 to help the

by *bailliages* in the eastern provinces, which demanded that measures be taken against them. On 15 April 1789, three weeks before the États Généraux convened, he wrote to Necker in his capacity as "syndic-general of the Jews of these three provinces," to warn him against "various proposals eager to tighten the chains of the Jewish nation."[24] He requested that the King's Council issue a decree authorizing the Jews of the East to appoint deputies to "discuss with [the king] the interests of the Jewish nation, and to invite one or more deputies of the États Généraux to defend their rights, which are those of oppressed humanity."[25] Cerf-Berr was now proposing that the Jews would choose Christian deputies to promote their interests in the États Généraux. Abbé Grégoire may already have agreed to undertake this role.

Comte de Puységur, whom Cerf-Berr also approached, wrote to Necker on 21 April: "There is no drawback in letting them be heard, and it would be unfair if they were denied it."[26] A commission of the King's Council, charged with overseeing elections to the États Généraux,[27] responded with an equally favorable opinion. On 23 April 1789 the minister of justice, Barentin, informed the intendants of the three provinces: "The king thinks it fair that the Jews be able to present in a collective memorandum their grievances and their wishes when the États Généraux convenes." The intendants were therefore instructed to ensure that assemblies were held "without commotion and without further ado," and that the Jews be given opportunities to lodge their memoranda of grievances and choose deputies who would gather in Paris at the residence of their syndic-general, Cerf-Berr. These memoranda were then to be compiled into a single petition, and submitted to the king, "who will judge whether there is cause to pass it on to the États Généraux."[28]

On 15 May 1789, when the États Généraux had already gathered at Versailles, Necker informed Cerf-Berr that this latest proposal had

---

kingdom avoid bankruptcy, he was dismissed on 11 July 1789, recalled 29 July and resigned in September 1790.

24   Cf. Roger Levylier, *Notes et documents concernant la famille Cerf-Berr, recueillis par un de ses membres.* 3 vol. (Paris: Plon, 1902-1906), 32.

25   Ibid.

26   In Liber, 271.

27   Archives nationales, B. II, packet 7, document 6, cited by Feuerwerker, *L'émancipation...*, 255.

28   Liber, 271–272.

been accepted.[29] In June, assemblies of Jews gathered, their registers of grievances were collected and edited,[30] and two representatives were elected from each province. Three of the six delegates who met in Paris at the beginning of August were members of Cerf-Berr's family. Along with Berr Isaac Berr of Nancy,[31] Cerf-Berr, "syndic-general of the Jewish nation," was now officially poised to conduct the political battle to emancipate the Jews of the East.[32]

The campaign ahead promised to be difficult. Improving conditions under which the Jews of the East lived was no longer a matter of convincing Malesherbes and members of his commission, who were enlightened and tolerant, to act. The stakes were higher and the political playing field larger. The États Généraux would now decide the Jews' future, and their cause would encounter resolute adversaries: deputies from the eastern provinces, whose constituents had submitted registers of grievances demonstrating deep hostility toward Jews.[33]

---

29 Levylier, 34. Necker's letter to Cerf-Berr concluded: "I am persuaded, sir, that you will give the king, on this occasion, new evidence of your usual zeal to serve him."

30 Robert Weyl and Jean Daltroff, "Le cahier de doléances des Juifs d'Alsace," *La Revue d'Alsace*, 109 (1983): 65–80.

31 Berr Isaac Berr (1740–1843) was son of a wealthy merchant from Nancy, cashier-general of the king's supplies, and the beneficiary of letters of naturalization which gave him all the rights of French subjects. Syndic of the Jews of Lorraine, he was a member of the delegation of Jews of the eastern provinces who arrived in Paris in August 1789. On 14 October 1789 he delivered an impassioned speech to the National Assembly in behalf of his coreligionists of the East. A writer and orator, he played an important role in the emancipation of the Jews under the Constituent Assembly. Surviving the Terror, he later took part in the two assemblies of Jewish notables convoked by Napoléon in 1806–1807. A municipal councillor during the Empire, he retained his offices during the Restoration.

32 Gouchaux Mayer-Cahn and Louis Wolf, who held important posts in the Jewish community, were appointed representatives for the Trois-Évêchés. Mayer Max, son-in-law of Cerf-Berr, and Berr Isaac Berr, syndic of the Jews of Nancy, represented Lorraine. Representing Alsace were David Sintzheim, another son-in-law of Cerf-Berr (as well as a future Grand Rabbi of France, and future president of the Sanhedrin), and S. Witterschein, who was soon replaced by Cerf-Berr's son, Théodore. Liber, 275.

33 Cf. Liber, 63 (1912): 186–210; 64: 89-108. Philippe Sagnac, "Les Juifs et la Révolution française (1789-1791)," *RHMC* [Revue d'Histoire moderne et contemporaine], 1 (1889): 215–217. Feuerwerker, *L'émancipation...*, 262–285. David Feuerwerker, "Les Juifs en France. Anatomie de 307 cahiers de doléances de 1789," in *Annales E.S.C.* [Économies, sociétés, civilisations], 1 (1965): 45–61. Bernhard Blumenkranz, "À propos des Juifs dans les cahiers de doléances," *A.H.R.F.* [Annales historiques de la Révolution française], 130 (1967): 473–480.

THE REGISTERS OF GRIEVANCES AND THE JEWS

On the eve of the Revolution, the future of France's Jews did not interest the French. Of more than forty thousand *cahiers de doléances* submitted, about three hundred made mention of the Jews. Several, representing the views of the Third Estate,[34] mentioned minor grievances attributable to jealousy on the part of guilds. Other petitions, still fewer in number, came to the Jews' support. The Third Estate of Bar-sur-Seine, for example, expressed hope that Jews might be granted the same rights extended to non-Catholics in 1787.[35] More important, politically, was the favorable position taken by the Nobility of Paris, who declared that "the États Généraux should take into consideration the future status of the Jews."[36] It was a significant statement because many of those who participated in editing this petition would soon be in the forefront of the political battle in favor of Jewish emancipation: Stanislas, comte de Clermont-Tonnerre, Adrien Du Port, the duc de La Rochefoucauld, and the marquis de Condorcet.[37]

The largest number of petitions which made reference to the Jews came from the eastern provinces, where the largest concentration of France's Jews lived.[38] Judging from the grievances noted, anti-Jewish hostility appears to have been inspired more by economic considerations than by purely religious prejudices, which were less intense at the end of the eighteenth century.[39] The most common in-

34 In the *généralité* of Rouen, two petitions, one from the guilds of Le Havre and the other from the Third Estate of Royville, near Arques, asked that the Jews who engaged in commerce in the region be compelled to pay taxes, as were other licensed merchants. In the *bailliage* of Bailleul, the Third Estate complained of Jewish merchants; cf. Feuerwerker, "Anatomie...," 50. Similarly, in Montpellier, petitions submitted by second-hand clothes- and sock-dealers and by gold- and silversmiths asked that measures be taken against the Jews; cf. Blumenkranz, "A propos...," 424.

35 Cf. Blumenkranz, "A propos..., 474.

36 Cf. Charles-Louis Chassin, ed., *Les Élections et les cahiers de Paris en 1789*. 4 vol. (Paris: Jouaust et Signaux, 1888-1889), 2:271.

37 Zalkind Hourwitz took care to send his memorandum to the Chamber of the Noblesse of Paris.

38 The most numerous came from the Trois-Évêchés, especially Thionville and Vic. Then followed Lorraine, with 138 petitions, of which seventy-two came from three *bailliages*: Bouzonville, Dieuze, and Exheim. In Alsace, only nineteen petitions found fault with the Jews.

39 Only seventeen petitions testify to a religious hostility; cf. Feuerwerker, "Les Juifs...," 52; Liber, 209.

dictment concerned usury, "one of the scourges most dreadful in the
countryside." Remarkably, of the more than two hundred petitions
that criticized the Jews for this practice, only a handful came from
Alsace, or more precisely the districts of Colmar and Sélestat, where
the "affair of the forged receipts" had spread and where anti-Judaism
was strongest. These petitions were the work of the Estates of the
Nobility and the Clergy of Alsace; the Third Estate did not raise
the matter because, in the absence of credit institutions, people of
modest means needed to be able to borrow money, even when it was
lent at inordinately high interest rates. Jews were also criticized for
excessive competition and for cornering markets in foodstuffs and
hard currency [40]—charges that were sometimes also lodged against
Christians in the petitions.

More telling were demands for measures to be taken against
the Jews. Petitioners in Lorraine asked that the restrictive measures
imposed on the Jews of Alsace in 1784 be applied in their province.
Similar calls were made by subjects living in Vic and Sarrebourg, in
the Trois-Évêchés. Some petitions wanted the Jews locked in ghettos; others suggested that they be dispersed throughout the kingdom.
Twelve of eighteen *bailliages* in Lorraine requested that the number
of Jews admitted as residents be severely limited, or "that the Jews be
expelled if they cannot be made useful." Suggestions about how to
make the Jews "useful" varied: thirty-two petitions advocated opening handicraft pursuits to Jews; nineteen recommended authorizing
Jews to engage widely in business or permitting them to pursue agriculture; twenty-eight proposed allowing Jews to enter the liberal arts.
Finally, eight petitions in Lorraine and in the Trois-Évêchés indicated
a willingness to support emancipation: if the Jews were to live in
France, then they ought to enjoy civil equality; allowed to follow other pursuits, they would abandon usury. For the most part, however,
the striking consistency in the rhetoric [41] in petitions emanating from

---

40   Cf. Feuerwerker, "Les Juifs...," 50–51; cf. B. Blumenkranz, "A propos...,"
478.

41   Liber: "One notes that in their petitions [of the farmers of Lorraine], many of
the clauses strangely resemble one another, and several are identical in expression,"
97. Cf. similarly, *Lettre d'un Alsacien sur les Juifs d'Alsace à M. Rewbell*, p. 9: "Who
has composed these petitions? Lawyers..., impassioned conspirators against human
rights, because few legal proceedings take place where these rights are respected," in
La Révolution française et l'émancipation des Juifs. 8 vol. (Paris: Edhis [Éditions d'Histoire
Sociale],1968). Vol. 8: *Lettres, Mémoires et Publications diverses, 1789-1806*.

the eastern provinces testify to an enduring anti-Judaism. Thus petitioners in Haguenau wished "to stop at its outset their astonishing
proliferation"[42] by permitting marriage only of the eldest son of each
Jewish family. In Thionville, petitioners wanted to refuse all right of
residence to Jews. In Colmar, members of the Clergy asserted: "The
Jews are the prime cause of the people's misery, of the loss of all sense
of energy, of moral depravation…";[43] and the Nobility of that city
echoed: "It is about time to take sides, definitely and decisively…"[44]

Nothing in these petitions surprised the royal government,
which was well-informed of such sentiments thanks to reports submitted by its provincial administrators and governors.[45] But in the
National Assembly, where deputies were obliged to act according to
the instructions of their electoral assemblies and where public opinion reigned, these renewed denunciations against the Jews of the East
and the demands to tighten rather than loosen constraints placed
upon them amounted to a set of formidable political obstacles.

Prudently the Jews decided against demanding complete equality
of rights in their own petitions composed at the end of the spring of
1789. Instead they developed a common agenda of requests: equality
of taxation; abolition of all special taxes, notably "of residence and
protection," as well as the right to engage in all professions, purchase
land and real estate, and to settle freely anywhere in the kingdom.
They also asked for freedom of worship and freedom to maintain
their communal organizations. Thus they repeated requests they
had presented to Malesherbes a year earlier: complete civil—if not
civic—rights, and the right to retain their religious and community
autonomy.[46]

Each community added its own demands to the general text. The
Jews of Metz called for abolition of the twenty thousand livres paid
each year to the Brancas family. The Jews of Alsace asked for liberty
to wed without prior authorization and the right to hire Christians
for agricultural labor, and requested that "all public figures should

42 Third Estate of Haguenau, Article 39; in Sagnac, 216.
43 Third Estate of Thionville; ibid., 280,
44 Petitions of the Clergy of Colmar and Schlestadt, in *Archives parlementaires de 1787 à 1860. Première série (de 1787 à 1799). Recueil complet des débats législatifs et politiques des Chambres françaises.* Jules Mavidal and Émile Laurent, eds. 32 vol. (Paris: P. Du-pont, 1862-1888), 3:55.
45 Nobility convened from the districts of Colmar and Schlestadt, ibid., 3:8.
46 Cf. Liber, 99–109.

be forbidden to employ hurtful epithets toward the Jews."[47] The Jews of Lorraine sought access to secondary schools and universities for their children.[48] Worried about protecting themselves against an influx of impoverished Jews, they also asked that Jews who wished to settle in Lorraine be required to present proof of possessing a certain amount of capital: ten thousand livres if they wished to live in Nancy, or twelve hundred livres if they wished to reside in a village. In hindsight, Berr Isaac Berr noted: "We contented ourselves with asking to leave the slavery in which we were singularly held and to preserve the slight privileges we enjoyed."[49]

Under Cerf-Berr's authority, these diverse petitions were melded in Paris into a single text and forwarded to the minister of justice, who in turn transmitted it to Abbé Grégoire, who thus became the Jews' advocate in the National Assembly. But before Grégoire was able to act upon their requests, political developments changed course yet again. After July 1789 France's Jews found themselves facing a radically different situation.

---

47 Ibid., 115.

48 Cf. Berr Isaac Berr, *Mémoire adressé à Malesherbes en 1788*: "As the morale of the Jews has been affected due to long persecutions and degradations, it is absolutely necessary to provide them the means to enable them to provide education to their children." Archives nationales, p. 154, II, 135.

49 "Lettre du S^r. Berr Isaac Berr, négociant à Nancy, Juif, naturalisé en vertu des Lettres-patentes du Roi, enregistrées au Parlement de Nancy, Député des Juifs de la Lorraine; à Monseigneur l'évêque de Nancy, Député à l'Assemblée Nationale," p. 4, in *La Révolution française et l'émancipation des* Juifs. Vol. 8: *Lettres, Mémoires....*

CHAPTER 4

A LONG HOT SUMMER

Six delegates representing the Jews of the East arrived in Paris at the beginning of August 1789 to meet again with Cerf-Berr. Since they had last gathered in June, however, the deputies elected to the États Généraux had voted to transform the body into a National Assembly. Reform had given way to revolution. With a vote on the evening of 4 August 1789, and a decree adopted over the course of 6-11 August, feudalism was abolished. The social order of the Ancien Régime was destroyed, and with it the privileges enjoyed by the nobility, some of which had weighed heavily upon the Jews. The most significant development of all was enactment of the Declaration of the Rights of Man and of the Citizen, during 20-26 August, which proclaimed that all men are born and live freely and equally in rights, and are guaranteed freedom of opinion, "even religious [opinion]."

During discussion in the Assembly on 23 August, as it was considering the Declaration, Pastor Jean-Paul Rabaut de Saint-Étienne [1] rose to speak, "more as a supplicant" than as a legislator: "I ask, for French Protestants, for all non-Catholics of the realm, that which you request for yourselves: liberty and equality of rights." On behalf of the Jews he added: "I ask it for this people torn from Asia, always wandering, always banished, always persecuted for nearly eighteen centuries; who would adopt our customs and habits if, according to our laws, they were integrated with us; and whom we ought not at all blame for its ethics, which are the product of our barbarousness and of the humiliation to which we have unfairly condemned them." [2]

The Assembly did not react directly to Rabaut's words, but in

---

1 Jean-Paul Rabaut de Saint-Étienne (1743–1793) was a deputy of the Third Estate of Nîmes. A *patriote*, he played an important role in the debates on religious questions. A deputy at the Convention and close to the Girondists, he was guillotined on 5 December 1793.

2 *Archives parlementaires de 1787 à 1860. Première série (de 1787 à 1799). Recueil complet des débats législatifs et politiques des Chambres françaises.* Jules Mavidal and Émile Laurent, eds. 32 vol. (Paris: P. Dupont, 1862-1888), 8:479.

voting the Declaration of the Rights of Man, it appeared to have responded to his eloquent hopes. Had not the Jews, like all men, been solemnly declared free and equal in rights? Their future in France seemed settled. Berr Isaac Berr recalled the emotion which gripped the Jewish delegation of the East: "We heard with great joy that the first article of the Constitution, which issued from the wisdom of the National Assembly, established human rights, declaring that all men are born equal and free. We then found not only that our mission was superfluous, but we thought that this decree, the foundation for the happiness of the French people, granted us rights even greater than those for which our petitions had instructed us to ask…"[3]

VIOLENCE AGAINST THE JEWS

Hope reigned in Paris. In the east, however, Jews were targets of popular violence. During the night of 1-2 August in Lixheim, Lorraine, a mob stormed the homes of Jews who had been denounced as hoarders. A dozen residences were looted, and the mounted police of Sarreguemines were called in to restore order. The troubles spread. On 6 August the Intermediary Commission of Lorraine wrote to the National Assembly: "The Jews were driven out of their homes, stripped of their property and even their clothes, and treated, especially in Lixheim, with unprecedented fury."[4]

The "Great Fear" spread in Upper Alsace. Farmers attacked châteaux and abbeys in order to destroy all tax records of their rents and fees. In Sundgau, they also attacked the Jews. Homes in nineteen villages were set ablaze or pillaged. Jews were pursued and mauled and had to flee, sometimes half-naked. Hundreds sought refuge across

---

3   Cf. Berr Isaac Berr, "Lettre du S^r. Berr-Isaac-Berr, négociant à Nancy, Juif, naturalisé en vertu des Lettres-patentes du Roi, enregistrées au Parlement de Nancy, Député des Juifs de la Lorraine; à Monseigneur l'évêque de Nancy, Député à l'Assemblée Nationale," p. 4, in *La Révolution française et l'émancipation des Juifs.* 8 vol. (Paris: Edhis [Éditions d'Histoire sociale], 1968. Vol. 8: *Lettres, Mémoires et Publications diverses, 1789-1806.* On 24 July 1789, several days after the Bastille was stormed, Berr Isaac Berr, at the head of a delegation of the community, had announced to the new municipal administration of Nancy that, in order to attest to its civic duty, the Jewish community would contribute to the urgent measures to supply the city. Cf. Jacques Godechot, "Les Juifs de Nancy de 1789 à 1795," *Revue des études juives,* 86 (1928), 87.

4   In David Feuerwerker, *L'émancipation des Juifs en France de l'Ancien Régime à la fin du Second Empire* (Paris: Albin Michel, 1976), 282. [On intermediary commissions, see chap.1, fn. 61, above.—TRANSL.]

the border in Basel, Switzerland, where they remained through the last days of August,[5] given humanitarian welcome by local authorities. The city of Mulhouse took in several hundred refugees as well. Anxiety reigned throughout the Jewish communities of the east.

When reports of these outbursts first reached the National Assembly, Abbé Grégoire spoke during the evening session of 3 August to denounce the violence. For the first time, a deputy raised his voice in favor of the Jews from within the well of the Assembly. After reviewing the situation the Jews of the East faced, he asked, "as a clergyman of a religion which looks upon all men as brothers…, that the Assembly exercise its power to intervene on behalf of this exiled and unfortunate people."[6]

Grégoire's defense of the Jews of the East alarmed the "Portuguese." Informed about developments in the Assembly through their personal relations with Bordeaux's deputies, as well as through David Silveyra, their representative in Paris, they thought that the wisest course, politically, was to avoid arousing any debate specifically focused on the Jews' situation. It was sufficient, they believed, to invoke the general provisions of the Declaration of the Rights of Man, and thereby gain recognition of their rights as citizens. The abbé's zeal had put Bordeaux's "politics of discretion" at risk.

On 14 August four representatives of Bordeaux's community published an open letter addressed to "M. Grégoire, curé of Embermesnil, deputy of Nancy." The text was revealing. The representatives began by paying Grégoire "a just tribute of praise and acknowledgment…," adding, "how we congratulate ourselves, sir, to have found in you a champion so courageous and so zealous. Providence seems to have brought you to ease our plight."[7] Homage rendered, the Bordelais moved on to political considerations: "We do not assume that, in the current state of affairs, we need, in order to regenerate the Jews, laws other than those which will serve to regenerate the entire king-

---

5 On 30 August 1789 Cerf-Berr wrote to the municipality of Basel: "Esteemed lords, I am filled with intense and respectful gratitude for the token of humanity and charity which you have showered upon the Jews of Alsace, victims of the current anarchy." Quoted in Feuerwerker, 29.

6 Ibid., 292.

7 "Lettre adressée à M. Grégoire, curé d'Embermesnil, député de Nancy, par les députés de la Nation juive portugaise de Bordeaux, le 14 août 1789" (Versailles: Baudouin, 1789), p. 1, Bibliothèque nationale, 8° Ld. 184–29. [See also: *La Révolution française et l'émancipation des Juifs*. Vol. 8: *Lettres, Mémoires…—Transl.*]

dom..."[8] They then requested that no measures be taken regarding the Jews of the East that would apply to all Jews without distinction: "If the conduct or the unfortunate plight of the Jews of Alsace and the Trois-Évêchés motivates the National Assembly to make some rule that ought to apply to all Jews of the kingdom, the Jews of Bordeaux would regard it as an injustice that would be as unwarranted as it would be cruel."[9] The "Portuguese" had issued a clear warning to Grégoire and to the representatives of the Jews of the East.

Given the "Portuguese" Jews' circumstances, their political argument was flawless. So far as they were concerned, the fact that they had been able to participate in elections to the États Généraux amounted to recognition of their status as citizens. Were the rights of citizens to be expanded, Bordeaux's Jews would benefit along with all other French citizens.[10] The good fortune of Bordeaux's Jewish notables, however, was irrelevant to Jews upon whom torment was now raining down in some communities in the eastern provinces. A wealthy Bordeaux Jew, elected an officer of the National Guard, shared little in common—other than the word "Jew"—with an impoverished second-hand clothes dealer from Lixheim who had to flee into the night to escape arson and looting. In Bordeaux "Jew" was only a term that described a religion; in Sundgau it was an insult and a threat. Finding themselves once again jumbled together with the wretched mass of Ashkenazim of the East aroused more unease than solidarity among the illustrious Sephardim of the Southwest.

Paris's Jews rejected Bordeaux's policy of reserve and silence. Along with all other Parisians, they had lived through key revolutionary events; many had enlisted in the National Guard [11] and had

---

8 Ibid., 2 and 3.

9 Ibid., 3.

10 For Grégoire's benefit, the "Portuguese" noted with satisfaction "the salutary effects produced by equality of rights in Bordeaux; our fellow citizens gathered with us in parish churches to form revolutionary regiments, and freely elected us to officerships, up to the rank of captain; does one need other examples of good fellowship between Christians and Jews?" Ibid., 4.

11 "Of five hundred Jews who live in Paris, there are more than one hundred who were enrolled in the National Guard," in "Discours prononcé par M. Godard, le 28 janvier 1790, en présentant à l'Assemblée générale de la Commune de Paris une députation des Juifs de Paris," p. 6, in *La Révolution française et l'émancipation des Juifs.* 8 vol. Vol 6: *La Commune et les Districts de Paris. Discours, Lettres et Rapports, 1790-1791.*

contributed funds to patriotic projects.[12] Their outlook on the political situation was more refined than that of their fellow Jews of the East, and even of the Southwest. Lacking a formal community structure, Paris's Jews were able to create new institutions better adapted to new circumstances, and in the summer of 1789 they formed a representative committee charged with defending and promoting their own interests. The committee's members reflected the diversity of their origins and obvious concern for stability: of eleven representatives, six, including its chairman, were Ashkenazim; five, including its vice-chairman, were Sephardim.[13]

On 26 August the same day that the Declaration of the Rights of Man was formally adopted, the Paris committee issued an address to the National Assembly. Since it was a joint effort of "Portuguese" and "Germans" who had intimate knowledge of the Revolution's developments, their statement had symbolic force and attracted political attention. After congratulating the Assembly, the Jews of Paris associated their appeal with principles enunciated in the Declaration of the Rights of Man: "In restoring to mankind its original dignity, in restoring to mankind enjoyment of its rights, you intended to make no distinction between one person and another... In this empire that is our homeland, the status of 'human being' guarantees us the status of 'citizen,' and the status of 'citizen' will give us all the rights of citizens, all civil rights..."[14] The Parisians then went further: "In order that the people break the habit... of regarding us, so to speak, as foreigners in the French nation and judging us unworthy of any other status, we come to beseech you, Your Lordships, to make particular mention of the Jewish nation in your decrees, and thus to sanction our status and our rights as citizens."[15]

---

12 Elie Mardochee offered 1,500 livres, in September 1789, in the name of the Jews of Paris. Cf. Léon Kahn, *Les Juifs de Paris pendant la Révolution* (Paris: P. Ollendorff, 1899), 153. On 14 September Trenel made a patriotic offering of 660 livres. "When the chairman announced that this gift had been made by a Jew, there was applause." In Abraham Spire, *Le Journal révolutionnaire d'Abraham Spire*. Introduction and translation by Simon Schwarzfuchs (Paris: Institut Alain de Rothschild; Lagrasse: Verdier, 1989), 59.

13 Cf. Maurice Liber, "Les Juifs et la convocation des États Généraux," *Revue des études juives* 63-66 (1912-1913): 176–181, who closely examines the committee's composition and its members' origins. Two of them, Lazare and Trenel, had previously represented the community in dealings with Malesherbes.

14 Cf. Liber, 182.

15 Ibid., 121.

Such a declaration seemed useless to the Jews of Bordeaux, since they were already integrated in the life of their larger community. But the Jews of Paris knew that the Jews as a whole had to be declared citizens if they were to be considered by others as such. To demonstrate their intention to integrate, they declared themselves ready to renounce any autonomous communal organizations, such as the judicial authority of rabbinic tribunals.[16] It was an easy sacrifice: there was no organized Jewish community in Paris.

Cerf-Berr and the six representatives of the Jews of the East, in the capital throughout August, could not ignore the Parisians' stance, and they issued their own address to the National Assembly. As they were drafting it, anti-Jewish agitation continued in some *bailliages* in Alsace and Lorraine. The king, in response to a motion the Assembly adopted at Grégoire's request, issued an edict on 26 August[17] that placed Alsace's Jews under his protection. On 28 August the Intermediary Commission of Lorraine sent a decree to localities in which Jews resided, denouncing "the excesses committed in several communes of the province against Jewish families that are settled there." The commission invited local authorities to grant Jews shelter and assistance, and "to make sure that when they returned to their homes they would be sheltered from the persecutions they have suffered."[18]

Bordeaux's politics of discretion was out of place in the face of this threatening situation. On 30 August the Jews of the East asked the Assembly, as had the Parisian committee, to "speak specifically to the plight of the Jews by giving them the status and rights of citizens,"[19] for "when popular fury recently sought out victims, it turned against the Jews…"[20] Only an explicit declaration that Jews enjoyed all the rights of citizens would save them from "attacks of prejudice

---

16 "We are so convinced," they wrote, "of the necessity whereby all members of a great empire submit to a uniform plan for police and a system of law, that we ask to be subject, as all the French, to the same system of law, the same police, the same courts, and that we relinquish…privileges which we have been granted to have our own leaders drawn from within our ranks."

17 Cf. Feuerwerker, *L'émancipation…*, 301.

18 Ibid., 297–298.

19 "Adresse presentée à l'Assemblée nationale par les députés des Juifs, le 31 août 1789, par les députés réunis de Juifs, établis à Metz, dans les Trois-Évêchés, en Alsace et en Lorraine," p. 13, in *La Révolution française et l'émancipation des Juifs*. Vol. 5: *Adresses, Mémoires et Pétitions des Juifs, 1789-1794*.

20 Ibid., 4.

or the traps of fanaticism."[21] The Jews of the East, however, unlike the Jews of Paris, intended to preserve "our synagogues, our rabbis and syndics in the same way that they exist today," and "to retain the free exercise of our laws, rites and customs."[22]

This deep, almost visceral, attachment to their customs and traditional institutions could only serve to offend sensibilities within the Assembly. What—abolish all privileges, and allow the Jews' to retain theirs? Make the kingdom's laws uniform, but permit the Jews to preserve theirs, along with their own communal structure? Politically unwise though it was under the circumstances, this request expressed the Jews of the East's unease in the face of persecutions that continued even as the Assembly proclaimed the Declaration of the Rights of Man. They longed for emancipation with all their might; but they were not ready to undertake radical integration, exchanging their status as a community for an abstract identity whose nature they could not grasp, and destruction of institutions they had long maintained through many hardships. Had they preserved intact their traditions, their laws, their communities for so long only to be obliged to relinquish them for a notion of citizenship that had no substance for these stubborn and frightened people?

The Jews of the East could not confide these profound anxieties to the National Assembly during these remarkable days when the Declaration of the Rights of Man was being framed and the promise of liberation filled the air. Berr Isaac Berr and the other representatives therefore advanced other, more utilitarian reasons: because their community structure fostered respect for religion, it therefore promoted "respect for society." "It is in order to be better citizens that we ask to preserve our synagogue, our rabbis and our syndics."[23] They noted also that their communities were crippled with debt, which they could only repay if they were able to maintain their communities' institutional structures.[24] This was far different from the elegant phrases marshaled by the Jewish notables of Bor-

21 Ibid.

22 The other demands of the address of 31 August were those already inscribed in the common petition of grievances drafted by the deputies of the Jews of the East. They asked, notably, the right to settle freely within the kingdom, and abolition of all special and unfair taxes. Ibid., 4.

23 Ibid., 11.

24 In order to guarantee settlement of its debt, the Jewish community of Metz requested that, in a private capacity, "there should be a law explaining that no Jew

deaux's Chartrons district.[25]

Then toward the end of August 1789, two Jewish communities in Lorraine—Lunéville and Sarreguemines—added still more complexity to the variety of requests the Jews had made. The two communities broke ranks with Cerf-Berr's group and presented to the Assembly a separate memorandum and their own demands. Enmeshed in a quarrel with their fellow Jews in Nancy,[26] the dissidents refused to be represented by the Jewish delegates of that city, and asked that "in the future, the Jews settled in Lunéville and Sarreguemines no longer be set apart from other citizens of their cities. May they cease to be organized as a separate *corporation* and thus be foreigners in their cities." The Jews of Paris had made the same request, but in this instance the dissidents' motive was different: once they ceased to be a "separate *corporation*," they would no longer be linked to the Jewish community of Lorraine—or subject to the authority of its syndics. Concealed behind this demand for emancipation and integration was a desire to break with Nancy; and to signal their support for France's emerging new order, the Jews of Lunéville attached to their memorandum a certificate from the city's committee, attesting that on 3 August the Jewish community had offered to contribute funds for public projects, thereby earning a place among the front ranks of "zealous donors."[27]

August 1789 was thus a month marked by great principles and petty maneuvers, solemn appeals and disputes among neighbors. France's "Jewish nation" appeared less than one and indivisible during these opening days of the Revolution.

---

will be able to leave the [Jewish] quarter without having paid his portion of the community debt." Ibid.

25 Numerous middle-class Jews, bankers and merchants, had taken up residence in this elegant neighborhood of Bordeaux.

26 When in 1788 the sixteen Jewish families of Lunéville had asked to choose their rabbi, the syndics of Nancy, upon whom they depended, refused permission. Frustrated, the Lunéville community involved the Sarreguemines community, where there was a significant number of Jews, in their opposition to Nancy. When the Revolution began, both communities saw in it an opportunity to free themselves of Nancy's supervision.

27 Cf. "Mémoire pour les Juifs de Lunéville et de Sarreguemines," p. 5, in *La Révolution française et l'émancipation des Juifs.* Vol 5: *Adresses, Mémoires....*

OPPOSING POLITICAL FORCES

Upon whom could the Jews rely during this summer of revolutionary fervor? The events shaking France captivated popular attention; but, save in the eastern provinces, where opinion was hostile, the plight of the Jews aroused little concern. Still, if the majority of deputies in the Assembly was more interested in the views of the voters who had elected them than in the Jews, within the ranks of a group of deputies known as *patriotes* were some of the Jews' staunchest advocates. Alongside Abbé Grégoire were several eminent representatives of Paris's open-minded Nobility—Stanislas, comte de Clermont-Tonnerre; Adrien Du Port; Louis-Alexandre, duc de La Rochefoucauld d'Enville, and Boniface, comte de Castellane—who firmly supported Jewish emancipation. Mirabeau, who exercised substantial influence in the Assembly and over public opinion during these first months of the Revolution, supported their cause. Other celebrities of the moment, such as the marquis de La Fayette and Abbé Emmanuel Sieyès, had not publicly indicated their views on emancipation; but La Fayette became the champion of the Declaration of the Rights of Man, joined the Society of Friends of Blacks, revered George Washington as his lodestar, and the United States had awarded the Jews complete civil and political rights;[28] and while Sieyès had excluded women and aliens from "active" citizenship in his influential political treatises, he had not barred Jews.[29] On the extreme left, democrats such as Maximilien de Robespierre and Jérôme Pétion de Villeneuve advocated Jewish emancipation, as they did abolition of black slavery.

Deputies representing the eastern provinces formed the nucleus of opposition to Jewish emancipation. Their electors were more inclined to exclude the Jews from public life than to integrate and to

---

28 Cf. George Washington's letter to the Jewish community of Rhode Island, 17 August 1790: "The citizens of the United States of America have a right to applaud themselves for having given to mankind examples of an enlarged and liberal policy—a policy worthy of imitation. All possess alike liberty of conscience and immunities of citizenship . . . for happily the Government of the United States, which gives to bigotry no sanction, to persecution no assistance, requires only that they who live under its protection should demean themselves as good citizens . . ." (Document communicated by the Hon. Antonin Scalia, Associate Justice of the Supreme Court of the United States.)

29 Cf. Jean-Denis Bredin, *Sieyès, la clé de la Révolution française.* (Paris: Fallois, 1988), 130–131.

accept them, and these deputies were aware of the hostility that encircled the Jews in certain *bailliages*. They viewed the violence that had broken out in July 1789 as a precursor of more trouble, and perhaps massacres, were the Jews declared to be citizens. The deputies' own anti-Jewish sentiments combined with those of their constituents to generate energetic opposition to initiatives undertaken by Abbé Grégoire and partisans of emancipation. Otherwise, their political leanings were mixed: a *patriote* like Jean-François Rewbell,[30] a right-wing monarchist like François-Joseph Hell, a liberal like Victor-Claude, prince de Broglie,[31] and a conservative like Bishop Anne-Louis-Henri de La Fare[32] of Nancy, all coalesced to unite against the Jews. Later the Revolution's radical turn would bring them the support of Abbé Jean-Sifrein Maury,[33] a brilliant orator associated with the "blacks" of the monarchist right. Finally, many deputies who had been elected by the upper ranks of the Catholic Church's hierarchy remained loyal to the tradition of anti-Judaism. Some ecclesiastics, to be sure, were among the Jews' most ardent supporters: Abbé Grégoire; Abbé Antoine-Adrien Lamourette, grand vicar of Arras and a friend of Mirabeau, and Abbé François-Valentin Mulot, a member of the Paris Commune. Nonetheless, most of the

---

30 Jean-François Rewbell (1747–1807) was an attorney and deputy to the États Généraux who sat on the left with the *patriotes*. He was elected prosecutor-syndic of Haut-Rhin during the Legislative Assembly, and also served as a deputy to the Convention. Charged with defending Mayence, he was obliged to surrender. He was a member of the Committee of Public Safety after Thermidor; served as a member of the Directory, specializing in foreign relations, and was elected to the Council of Anciens. The coup d'état of Brumaire ended his political career.

31 Victor-Claude, prince de Broglie (1757-1794) was a deputy of the Nobility of Colmar to the États Généraux. A liberal, he was a member of the Society of Friends of the Constitution. During the Legislative Assembly, he served as brigadier of the Army of the Rhine, but resigned after 10 August. He was guillotined on 27 June 1794.

32 Anne-Louis-Henri de La Fare (1752-1829) was a bishop, and a deputy of the Clergy of Nancy to the États Généraux who opposed the Revolution's principles. In 1790 he, along with Pierre-Victor Malouet and Clermont-Tonnerre, founded the Impartials' Club. An émigré in 1791, he returned to France after the Restoration and became a peer of France, archbishop of Sens and a cardinal in 1823.

33 Jean-Sifrein Maury (1746-1817) was a celebrated preacher, writer and academician. Elected to the États Généraux by the Clergy of Péronne, he was a relentless defender of royal prerogatives and a brilliant orator. He emigrated after the dissolution of the Constituent Assembly. Named bishop, later cardinal, by the pope, he supported Napoléon after his coronation, was ennobled, named to the Institute and received the diocese of Paris. Rejected by Louis XVIII after the Restoration, he was imprisoned for six months in Rome, where he appealed to the pope for pardon.

deputies in the Assembly elected to the États Généraux to represent the clergy opposed Jewish emancipation.

Such were the political battle lines drawn in the summer of 1789 between advocates and adversaries of emancipation. In the center were numerous deputies who remained uncertain. As for the king and his ministers, the Jews were of little concern during the summer when absolute monarchy was collapsing. But their stance had not changed since Malesherbes's departure. Louis XVI wrote to the Assembly at the end of September 1789: "I have already indicated my intentions on behalf of the Jews of Alsace, and I shall continue to protect them against the persecutions of which they are victims."[34] Now, however, it was the Assembly's task to emancipate them, not his.

Given popular hostility in the eastern provinces and the resolute opposition mounted by its region's representatives, the greatest chances for the success of the Jews' cause during summer of 1789 hinged on a principle—the Rights of Man[35]—and the ardor of one deputy: Abbé Grégoire.[36] The Assembly's majority had not explicitly troubled itself to address Jewish emancipation when it voted to adopt the Declaration. Nonetheless civil equality and religious liberty for Jews seemed implicit in its articles. To partisans of Jewish rights, the struggle appeared to have been won; all that remained was a matter, in Clermont-Tonnerre's words, "of a cause in which one sees no objections that give reason for dispute..., which, in a word, comes down to proving that it is enough to be human and to be a civilized being in order to enjoy the right to be a citizen."[37]

Grégoire—ever impatient, ever impulsive—pressed the Assembly for a decree acknowledging that all Jews had the rights of citizens. On 1 September, only five days after the vote on the Declaration, during an evening session chaired by Clermont-Tonnerre, he rose to call attention to the threats facing the Jews of Alsace and to ask that

---

34 *Archives parlementaires*, 9:242.

35 Cf. Clermont-Tonnerre, to the National Assembly, 28 September 1789: "It was held in store for this century of tolerance and reason to behold an honorable minister of the altars raise his voice in this assembly...in favor of the unhappy remnants of Israel...I will not usurp the holy work that he has undertaken!" *Archives parlementaires*, 9:201.

36 Cf. *La Déclaration des droits de l'homme et du citoyen*. Introduction by Stéphane Rials (Paris: Hachette "Pluriel," 1989), 236–246.

37 Clermont-Tonnerre, session of 28 September 1789. *Archives parlementaires*, 9: 201.

a special session be devoted "to consider the status of the Jews in France."[38] The Assembly agreed to do so but Grégoire's political timing was poor. That same day Mirabeau declared himself in favor of allowing the king to retain a veto over legislation, which created political turmoil. Two days later, on 3 September, when the addresses published by the Jews of Paris and the Jews of the East were presented to the Assembly, legislators moved to refer the documents to a committee for study.[39] When the Assembly reconvened on 7 September, "We awaited," wrote the *Courrier français*, "to see discussed this great, important issue, and the Assembly was therefore very crowded. But two decrees [on taxation]...entirely occupied the session, and Abraham's children were never heard."[40]

Such temporizing did not please partisans of Jewish rights while threats against the Jews continued. On 15 September a strange pamphlet, attributed to "Martin, former consul of Avignon," began circulating in Paris, denouncing "a dark plot hatched by the Jews in the city of Avignon against the vice-legate."[41] The *Courrier de Versailles,* published in Paris, quickly unmasked the allegations as falsehoods, but the tract's intent was clear: to incite passions against the Jews just as the National Assembly was beginning to take up the question of their emancipation.

TENSION IN ALSACE

As the rumor of a Jewish conspiracy in the south of France made its rounds in Paris, anti-Jewish agitation once again roiled the kingdom's eastern provinces. Peasant violence in the Alsatian countryside— the "Great Fear" that dominated the summer of 1789—focused on Jews as much as on the nobility, and was fed by hatred and fear: hatred of Jewish usurers and fear of seeing them seize land. The prospect that

---

38 *Archives parlementaires*, 8:542. Cf. *Journal des débats et des décrets*, no. 6: 3.

39 The deputies of Strasbourg were equally pessimistic about it. They wrote on 4 September to their constituents: "We are threatened with another curse. The Jews are asking for civil status throughout France, and the matter, which ought to have been dealt with today, will without fail be dealt with next week. Alsace will defend itself, but we do not guarantee success..." Printed by R. Renso, *Revue d'Alsace* (1879), 415.

40 *Courrier français*, no. 66 (9 September 1789): 326. Cf., regarding Grégoire: "The honorable member declared himself a champion of the Asiatic people and he has long requested a session for his clients." Ibid.

41 Cf. Feuerwerker, *L'émancipation...*, 303.

thousands of Jews there might gain all the rights of citizens revived fears of competition among merchants and artisans at a time when economic crisis was rampant. Farmers thought the idea unbearable that Jews might freely purchase land. Debtors, who had been granted mortgage guarantees by front men for Jewish usurers, imagined their properties being sold and Jews settling in as owners. If people burned Jews' wretched homes the way they torched nobles' châteaux, it was in the hope that fire would destroy documents recording debts as well as documents recording hereditary nobility.

On Rosh Hashanah, the Jewish religious new year, celebrated during 21–22 September 1789, shots were fired in front of some synagogues and some Jewish homes were attacked. As Yom Kippur, the Day of Atonement, neared, syndics David Sintzheim and Théodore Cerf-Berr asked maréchal de Rochambeau, commander in chief in Alsace, to provide protection. Rochambeau referred them to the civil authorities, who in turn requested troops to ensure protection, if necessary, for the Jews.

Sintzheim and Théodore Cerf-Berr again called the National Assembly's attention to the appalling situation of the Jews, especially in upper Alsace: "They have all been driven out and they are in continual expectation of being exterminated."[42] On 28 September, the Assembly took up "the matter of the Jews of Metz (*sic*) who request the Assembly's protection."[43] The session, held during the evening, ran late and fewer than two hundred deputies were present. Referring to the threats confronting the Jews, Clermont-Tonnerre declared: "Already, their houses have been pillaged, their persons exposed to outrages and violence. The approaching feast of expiations [Yom Kippur], by gathering them in their synagogues, exposes them without defense to widespread hatred."[44] He asked the Assembly to place the Jews' persons and property under protection of the law. Abbé Grégoire vigorously supported Clermont-Tonnerre's motion. The Assembly agreed and authorized its president to write to all public officers in Alsace, informing them that the Jews were placed under protection of the law, and called on the king and the government to take protective measures. The press published extracts of a letter from the Assembly's chairman, Jean-Joseph Mounier, to Alsatian authori-

---

42 Ibid., 305.
43 *Archives parlementaires*, 9:200.
44 Ibid.

ties. The next day, 29 September, the king informed the Assembly that he had placed the Jews of Alsace under his protection.[45]

The six Jewish representatives of the eastern provinces, however, were at the end of their patience. On 4 October they wrote to the Assembly's president: "Our lives have never been so turbulent or disquieted as during these past several months. The provinces in which we live have seen us, for nearly two months, at the door of the National Assembly, the sanctuary of justice, without ever obtaining a hearing. They [the provinces] do not attribute this delay to the important work which occupies the Assembly,[46] but to the scorn in which the Jews are customarily held…"[47]

They were finally given a hearing on the evening of 14 October, when the National Assembly was holding its next-to-last session at Versailles before relocating to the Salle du Manège in Paris. It was an extraordinary moment. Berr Isaac Berr, a Jew from Lorraine who represented the most despised communities of France, accompanied by six other Jews from the eastern provinces, addressed the National Assembly in the Salle de Menus Plaisirs, where five months earlier His Most Christian Majesty, the absolute ruler of the kingdom of France, had opened the États Généraux.

Berr Isaac Berr's remarks suited the occasion. A religious believer, he began by invoking God's name: "In the name of the Eternal, author of all justice and of all truth; in the name of this God who, in giving to each the same rights, prescribed to all the same duties…" He then called the Assembly's attention to "a people insulted throughout so many centuries by ignominious treatment, which the unfortunate descendants of the most ancient of all peoples have endured in nearly all countries of the earth…everywhere persecuted, everywhere debased, and who, however subjugated, never rebel. Objects of indignation and scorn among all peoples, when they ought only to have

---

45 *Le Moniteur*, 28 September 1789; *Le Courrier de Versailles à Paris*, vol. 4, no. 88: 16–22; *Les Révolutions de Paris*, no. 12 (4 October 1789), 17; *Le Point du jour* (30 September 1789): 150–161; *Le Journal de Paris*, vol. 2, no. 271: 122.

46 Throughout September 1789 the National Assembly was occupied with basic constitutional issues: creation of an "upper chamber," refused on 10 September; the king's right to a suspensive veto, recognized by the king on 11 September; and the monarchical form of government, affirmed on 22 September.

47 In Feuerwerker, *L'émancipation…*, 311.

been the object of tolerance and pity…"[48] Recalling his delegation's request, formally submitted on 31 August, that the Assembly grant Jews their rights as citizens, Berr Isaac Berr concluded with emotion: "May we owe to you a less sorrowful life than the one to which we are condemned…may men look upon us as their brothers…; may a total reformation take place in the institutions to which we are ignominiously enslaved; and may this reformation, until now too vainly wished for, which we ask with tears in our eyes, be your kind deed and your handiwork!"[49]

The session's president, Emmanuel-Marie-Philippe Fréteau de Saint-Just,[50] whose sympathies lay with the *patriotes*, responded with words of good will to this speech laden with suffering and hope: "The Assembly will take your request into consideration and will be pleased to bring tranquility and happiness to your brethren…"[51] But Abbé Grégoire was dissatisfied with these vague assurances. He rose to ask that the Assembly make a commitment to decide on the citizenship of the Jews during the course of the session, and that the Jews' representatives be invited to attend the session, as were other delegations. Despite protests by several elected members,[52] the Jewish delegation, no doubt with great emotion, took seats in the meeting hall alongside representatives of the nation.

48 *Procès-Verbal* [minutes] of the Assembly, 14 October 1789, evening session, 6, no. 100: 5. *Archives parlementaires*, 9:765.

49 Ibid.

50 Emmanuel-Marie-Michel-Philippe Fréteau de Saint-Just (1738–1794) was an advisor to the Parlement of Paris, and a deputy of the Nobility of Melun. He supported abolition of the religious orders and the Noble estate, and in 1791 was elected judge of the Paris court. He was guillotined on 14 June 1794.

51 Ibid.

52 According to *Le Courrier* of Gorsas, 4:243 (17 October 1789), "there were several members of the Clergy who murmured."

CHAPTER 5

PROTESTANTS, ACTORS, EXECUTIONERS AND JEWS

DEBATE BEGINS

As the autumn of 1789 began, the National Assembly prepared for a crucial debate. The people, now sovereign, had to choose not only deputies for the Legislative Assembly, but also judges and administrative, municipal and departmental officials. The election was therefore a political act par excellence, and it raised two key questions: Who would be eligible to vote, and who would be eligible to hold public office?

A majority of the Assembly rallied behind an ingenious proposal Abbé Sieyès had offered in July. All inhabitants of a nation, said Sieyès, had "the right to protection of their person, property, liberty, etc."; these he called "passive citizens." But "all do not have the right to take an active role in forming governments"; those who possessed this right were "active citizens."[1] The distinction allowed legislators to pay formal respect to the Declaration of the Rights of Man and of the Citizen, since Sieyès' formulation recognized that all inhabitants were citizens; but it adroitly cordoned off from political life all those whom the majority considered unfit or unworthy. The Assembly would now have to define who were unfit and unworthy.

Discussion began on 10 October when the Committee on the

---

1 Thus, "women (at least in the current situation), children, aliens, those who contribute nothing to the support of public institutions should not actively influence public matters." Cf. François-Alphonse Aulard, *Histoire politique de la Révolution française* (Paris: A. Colin, 1901), 61. [Abbé Emmanuel-Joseph Sieyès (1748-1836) was the author, in February 1789, of the celebrated pamphlet, *Qu'est-ce que le tiers état?* (What Is the Third Estate?). He was subsequently elected to the États Généraux as a member of the Third Estate, representing Paris. He served on the committee that drafted the Declaration of the Rights of Man and of the Citizen. A political survivor, he went on to serve on the Committee of Public Safety following Robespierre's overthrow; was elected a member, and later president, of the Consulate; and was a key player in the coup d'état that led to Napoléon's rise to political power. Thereafter Bonaparte heaped honors upon him while ignoring his advice.—TRANSL.]

Constitution proposed to base suffrage upon ability to pay a certain level of taxes.[2] Among five deputies who denounced the plan, three— Abbé Grégoire, Adrien Du Port[3] and Maximilien de Robespierre— would play active roles in the struggle for Jewish emancipation.[4] However, the Jews were never mentioned during the ensuing debate on the nature of active citizenship, which concluded on 29 October with adoption of the committee's proposal. The Declaration of the Rights of Man's acknowledgment of freedom of conscience made it impossible to write a provision into the Constitution which explicitly denied active citizenship based on religion, and the only criteria for exclusion retained were those of gender, age, income or domestic service. Bordeaux's strategy of silence seemed to bear fruit: since Jews were not mentioned in the legislation, the drafters apparently assumed that Jews were citizens like everyone else. Moreover, the Jews of the Southwest had already participated in elections for deputies to the États Généraux.

In October Abbé Grégoire introduced a lengthy "Motion in Favor of the Jews, Preceded by a Historical Note."[5] It reprised themes and arguments in his *Essai sur la régénération des Juifs* and set forth requests Alsace's Jews made in their address of 31 August.[6] He con-

---

2 The Committee on the Constitution proposed to limit voting eligibility to French males of at least twenty-five years of age who paid a direct contribution equal to the value of three days' labor. Excluded were women, domestic servants and those who could not prove residence in their district for at least one year.

3 Adrien-Jean-François Du Port (1759–1795) was an attorney with a practice before the Parlement of Paris, founder of the Society of Thirty in 1788, deputy of the Nobility of Paris in the États Généraux, and a *patriote* who played an important role in development of the judiciary. With Barnave and Alexandre de Lameth, he was part of the Triumvirate, whose influence grew during the period of the Constituent Assembly. Founder of the Club des Feuillants, he reconciled with Louis XVI after the king attempted to flee the country with his family in June 1791. Fleeing Paris after 10 August, Du Port was arrested, then freed when Danton intervened in his behalf. Du Port emigrated, returned to France after 9 Thermidor [27 July 1794, when Robespierre was deposed], was exiled again after 18 Fructidor, and died in Switzerland.

4 According to Gorsas, Grégoire said that in order to be able to be a voter or to be able to vote, "one only need be a good citizen, and have sound judgment and a French heart"; Aulard, 69

5 *Archives parlementaires de 1787 à 1860. Première série (de 1787 à 1799). Recueil complet des débats législatifs et politiques des Chambres françaises.* Jules Mavidal and Émile Laurent, eds. 32 vol. (Paris: P. Dupont, 1862-1888), 9:764.

6 "That the Assembly acknowledge that Jews possess all rights and duties of citizens, and that they enjoy liberty of worship; that the Assembly abolish the Brancas tax collected in Metz; that it make arrangements to guarantee payment of the debt

cluded his "Motion" with the final words of his essay: "May at last the Jew, granting to the Christian a return of his love, embrace me as his fellow citizen and friend."[7] The *Gazette de Paris* approved of Grégoire's initiative in its 16 November issue: "A priest of the Gospel, a curé of the Roman Church has become a defender of the Jews, leading their cause in the National Assembly…Who, even in the eighteenth century, would ever have been able to foresee that such homage would be paid to truth, to justice, to human rights, and by such a person…?"[8] However, Grégoire's "Motion" did not go unanswered. Abbé François-Martin Thiebaut,[9] a Catholic priest and deputy from Metz, retorted by repeating arguments Michælis had made in his polemic against Dohm: Jewish religious law, with its litany of prohibitions, made Jews incapable of fulfilling the duties of ordinary citizenship, which doomed them to remain aliens.[10]

Debate on emancipation promised to be passionate, but the topic never found its way onto the Assembly's formal agenda because the body's attention was focused on many other matters. As 1789 drew to a close, the Assembly had not acted on its pledge to examine the future status of the Jews. It was almost incidental that the matter came up in debate. In the meantime, when legislators made reference to France's Jews, a number of crucial themes were advanced, which shaped the Assembly's thinking about Jewish rights.

On 21 November Charles Bouche,[11] deputy from Aix, addressed the Assembly regarding "restitution for the Comtat Venaissin, its cities and the [papal] state of Avignon."[12] Noting that the Jews' "number there is considerable," Bouche asked that all special taxes imposed upon them, as well as of requirements that they wear distinctive cloth-

contracted by the Jewish community of Metz; finally, that it forbid insults to members of the Jewish nation." Ibid.

7 Ibid.

8 *La Gazette de Paris*, 2:29. Cf. ibid., (15 November 1789): 45, 46; (16 November): 49, 50; (17 November): 54, 55.

9 François-Martin Thiebaut (1749–1795) was a doctor of theology and militant monarchist who died during the emigration.

10 Cf. Maurice Liber, "Les Juifs et la convocation des États Généraux," *Revue des études juives* 63-66 (1912-1913): 199, 200.

11 Charles Bouche (1737–1795) was an attorney, deputy of the Third Estate from Aix, a centrist *patriote*, and member of the Society of Friends of the Constitution and then of the Club des Feuillants. Following the Constituent Assembly, he served on the Court of Appeal.

12 *Archives parlementaires*, 9:208.

ing or badges, be abolished, and suggested that they be permitted to purchase real estate. He also declared himself in favor of recognizing the Jews as citizens—when the Assembly thought it appropriate to do so. Thus, while Bouche spoke favorably about Jewish emancipation, he also expressed his electoral constituents' reluctance to acknowledge complete equal rights for Jews.

In December, the Assembly made some essential decisions: to issue assignats [which became the basis for a paper currency], to sell Church and royal properties, and to divide the kingdom's provinces into departments. During an evening session on 21 December Pierre Brunet de Latuque, deputy from Nérac, took to the rostrum to speak about the status of the nation's Protestants. Reminding the deputies that there were many Protestants in his southern province of Guyenne, he reported that in certain communes where Catholics were in the majority, calls had been made to deny Protestants access to elective office. Invoking the Declaration of the Rights of Man and the legal definition of "active" citizenship, Brunet de Latuque declared, "Gentlemen, you did not want religious beliefs to be a basis for excluding others,"[13] and proposed that the Assembly adopt a decree declaring that non-Catholics, "like all other citizens," were voters, eligible to serve in office and free to seek employment in all fields.[14] That brought Pierre-Louis Rœderer to the podium to request acknowledgment that the same rights should be granted "to a class of citizens who are spurned in polite society and yet who have their value and importance: actors..."[15]

Clermont-Tonnerre[16] responded in an attempt to redirect debate to Brunet's original motion and offered a text intended to express a general principle: no active citizen "can be removed from the roll of eligible voters or excluded from public employment on grounds of

---

13 Ibid.

14 Ibid.

15 Ibid.

16 Stanislas-Marie-Adélaïde, comte de Clermont-Tonnerre (1757–1792) was a deputy of the Nobility of Paris to the États Généraux and an admirer of England's constitutional monarchy. He was a leader of the forty-six deputies of the Nobility who went over to the Third Estate on 25 June 1789. After the events of October 1789, when the king and the National Assembly moved from Versailles to Paris, he reconciled with the monarchists. With Malouet he created the Club des Impartiaux in January 1790. Following the royal family's flight to Varennes in June 1791 he published an extremely critical study, "An Analysis of the Constitution." Clermont-Tonnerre was murdered by a mob on 10 August 1792.

profession or religion."[17] Without explicitly saying so, his proposal acknowledged Jews as full citizens.

The implications of Clermont-Tonnerre's text did not escape Jean-François Rewbell, who sat on the left of the Assembly with the *patriotes* as deputy from Colmar. Rising to question Clermont-Tonnerre he asked whether his colleague intended to include Jews among "active" citizens. "Yes," Clermont-Tonnerre proclaimed. "That is my intention, and I take pride in it."[18] The Assembly erupted in commotion. Rewbell immediately took the floor again, and his retort was harsh: "I think what the Jews themselves think: they do not think of themselves as citizens..."[19]

Rewbell had broached a key argument: do not give those who wish to be aliens within France the same rights granted to the French. Newspaper accounts reflected the muddled discussion that followed. "The *patriotes*," wrote a journalist in *Le Patriote français*, "were impatient to vote [on Brunet's motion] in order to do justice on a matter of principle. But with the usual shilly-shallying over previous business and postponements, the clock ran out and the session was adjourned."[20] Writing in the *Journal de Paris*, Jacques-Pierre Brissot expressed indignation regarding Rewbell's comments: "It takes courage to put forth paradoxes so foreign and so at odds with sound politics and *philosophie*."[21] The *Journal de Versailles* noted

---

17 *Archives parlementaires*, 10:695.

18 *Le Courrier français*, no. 170 (22 December 1789). "If M. de Clermont-Tonnerre had only used his talent to put forth similar decrees," wrote Camille Desmoulins, "his reputation today would not be so doubtful. We must never despair of intelligent men." *Révolutions de France et de Brabant*, no. 5: 204–205.

19 *Archives parlementaires*, 10:695. According to the *Moniteur*, 1:116, Rewbell had said that "there are 300,000 Jews in this province." This was more than ten times their actual number in Alsace. On 5 January 1790 Rewbell wrote to Camille Desmoulins to explain his attitude at the time of the debate on 21–24 December 1789: "Would you go to the trouble of reading the 'Address of the Jews of Metz, Trois-Évêchés, and Lorraine,' issued last 31 August? What do you think of those who wish to become French [citizens] and nevertheless retain their own system of governance, their own lawyers; who wish to follow laws of inheritance, legal trusteeship and age of majority, etc., other than those of the French, their neighbors... You see that it is not me who excludes the Jews. They exclude themselves..." Quoted in Liber, 193.

20 *Le Patriote français*, 23 December 1789.

21 *Journal de Paris*, no. 358 (24 December 1789). [Jacques-Pierre Brissot de Warville (1754-1793) was a journalist and edited the newspaper *Le Patriote français*. He was prominent in calling for confiscation of property owned by the émigrés, members of the nobility who fled France during the opening stage of the Revolution. In 1792 he supported war against European nations that provided refuge to the émigrés as

that Rœderer expressed regret that Clermont-Tonnerre had posed the issue of Jewish rights so baldly: "We know that many people, who agree to admit a truth when it is set forth in vague and general terms, tremble and shudder once they begin to understand its practical consequences. That is what happened when M. de Clermont-Tonnerre realized the far-reaching consequences of the principle to which he appealed."[22]

THE CONFRONTATION

After several parliamentary skirmishes on 22 December, discussion resumed on 23 December regarding "admission of non-Catholics to all municipal and provincial public offices, and to all civil and military posts, like all other citizens."[23] Two days previously Rœderer had reminded the Assembly of the social indignities actors traditionally suffered, and some monarchist deputies, in response to Clermont-Tonnerre's motion, had invoked in ironic tones the evil reputation that afflicted executioners. Debate now broadened to include these occupations' status as speakers randomly discussed Protestants, actors, executioners and Jews in order to decide whether members of these groups would be eligible to vote and to hold public office.

The mixture was, to say the least, odd. No common thread tied together the ancient prejudice that affected several hundred actors (some of whom were idolized by the public), the dread that executioners inspired, and the plight of the Jews, whose fate was, as Brissot noted, "a matter of interest to people concerned with *philosophie*, humanity, justice, love of country and religion."[24] No one in the Assembly—not even the most hard-line conservatives—seriously thought, two years after the edict of toleration issued in 1787 and four months after promulgation of the Declaration of the Rights of Man, that Protestants, who were encountering difficulties with groups of Catholic fanatics in the Southwest, could be excluded from any public posts.

---

part of a conspiracy to launch a counterrevolution. His political followers, known to contemporaries as "Brissotins," were the nucleus of the "Girondin" opposition to Robespierre's "Montagnards." Brissot died on the scaffold when the Girondins were purged during the Terror.—*TRANSL.*]

22 *Journal de Versailles*, no. 8 (26 December 1789).
23 *Archives parlementaires*, 10:754.
24 *Le Patriote français*, 23 December 1789.

Clermont-Tonnerre, rising to open the discussion, attempted to redirect the legislature's attention to emancipation in general terms, as a matter of religious liberty. The Assembly, he noted, could not refuse to one group the benefit of religious liberty granted to others; nor could it justify, given the Declaration of the Rights of Man, denying to Jews rights to which Protestants were entitled. "There is no middle course possible," he declared; "either you acknowledge a national religion..., and cast from your midst those who follow another religion, whereby you blot out the Declaration of Rights's article concerning religious freedom; or, better, [you] allow each individual to have his own religious opinion and not exclude from public offices those who exercise this right. That is justice, that is sensible."[25]

The principal opponents of Jewish emancipation—Abbé Jean-Sifrein Maury; Bishop Anne-Louis-Henri de La Fare, of Nancy; François-Jean Hell, and Charles-Louis-Victor, prince de Broglie—retreated from questioning the rights of France's Protestants. That issue was settled and abandoned once the Jews' champions shifted the debate to the high ground by invoking the Declaration of the Rights of Man. Instead Jewish emancipation's opponents now argued that rights, equal to those granted to Christians, should not be given to Jews because the Jews were aliens by virtue of their religion and their way of life.

Clermont-Tonnerre was a gifted politician. He rallied support for his motion, noted Adrien Duquesnoy, a moderate *patriote* and close observer who served as deputy for Bar-le-Duc, "with all the intelligence, all the skill, all the assurance and ease that he knew how to muster—if need be with that amiable charlatanism of which he is capable and which is hardly becoming to anyone but himself."[26] Clermont-Tonnerre knew he could win over the Assembly's moderates only if he convinced them that they had a pressing moral obligation not to abandon the Declaration of the Rights of Man. But he also wanted emancipation to remove everything that branded the Jews as different, everything that made them a community distinct from others—in a word, everything that made them a "nation." That

---

25 *Archives parlementaires*, 10:755.

26 Adrien-Cyprien Duquesnoy, *Journal d'Adrien Duquesnoy, député du Tiers état de Bar-le-Duc, sur l'Assemblée constituante, 3 mai 1789–3 avril 1790*. Published for the Société d'histoire contemporaine by Robert de Crèvecœur. 2 vol. (Paris: Alphonse Picard et fils, 1894), 2:209.

STA. CLERMONT-TONNERE

Députe de Paris à l'assemblée Nat.^{le} en 1789

Moreover, is there a law that obliges me to eat hare,
and to eat it with you?
— Stanislas, comte de Clermont-Tonnerre

was why he advocated that the Jews be granted citizenship, as Lacretelle had done when in 1775 Lacretelle had argued a lawsuit on
behalf of Jewish shopkeepers in Thionville.

Clermont-Tonnerre opened his rebuttal by reminding the Assembly of the criticisms directed toward Jews: "They say these people
are unsociable. They are commanded to practice usury. They cannot
associate with us either by marriage or in ordinary social intercourse;
the delicacies on our tables are forbidden to them; our armies will
never see Jews serving the homeland."[27] These criticisms, he declared,
were "either unjust or specious." With a spark of eloquence, he cried
out: "Subdue your hatreds and open your hearts to reason: this usury, justly condemned, is the result of our own laws. Men whose only
possession is money can make their livings only by lending money.
That is the cause of the evil. Let them have land and a homeland, and
they will no longer lend money. That is the remedy."[28]

As for the matter of the Jews' "unsociability," Clermont-Tonnerre suggested that it would disappear by itself under the impact of
education and as Jews learned new customs. "Moreover," he added
in an aside, "is there a law that obliges me to eat hare [a non-kosher
animal], and to eat it with you?"[29] Then he arrived at the heart of his
argument: France's Jewish communities were self-governing in civil
matters pertaining to marriage and inheritance, according to their
own religious legal codes and customs. Clermont-Tonnerre rejected
these privileges, and in doing so revealed exactly what he thought:
"*We must refuse everything to the Jews as a nation, and grant everything to the Jews as individuals.* They must not constitute within
the state either a political body or a caste. They must be citizens as
individuals..."[30]

This, then, was Clermont-Tonnerre's doctrine of integration:
the Jews' failings were the result of injustice practiced by Christians.
Christians were guilty, not the Jews. Let the Jews be given equal
rights and they will, thanks to the Enlightenment, cease their fanatical or appalling practices. At the same time, do not permit them to
maintain their own communal institutions and laws. If the Jews wish
to be citizens, then let them be citizens, completely, like others. But

---

27 *Archives parlementaires*, 10:765.
28 Ibid.
29 Ibid.
30 Ibid., emphasis in the original text.

there cannot be a special category of citizens who have their own rights and institutions. Everyone should be equal and identical in the eyes of the law. Let the Jews be citizens as individuals. There must no longer be an *imperium in imperio*, a Jewish nation within France.

Clermont-Tonnerre evoked Malesherbes's thinking but went further. He wanted Jews to be full citizens. Just a year before they had not dared to make that demand; but the Revolution had passed that point. Now, as a result, one of their most eloquent defenders rejected the other component of their requests: that they be allowed to maintain their own laws and religious courts. Clermont-Tonnerre's eloquence and his humane regard for a humiliated people [31] reveals the political motive that drove supporters of emancipation: to lay to rest the "Jewish question" by granting Jews equality but refusing to grant them special treatment; to recognize them as citizens but not as Jews per se.

Abbé Maury, parliamentary leader of the monarchist right, responded to Clermont-Tonnerre. Their confrontation was all the more startling because, in the wake of events during October 1789, when a Parisian mob forced the king and the National Assembly to relocate to Paris from Versailles, Clermont-Tonnerre had rejoined the monarchist camp. He went on to join with Pierre Victor Malouet in creating the Club des Impartiaux to counter the growing influence of the Society of Friends of the Constitution (a forerunner of the Jacobin Club), where advocates of emancipation, including deputies such as Adrien Du Port and other important figures, such as Condorcet, met.

A brilliant and skillful orator, and a leader of the monarchist "blacks," Maury answered Clermont-Tonnerre with arguments based on traditional anti-Judaism, rather than attempting to refute the principles of the Declaration of the Rights of Man. The Jews, the abbé declared, could not be citizens like others: they "have spent seventeen centuries without mixing with the other nations." [32] They could not be farmers because "they prefer trade to toil," and because "the law they observe does not allow them time to devote themselves to agriculture. Over and above their sabbath, they have fifty-six

---

31 Cf. Charles Du Bus, *Stanislas de Clermont-Tonnerre et l'échec de la révolution monar-chique (1757-1792)* (Paris: F. Alcan, 1931), 210–215.

32 *Archives parlementaires*, 10:757.

more religious holidays than do Christians."[33] They were no more capable of being artisans than soldiers because their sabbath kept them from engaging in work or combat. Truly, "they have never engaged in anything except trading in money." And Maury, in order to sway the Assembly majority, which was hardly well-informed in such matters, asserted: "In Alsace they [the Jews] hold twelve million mortgages on landed properties. In a month they could possess half the province. In ten years, they could completely take over; Alsace would be no more than a Jewish colony..."[34] Maury's statistics were wildly exaggerated, but he exaggerated in order to evoke the image of a French province, long a Catholic stronghold, menaced with falling into the hands of the Jews. Traditional Christian anti-Judaism fed such fantasies.

The political conclusion Maury drew from these premises was that Jews were ineligible to enjoy the rights of citizenship because their religious laws prohibited them from carrying out the duties of citizenship. They were not really French; they were aliens residing in France. "To call Jews citizens," he declared, "would be like saying that, without letters of nationalization and without ceasing to be English or Danish, the English and the Danes can become French."[35] Abbé Maury thus excluded Jews from participation in national life by declaring them, by definition, alien to it. In so doing, he prefigured the transition from classic anti-Judaism to modern anti-Semitism.[36]

The *patriote* press gave Maury's ideas a critical though mixed response. "Unfortunate Jews," declared Gorsas in *Le Courrier*, "remain forever strangers in the nation from which you seek fairness! Hear your sentence: It is Abbé Maury who pronounces it." That same day, Rœderer's *Le Journal de Paris* was more temperate in its criticism of a "speech whose eloquence grew as it slipped away from the bounds of rigorous logic."[37] While refuting Maury's reasoning, the newspaper concluded: "What would happen if they became active citizens and wanted neither to fight nor to work on their sabbath days? It is impossible to make them join the armies, or to imagine

---

33   Ibid.
34   Ibid.
35   Ibid., cf. Maury: "Therefore may they be protected as individuals, and not as Frenchmen, since they cannot be citizens..."
36   *Le Courrier*, ed. by Gorsas, no. 14 (25 December 1789).
37   *Le Journal de Paris*, no. 359 (25 December 1789).

them serving on administrative bodies or in the legislative Assembly. They would remain more or less as they are, and we would act properly toward them. They would lose nothing, and we might gain much."[38]

Robespierre responded to Maury on behalf of the *patriotes*. He was succinct. He denounced the lies: "You have been told things about the Jews that are grossly exaggerated and often historically incorrect." He reiterated themes Clermont-Tonnerre and Grégoire had previously developed: "How can we deny the persecutions to which various peoples have subjected them? On the contrary, these are national crimes for which we ought to atone by restoring to them the inalienable human rights of which no human power can rob them ..." Ever the moralist in political matters, Robespierre urged the Assembly: "Let us give back to them happiness, their homeland, their honor in giving them the dignity of men and citizens; let us consider that it can never be politically wise, whatever one might say, to condemn to debasement and oppression a multitude of people who live among us."[39] *Le Moniteur* commented: "M. de Robespierre championed M. de Clermont-Tonnerre's motion; but he gave weak justification for his point of view."[40]

When Msgr. de La Fare, bishop of Nancy, took the floor, he resumed where Abbé Maury had left off, asserting that "the Jews' religious laws make them strangers among all nations."[41] In a display of magnanimity, he acknowledged that "To be fair...the Jews have rendered Lorraine and, above all, the city of Nancy, great service..."[42] But the reality was that "the people loathe them...," and "a decree that gave the Jews the rights of citizens would arouse a grave conflagration."[43] Prudence therefore dictated that the Assembly make no decision, and Bishop La Fare recommended appointing a committee to revise all legislation concerning the Jews. It was an

---

38 Ibid.

39 *Archives parlementaires*, ibid.

40 *Le Moniteur*, 1 (26 December 1789): 124.

41 *Archives parlementaires*, ibid.

42 Ibid.

43 *Archives parlementaires*, ibid. According to La Fare, "[F]our months ago, people in Nancy wanted to pillage their houses..., some claimed that the Jews were hoarding wheat; others that their numbers had grown too large, that they bought the most beautiful houses—and that soon they would own the entire city."

elegant way of shelving the question.[44]

La Fare's speech had greater impact than Robespierre's among the Assembly's moderates. Robespierre had appealed to principles: the Declaration of the Rights of Man and its moral imperatives; La Fare had appealed to facts: open hostility toward Jews in the eastern provinces. The deputies were struggling with a host of basic issues: eradicating the deficit, finishing work on the Constitution, organizing the country's administrative structure, creating a new legal system—in short, giving birth to a new France. Granting the Jews civil rights by recognizing them as citizens risked sparking new riots; granting citizenship to a few thousand Jews who a month previously had not asked for it risked eroding support for the Revolution. Human decency demanded that they be protected from all violence; but as to their rights as citizens, prudence suggested that nothing be decided. Surely the matter of the Jews' political status could wait.

Sensing that a decision in favor of Jewish emancipation was slipping away, Adrien Du Port, a moderate *patriote*, skillful parliamentarian and clever politician, attempted to recapture the initiative in the debate. As 1789 was drawing to a close, his political influence was growing in the Assembly. With Antoine Barnave and Alexandre de Lameth, he was part of the "Triumvirate" that controlled the Society of Friends of the Constitution, a forerunner of the Jacobin Club. Although legislative luminaries such as Mirabeau and Sieyès heartily detested him, Du Port was acknowledged as an excellent jurist, a friend of freedom and a man of principle. An influential figure in the Committee on Legislation and an author of the new penal code, he now threw his weight into the discussion, proposing that no Frenchman could be excluded from citizenship for a reason that had not been expressly articulated in a law passed by the Assembly.[45] Du Port's motion was clever because he knew that the Assembly, author of the Declaration of Rights, would never adopt a decree that explicitly excluded the Jews from citizenship.

Clermont-Tonnerre immediately attempted to rally support for consideration of this new motion. The Assembly's rules of proce-

44 "Some banal arguments, some trivial ideas...," wrote Adrien Duquesnoy regarding La Fare's speech; "a man of great mind lowers himself when he fights for a bad cause." Duquesnoy, 203.

45 "M. Du Port," wrote *Le Moniteur*, "spoke to the same principles as those which M. de Clermont-Tonnerre had put forward. His speech seemed thin..." *Le Moniteur*, 1 (26 December 1789): 131.

dure, however, dictated that, unless its members decided otherwise, Brunet de Latuque's more narrowly framed motion in favor of rights for non-Catholics, i.e., Protestants, would have to be voted on first. The Assembly decided to vote on whether to give Du Port's motion precedence. A favorable vote for Du Port's motion would presage its ultimate adoption. It was a crucial moment in the struggle for Jewish emancipation. "Two rounds conducted by standing-and-sitting yielded uncertain results. When a roll-call voice vote was finally taken the body refused, by a majority of 408–403, to give precedence to Du Port's wording.[46]

Despite this outcome, the *patriote* press remained optimistic. "It may be astonishing," wrote a journalist, "that the clergy and other opponents had obtained only five votes needed to block this motion."[47] Rœderer, writing in the *Journal de Paris*, noted: "The tiny margin was a most uncertain measure of the Assembly's general will."[48] Brissot regretted "not having seen the eloquent Abbé Grégoire stand up for these unfortunates whom he had so well defended with his pen."

Indeed, Grégoire, after having widely circulated his essay and publicized his motion in favor of the Jews of the East, had not participated in the debate. His silence, so out of character, was a judgment about the political environment. Earlier that month on 3 December he had attempted to convince the Assembly to recognize the citizenship of mixed-race people of color; and on 10 December he had published his "Memorandum in Favor of the People of Color of Saint-Domingue."[49] Spokesmen for France's colonial lobby had lashed out against him. In this highly emotional climate and in the wake of his defeat on behalf of the rights of people of color, his participation in that month's debate on Jewish rights might have proven counterproductive. Nonetheless it was regrettable, as Brissot noted, that at this critical moment Grégoire did not lend his impassioned voice to tell the Assembly about the long suffering of the Jewish people and of his hope that justice might finally be done.

---

46 *Archives parlementaires*, 10:738.

47 *Le Journal d'Etat et du citoyen*, ed. by Kéralio, no. 13, 2d trimester (27 December 1789).

48 *Journal de Paris*, no. 359 (25 December 1789).

49 Cf. Yves Benot, *La Révolution française et la fin des colonies* (Paris: La Découverte, 1988), 66.

The Jews of Paris had paid close attention to the debate. Seeing Du Port's defeat on 22 December and the thin margin of votes
that separated advocates and opponents of Jewish emancipation, they
decided to renew their efforts to sway both the Assembly and public
opinion in their favor. On 23 December they drafted and printed a
"New Address of the Jews to the National Assembly." Responding to
the charge that sabbath observance rendered Jews incapable of fulfilling a citizen's duties, they emphasized that Jews who served in the
National Guard had left work at great cost, "for they had to bear
arms to protect the public, day and night, even during our day of
rest." Invoking the arguments advanced by Abbé Grégoire, the "gen-
erous and eloquent pastor of Metz," and "other equally distinguished
members" of the Assembly, they put the deputies on notice that in
view of the Assembly's "well-known reverence for human rights...,"
Paris's Jews expected the Assembly to take no action that would "con-
tradict the acts of wisdom and justice that have issued forth [from
the Assembly]..."[50] Whether this address, dated 24 December, was
delivered to the deputies before the start of that morning's session is
unknown. Nonetheless, it is evidence of the maturity and activism
Paris's Jews brought to this political struggle.

WE MUST WAIT...

When debate resumed on 24 December, the deputies of the eastern provinces sensed that the five-vote margin by which Du Port's
motion had lost still indicated strong support for Jewish rights. They
decided to respond in force. François-Jean Hell, who represented
Haguenau, in Alsace, and who was the most passionate opponent
of the Jews and instigator of the "affair of the forged receipts," led
off. In a skillful feint to disarm the Assembly's majority, this ultraconservative monarchist paid his respects to the ideological currents
of the day, conceding that "The Jews are men, and they should enjoy
the Rights of Man." But he immediately added: "They will make
themselves worthy of this if you enact legislation declaring what you
expect of them." It was up to the Jews to deserve the Rights of Man,
he argued, and we must make them ready for those rights with ap-

---

50 "Nouvelle Adresse des Juifs à l'Assemblée nationale," 24 December 1789, p.
3, in *La Révolution française et l'émancipation des Juifs* (Paris: Edhis [Éditions d'Histoire
Sociale], 1968) 8 vol. Vol. 5: *Adresses, Mémoires et Pétitions des Juifs, 1789-1794*.

propriate measures. "As it would be dangerous for Alsace—and for the Jews themselves—to declare that from now on Jews are capable of attaining all positions, the Assembly should take care in order to prepare them."[51]

Hell therefore offered the Assembly a series of restrictive proposals which, in 1788, he had convinced Alsace's intermediate commission to adopt.[52] Among these was a limit on the Jewish population, which took the form of forbidding Jews to marry without authorization. Permission would be granted only if Jewish households in a district "do not exceed a sixth of the other faiths, and if the Jew has a useful occupation and gives proof of being the owner of at least one acre of land." As for the intended bride, she had to be able to "sew a straight line, knit [and] spin flax, hemp, cotton and wool." With this idyllic vision of a handful of Jews regenerated by agricultural and handicraft pursuits, cultivating their fields beside wives who worked at their spinning wheels, Hell concluded this astonishing motion—introduced four months after the adoption of the Declaration of the Rights of Man—by adding that it would accomplish "the double objective that you seek: to root out usury and to make all individuals born and living in the French empire equally happy..."[53]

Then prince Claude de Broglie followed Hell at the rostrum. A moderate liberal, he was closer to the *patriotes* than the conservatives, but he was also a deputy from Colmar. The prince began by noting, courteously, that his remarks applied only to the Jews of Alsace, and that he was "far removed" from wishing to place obstacles in the path of acts of kindness which the Assembly sought to bestow "on the people of this unfortunate nation."[54] What followed, however, were classic arguments against emancipation: "The Jews

---

51 *Archives parlementaires*, 10:778.

52 Among its measures, Hell's proposals also called for participation by the Jews in taxation like other citizens, while "continuing to pay the current fees of protection"; abolition of all community organizations and of all rabbinic jurisdiction; prohibition of legal documents drawn up in any language other than French; the possibility of acquiring land on condition that it be cultivated personally; and the right to engage in all occupations, but without the right to sell on credit or to lend money.

53 *Archives parlementaires*, 10:778. It is striking to note that in the same speech Hell observed "that, throughout the empire of France, all Mohammedans, especially the subjects of the Turkish emperor (*sic*), enjoy all rights, honors and advantages enjoyed by French citizens." Who, after such a declaration, could deny Hell's devotion to the Rights of Man?

54 Ibid., 10:779.

are aliens in France, a sort of temporary residents, or rather cosmopolitans, who have never enjoyed or ever even laid claim to status as French citizens, [and] to whom it would be dangerous to grant [citizenship] without caution ... Even in the smallest villages they are concentrated in a body as a nation; and this political existence of a nation within a nation is certainly as dangerous in its consequences as it is antisocial in principle."[55] Confronted with enormous growth in the number of Jews in Alsace, which had increased from ten thousand to twenty-six thousand in fifteen years, what was to be done at a time when "their idleness, their lack of tact, which necessarily follows from humiliating laws and conditions to which they were subjected in many places, contribute to making them odious?"[56]

A man who liked to think of himself as both compassionate and practical, prince de Broglie declared that it was necessary to admit the Jews to all trades and agriculture without delay. After a certain number of years of "apprenticeship or testing, we will be able to allow Jews—individually, on favorable testimony from the district's inhabitants—to take the civil oath which will admit them to all the privileges of French citizens." Moreover, it was necessary to grant an extension of at least ten years to the Jews' debtors, in order to allow them time to discharge their debts. Such measures would prevent the outbreak of violence that threatened the Jews were they to be given the rights of citizens.[57]

Then Rewbell, who represented Colmar's Third Estate and sat on the Assembly's left, took up the same theme. Hatred against the Jews in Alsace was such, he said, that it "would be imprudent, for the Jews themselves, to grant the Jews, at least at present, the same rights as other citizens..."[58]

The Assembly heard the consensus among Alsace's deputies—an ultraconservative like Hell, a liberal like prince de Broglie, a committed *patriote* like Rewbell—each opposed to granting citizenship to the Jews. The National Assembly was being asked to deny applica-

---

55 Ibid., 780.

56 Ibid.

57 According to *Le Moniteur*, 27 December 1789, "M. de Clermont-Tonnerre supported prince de Broglie's motion," 1:128. Compared with the reception given Clermont-Tonnerre's speech of the previous evening, this had been a very clear setback. The *Archives parlementaires* make no mention of such a speech by Clermont-Tonnerre.

58 *Archives parlementaires*, 10:781.

tion of the Declaration of the Rights of Man to the Jews in order to accommodate local opinion in the eastern provinces.

Antoine-Pierre-Joseph-Marie Barnave then stepped in.[59] Associated with the *patriotes*, he was an eloquent speaker and his influence in the Assembly was growing. At this point in the debate, when the majority remained uncertain of what course to take, his remarks could be decisive in countering the Alsatian deputies' offensive. He began by invoking the Declaration of the Rights of Man, contending that no one could be denied its protections by reason of religious belief (the Jews) or occupation (actors). But rather than declaring outright support for Jewish emancipation, he suggested that "the Assembly should limit itself to specific statements in favor of Protestants."[60] An adroit politician, Barnave wished always to be a realist. He sensed that, for the moment, victory was eluding emancipation's supporters and he was anxious to avoid any head-on clash with the Assembly's majority. By deftly presenting the Assembly with a means to avoid making a direct statement about the citizenship of the Jews, Barnave opened the way for a vote that gained time for emancipation's supporters.

In succession De Barmal, bishop of Clermont, who was very conservative and hostile to the Jews, and Bon-Albert Briois de Beaumetz, a moderate, proposed to divide the questions submitted to the Assembly, and to postpone consideration of the one related to the Jews. Beaumetz supported this request with a simple argument: the Assembly risked giving the Jews rights which they did not want. He agreed, therefore, that it was better make inquiries before making a decision.[61] The Assembly, offered a way out of a difficult situation, greeted this proposal with lively applause. The game appeared to be over.

Then Mirabeau addressed the chamber. Curiously, the greatest

---

59 Antoine-Pierre-Joseph-Marie Barnave (1761–1793), a lawyer and deputy who represented Grenoble's Third Estate, formed the "Triumvirate" with Du Port and Lameth. Creator of the Society of Friends of the Constitution, which became the Jacobin Club, he left the Jacobins to found the Club des Feuillants. After the royal family's flight to Varennes in June 1791, he reconciled with the court and became a defender of the monarchy. Arrested after 10 August 1792, he was guillotined 29 November 1793.

60 *Archives parlementaires*, 10:781.

61 "Before deciding in favor of this long-unfortunate people, we need to know what they would like to be, at what cost they wish to obtain their liberty and, finally, that they are deserving of it." Ibid.

orator of the Assembly, a populist leader who more than anyone else was capable of winning votes from the undecided and courageous decisions from the fainthearted, had not yet taken part in the debate, despite his support for Mendelssohn's ideas and the cause of Jewish emancipation.[62] He had had several opportunities to throw his formidable influence and his oratorical talent behind emancipation, yet he had been reticent to do so. Deeply political and an exceptional parliamentarian, Mirabeau, like Barnave, calculated that in the wake of the Alsatian deputies' assault, a majority of the Assembly, despite its commitment to the Declaration of the Rights of Man, was indifferent to the plight of the Jews and was going to decide that there was no need to rule on their citizenship. Nothing was worse for a populist parliamentarian than to throw himself deeply into a debate only to be repudiated by the majority. Mirabeau's credit had already declined among the *patriotes* since the Assembly's debates about the king's veto. Political caution and personal interest had led him to maintain a low profile.

But the great orator could not allow to go unchallenged Beaumetz's remarks that perhaps the Jews did not want the rights which the Assembly might grant them. "So, gentlemen," Mirabeau declared, "could it be that because the Jews do not want to be citizens, you would not declare them to be citizens? In a government such as you are creating, all men must be treated as men."[63] Incidentally, he added, it was not true that the Jews did not wish to be citizens; and he proceeded to read to the Assembly the request by Jews of the East that they be granted citizenship. But that was as far as Mirabeau was prepared to commit himself in the current debate, and he joined the majority that was then taking shape: "I conclude that we must defer the question on the Jews because the situation is not clear enough; but I do not any less seek to destroy the previous speaker's impressions

---

62 His newspaper, *Le Courrier de Provence* (cf. no. 83, 23 and 24 December 1789), firmly supported the doctrine of emancipation: "All men have a homeland; this homeland is the place of their birth and education. Consequently, Jews born in France of parents settled in France are French; they are our compatriots, our fellow citizens. Do they wish to enjoy all rights of citizenship? Then they must submit to the political and civil laws of the kingdom. And if they submit to all the laws of the State? Then we cannot deny them their exercise of all rights granted to others. What does diversity of worship matter?"

63 *Archives parlementaires*, 10:781.

regarding this people, who are more sinned against than sinning."[64]

The question was finally brought to a vote. "After much debate, complaint and clamor,"[65] the Assembly declared that "non-Catholics will be able to be voters and eligible under set conditions; that they are fit to hold all civil and military posts, as are all other citizens...,without prejudice regarding the Jews, upon whose status the National Assembly awaits the proper time to declare its opinion."[66] After the decree was read, wrote a witness, "cries of 'Vive la Nation!' resounded throughout the chamber, and spectators in the gallery applauded along with the deputies."[67]

Remarking that the decree was adopted "against the wish of the Clergy,"[68] the *patriote* press readily approved the Assembly's decision to avoid addressing the issue of Jewish emancipation. *La Gazette de Paris* stated, "There are few questions so delicate...The Law of Moses has so linked politics to religion that it is nearly impossible for the Jew to be a French citizen, at least unless he abandons a large part of [that] law."[69] Brissot, writing in *Le Patriote français*, approved the Assembly's action: "This idea to delay was sensible because, without excluding the Jews, it prepared the way to see them one day as eligible; it allowed time for prejudices to dissipate, time for passions to calm, and for the Jews to make themselves worthy of the rights of citizens by giving up this system of isolation and intolerance which is peculiar to them."[70] Rœderer, having once before impugned Abbé Maury's arguments, wrote in the *Journal de Paris* of the decision to defer a decision: "A motive of caution, and no doubt of humanity, dictated the reservation about making a decision regarding the Jews; let us hope that it will be resolved soon...It is the only way to regenerate this wandering and persecuted tribe."[71] Mirabeau's newspaper, *Le Courrier de Provence*, approved this approach: "Our

---

64 Ibid., 782, and Mirabeau's newspaper, *Le Courrier de Provence*, no. 83: 18.

65 *Le Moniteur*, 1: 128.

66 *Archives parlementaires*, 10:781.

67 Duquesnoy, 2:208.

68 Ibid.

69 *Le Journal général de la Cour et de la Ville*, no. 99. Cf. Duquesnoy who, reporting on the session, concluded: "There are no maneuvers, chicaneries or subtleties that the high clergy did not employ today." Duquesnoy, 2:207.

70 *La Gazette de Paris*, 25 December 1789.

71 *Journal de Paris*, 26 December 1789. [See text referred to in fn. 37, above, regarding Rœderer's comments about Abbé Maury.—TRANSL.]

first duty, no doubt, is to be just; but in a matter of this importance we cannot separate justice from caution and moderation."[72] Jean-Paul Marat, however, considered the entire debate pointless. "I do not have the strength," he wrote, "to comment on the puerile things with which the National Assembly is busy at this moment..." Significantly, he praised Abbé Maury: "The most profound thing he ever said is his speech taking objection to the Jews..."; nonetheless, Marat concluded, almost with regret, in favor of granting them citizenship: "Though there are few indications that we will see them devote themselves to legitimate livelihoods available in society, there are no grounds to exclude them."[73] Camille Desmoulins preferred to take an ironic view: "Would it not be the height of absurdity if one had only to show proof of a foreskin in order to be eligible [for citizenship]?"[74]

The debate's outcome was truly a defeat for the Jews. The Assembly had not rejected their requests. But only several months after having proclaimed the Declaration of the Rights of Man, it had shied away from recognizing complete civil rights for Jews, as it had avoided doing the same for men of color. Prejudice remained stronger than principle. The Bastille of anti-Judaism still stood, rooted in the traditional hostility of the Church and collective perceptions of the racketeering and usurious Jew, irreconcilably a stranger in Christian society.

---

72 *Le Courrier de Provence*, no. 83: 18.

73 *L'Ami du peuple*, 25 December 1789.

74 Cf. *Révolutions de France et de Brabant*, no. 5: 204.

CHAPTER 6

EVERY MAN FOR HIMSELF

THE BORDEAUX DELEGATION TO PARIS

THE JEWS OF THE SOUTHWEST CONSIDERED THE NATIONAL AS-
sembly's decree of 24 December 1789 to be a disaster. Until then they
had attained all the objectives toward which they had worked for a
year: to participate in elections, to be recognized as eligible to hold office, to be welcomed into the National Guard and elected as officers,
to be admitted into political clubs—in short, to be treated equally
and as full citizens. And now, due to the unreasonable strategy that
the Jews of the East had pursued, *all* Jews in France, including the
"Portuguese," had no clearly defined status. Not only had the Jews of
the East *not* gotten what they wanted, but in defeat they had deprived
the Jews of the Southwest of their gains. That is where these fanatical,
starving Ashkenazim had led them—with their leaders Cerf-Berr and
Berr Isaac Berr, and their advocates, an activist and hotheaded abbé
and Parisian aristocrats whose knowledge of Jews consisted of what
they had read in books. Six months after the onset of the Revolution
the "Portuguese" looked upon their situation as more precarious than
it had been in 1788 when they had met with Malesherbes.

Bordeaux's Jews met in general assembly, chaired by the community's syndic, Dias Pereyra, on 30 December. They then composed an
address that forcefully expressed their displeasure with their Ashkenazi brethren. In it they recalled that "in our capacity as *regnicoles* in
Bordeaux, we have enjoyed without trouble, in this city and throughout the jurisdiction of Paris, the rights of citizens... We dare to believe
that our status in France would not today be under discussion had not
certain Jews in Alsace, Lorraine and the Trois-Évêchés given birth to
a confusion of ideas, which seems to envelop us..."[1] They criticized

---

1 "Adresse à l'Assemblée nationale" [31 December 1789], in *La Révolution française
et l'émancipation des Juifs.* 8 vol. (Paris: Edhis [Éditions d'Histoire sociale], 1968). Vol.
5: *Adresses, Mémoires et Pétitions des Juifs, 1789-1794.*

the desire of the Jews of the East "to live in France under a special system, to have laws of their own and to constitute a class of citizens separate from all the others."[2] Finally, they asked: "Should the poorly conceived requests of the Jews of Alsace, who enjoy few of the advantages which we possess, be allowed to deprive us of our rights? So far as we are concerned, *it is less a matter of acquiring* [rights] *than of not losing* [rights]."[3] The Bordelais minced no words in clearly delineating the differences—the chasm—that existed, between themselves and the "Teutons."

Dias Pereyra, his deputies and 215 heads of families signed the address, and a special delegation was authorized to present their case to the National Assembly in Paris.[4] Eight delegates were chosen; among them were the senior Gradis, Lopes Dubec, Abraham Rodrigues and the elder Furtado[5] who eighteen months earlier had traveled to Paris to meet with Malesherbes.

Three delegates left the next day for the capital by mail coach. After halting at Poitiers to observe the Jewish sabbath, they arrived in Paris on the morning of 4 January and lodged at the hôtel de la Chine on the rue Neuve-des-Petits-Champs. They set to work at once. Thanks to the "Journal de la députation,"[6] which has fortunately been preserved, it is possible to follow day by day, almost hour by hour, the campaign they waged in Paris. The journal provides a remarkable portrait of political canvassing during this period in the National Assembly's deliberations.

On the first day, the Bordeaux delegates met with their counterparts among the Jews of the East, who lodged with Cerf-Berr. "They appear fully confident of being admitted to the rank of citizens," wrote the "Portuguese" representatives in their journal.[7] During their second meeting, held the next day, the Jews of the East revealed their strategy. "They acknowledged that if they were granted the rights of citizens so as to be able to buy, sell and otherwise dispose of real estate at will, with freedom to engage in all forms of commerce,

2 Ibid., 2.

3 Ibid., 4. Emphasis added.

4 Zosa Szajkowski, "La délégation des Juifs de Bordeaux à la commission Malesherbes en 1788 et à l'Assemblée nationale en 1789," *Zion* 18 (1951): 64.

5 Furtado declined to participate.

6 "Journal de la députation de Bordeaux," in "Registre et répertoire des délibérations de la nation juive," 1790 n°. 4, Archives départementales de la Gironde.

7 "Journal de la députation...," op.cit., 66

arts and trades, they would be satisfied not to seek that extension of rights which would make them persons endowed with legal qualifications to vote and be eligible to hold administrative, civil service and military positions." [8]

The Bordelais' position was different. Emancipation of all of France's Jews mattered less to them than obtaining confirmation that they themselves were citizens: "For the rights and possession of professional station of Bordeaux's Jews are claims that no consideration can or should make us abandon."[9] Therefore the Bordelais refused to make common cause.

The two delegations parted, promising to provide each other with copies of their respective memoranda and to remain in touch. But from then on it was every man for himself, and God help them all.

Between 6 and 28 January the Bordeaux delegation, which now numbered seven members, crisscrossed the city to meet with anyone who might be able to serve their cause, calling upon all their friendships and seeking out all supporters in the Assembly and in political clubs. Their journal records encounters with their most ardent advocates. Abbé Grégoire, "at the top" of their list, gave them a most fraternal welcome: "He embraced us, assuring us that we could always rely on him."[10] But the Bordelais knew that if the abbé was the foremost champion of the Jews' cause, he was above all a defender of the poverty-stricken Jews of the East. Therefore, they also sought out others for assistance. Garat-aîné,[11] vicomte de Noailles[12] and

---

8 Ibid.

9 Ibid.

10 Ibid.

11 Joseph Garat (1749–1833), known as Garat-aîné (Garat the elder), was an attorney and writer. A friend of the Encyclopedists, he served as a deputy of the Third Estate to the États Généraux. A moderate *patriote*, he was named minister of justice on 9 October 1792, then served as interior minister until 19 August 1793. He was ambassador to Naples, and elected to the Council of Anciens. A supporter of Napoléon, he was made a count and academician. After the Restoration he was excluded from the Institute.

12 Louis-Marie, vicomte de Noailles (1756–1804) was brother-in-law of the marquis de La Fayette and fought in the American War of Independence. A deputy of the Nobility to the États Généraux, and a liberal, he proposed on 4 August 1789 the abolition of feudal privileges and rights. After the Constituent Assembly he rejoined the army, resigned on 27 May 1791, and emigrated. In 1802 he joined Rochambeau in Saint-Domingue, fought the English in the Caribbean, and died of wounds.

Jacques-Guillaume Thouret[13] received them with friendly regard. They also met with the marquis de La Fayette, who received them "with expressions of the greatest benevolence and declared himself very gratified with the zeal the Jews of Paris had shown during the Revolution."[14] They visited Rœderer, whom they knew from the Malesherbes Commission, and Clermont-Tonnerre, who suggested "that, for the time being, we ask only that the privileges we enjoy be preserved."[15] Barnave seemed "well predisposed in our favor," and Alexandre de Lameth pleaded their case before "the Committee of Friends of the Constitution at a gathering of more than three hundred deputies."[16] Oddly, despite presenting themselves on several occasions at Mirabeau's residence on the rue de la Chaussée-d'Antin, they never managed to find him at home; nor were they able to meet with Abbé Sieyès.

As the delegates made their round of visits, it is apparent that the core of their support was clearly among the Assembly's *patriote* deputies.[17] Members of the royal cabinet, too, were favorable. The minister of justice, Champion de Cicé, who was also archbishop of Bordeaux, assured them of his complete assistance and interceded on their behalf with Guy-Jean-Baptiste Target, who was then serving as president of the Assembly. At last, on 26 January, their parliamentary plan of action appeared to have succeeded. Charles-Maurice de Talleyrand-Périgord, bishop of Autun, who was to present the Committee on the Constitution's report to the Assembly, declared himself in favor of their goals. At that point the delegates drafted a memorandum in accordance with instructions they had received from Bordeaux's syndics: "Our matter is about to be decided."[18]

All that remained for the Bordelais was to determine what the Jews of the East—whose representatives were aware of the Bordeaux

---

13 Jacques-Guillaume Thouret (1746–1794) was an attorney and moderate *patriote* who served as a deputy of the Third Estate from Rouen. He played a major role at the start of the Revolution. Named to the Court of Appeals, he was guillotined during the Terror.

14 "Journal de la députation...," op. cit., 73.

15 Ibid., 70.

16 Ibid., 74.

17 While Clermont-Tonnerre remained faithful to the Jews' cause, he joined the monarchists and, with Malouet, founded the Club des Impartiaux, whose members opposed the *patriotes*.

18 Ibid., 76.

delegation's self-centered game—intended to do. "We have been assured," the Bordelais noted in their journal, "that they have been in a bad mood since they saw our printed memorandum... They will not delay printing their own; but after all the objections that continue to be made about the Jews of Alsace, there is a strong chance that the question regarding them will again be deferred."[19] At this point, however, the Bordeaux delegates cared little about the fate of the Jews of the East. On the other hand, they cultivated close ties with the Jews of Bayonne. Their representative in Paris, David Silveyra, intensified his activities, and submitted an address on behalf of "the Spanish and Portuguese Jews settled in Bourg-Saint-Esprit," in which he made arguments identical to those of the Bordelais.[20] He also defended the interests of the "Portuguese" settled in Marseille, Lyon and Paris. Thus the Sephardim of southern France allied themselves in a bloc against the Ashkenazim of the East.

The Jews of the East understood their southern brethren's strategy: to emphasize all the differences between them in order to obtain a decision in their own favor. On the other hand, the Jews of the East thought that their best chance to succeed was to convince the National Assembly to decide on the citizenship of *all* Jews, without making any distinctions among them. Not only did the interests of the two groups diverge, but their strategies were in conflict. The atmosphere was glacial during a dinner Cerf-Berr hosted on 26 January for the two groups' representatives and Grégoire, Rœderer, Claude-Antoine Thiéry and Jacques Godard. "We met with these gentlemen, and they with us, with much reserve," wrote the Bordelais in their journal. "But we knew indirectly that they had sought a delay in the decision of our matter, in order to be able to deliver their memorial which, as we are told, will be back from the printer only in another two or three days."[21]

That gave the Bordelais all the more reason to press ahead. The next morning, on 27 January, they met with Talleyrand, who in-

19 Ibid., 77.
20 Cf. Silveyra: "The fate of the 'Portuguese' Jews, who since 1550 enjoy the right of citizenship, who pay taxes like all their fellow citizens, who contributed to the election of deputies to the États Généraux, cannot be confused with the condition of the Jews of the East"; in "Adresse présentée à l'Assemblée nationale par le député des Juifs portugais et espagnols," in *La Révolution française et l'émancipation des Juifs*. Vol. 5: *Adresses, Mémoires et Pétitions des Juifs, 1789-1794*.
21 "Journal de la députation...," op. cit., 78.

formed them of his favorable views and read his report to them. He did not conceal the fact "that the Jews of Alsace had appealed to him not to write the report until he had read their memorial," but "that this was not his intention."[22] That evening, three members of the Bordeaux delegation went to the Jacobin Club, where they were introduced by Abbé Grégoire, and Lopes Dubec had their memorandum read to those present. Some Jacobins who spoke supported their requests. Only Thiéry, an attorney, whom the Jews of the East had authorized to serve as their legal counsel, spoke in their favor, presenting the proposition that "if they are denied the status of active citizens, that status must be denied equally to the Portuguese Jews or the matter once again deferred."[23] Isaac-René-Guy Le Chapelier,[24] who chaired the meeting, voiced opposition: the Assembly ought to acknowledge that it was unable to deprive the Jews of Bordeaux of their citizenship, and "only the matter of citizenship for the Alsatian Jews should be deferred."[25] Discussion ended on this note.

January 28 was the day of decision for the Bordelais: that afternoon, at two o'clock, the Assembly had scheduled the beginning of its discussion about Talleyrand's report. In the morning they met with Necker, who gave them "the most gracious welcome." The delegation had reason for optimism: they had prepared for the debate and knew that the Jews of Bordeaux were, in Necker's words, "well regarded in public opinion."[26]

AMONG THE JEWS OF THE EAST

Meanwhile, the Jews of the East's representatives had not remained idle. Fully aware of their reputation as usurers and religious zealots, they decided to appeal to public opinion before such ideas took firm root in the Assembly. In early January they published a

---

22 Ibid.

23 Ibid.

24 Isaac-René-Guy Le Chapelier (1754–1794), an attorney and deputy of the Third Estate of Rennes, presided over the session of 4 August 1789. He was the author of the law of 14 June 1791, which forbid professional associations. Founder of the Breton Club, which became the Jacobin Club, he resigned to rejoin the Club des Feuillants. During the Terror he fell under suspicion and was guillotined on 22 April 1794.

25 "Journal de la députation...," op. cit., 78.

26 Ibid.

pamphlet entitled "Impartial Reflections of a Citizen on the Question of the Eligibility of the Jews,"[27] which Berr Isaac Berr had commissioned Thiéry to write.[28] In it Thiéry advanced the suggestion that the Jews of the East were relinquishing eligibility for citizenship "until, by their labor and efforts, they may demonstrate themselves worthy of it, and until the people may become accustomed to this idea."[29] Berr Isaac Berr published, under his own name, a letter to Abbé Maury on 10 January, in which he refuted the assertion that their religious law prohibited Jews from fulfilling their duties as citizens and participating in common civic life, and cited Emperor Joseph II of Austria, who allowed Jews access to all occupations.[30]

The Jews of the East's delegates also decided to make their case directly to the Assembly in the form of a lengthy memorandum in which they refuted arguments raised against them during December's debates. Jacques Godard, a young attorney who resided in Paris's rue des Blancs-Manteaux, in the district where most of the Jews of the East lived, was engaged to assist in drafting the document. The memorandum's cover letter, signed by the Jews of the East's representatives and addressed to the president of the National Assembly, summarized its authors' political objective: "We are informed that an address of the Jews of Bordeaux has just been presented to the National Assembly... We have decided, therefore, to hasten in sending this memorandum, which we have the honor to address to you, in order that our future may be decided at the same time as that of our brothers from Bordeaux." Their principal requests, they noted, were identical with those of the Bordelais, "with the exception that that which they [the

---

27 "Réflexions impartiales d'un citoyen sur la question de l'éligibilité des Juifs, présentée et discutée dans les séances de l'Assemblée nationale des 23 et 24 décembre, et ajournée par la même assemblée," in La Révolution française et l'émancipation des Juifs. Vol. 8: Lettres, Mémoires et Publications diverses, 1789-1806.

28 "Journal de la députation...," op. cit., 65. Contained in Thiéry's memorandum are arguments he made in his essay submitted to the Metz essay competition: "The Jews are what we have made them... Why, since they are men, do they not enjoy the rights of man?" in "Réflexions impartiales...," op. cit., 10.

29 Ibid.

30 "Lettre de Berr Isaac Berr à M. l'abbé Maury, député à l'Assemblée nationale," in Naphtali Herz Wessely, Instruction salutaire adressée aux communautés juives de l'Empire; par le célèbre Hartwic Weisly, Juif de Berlin; traduite en François, en l'année 1782. Nouvelle edition, Augmentée de Notes, d'un Lettre à M. l'Abbé Maury, Député à l'Assemblée Nationale, par l'Éditeur, et de la réponse de M. l'Abbé Maury (Paris: Belin, 1790), 3-8. Cf. David Feuerwerker, L'émancipation des Juifs en France de l'Ancien Régime à la fin du Second Empire (Paris: Albin Michel, 1976), 330-331.

"Portuguese"] ask to preserve, we ask to gain." The Jews of the East's representatives concluded: "Therefore we trust that the National Assembly will not decide [the status of] one [group] without [deciding the status of] the other, because it does not appear to us that it [the Assembly] can have grounds to separate them."[31]

Intended for distribution to deputies before the Assembly reopened its consideration of Jewish rights on 28 January, the memorandum had still not been printed as of 26 January, and it is unclear whether the document reached the Assembly in time. In any event it was far too late for this attempt to influence the course of the debate. The Jews of the East's memorandum consisted of more than a hundred pages. How did they hope that the deputies, then in session, would read it; and what could a lawyer's brief, even a brilliant one, accomplish, given the tenacity and skill with which the Bordeaux delegates conducted their campaign to win over the most influential deputies belonging to the *patriote* party, including the Society of Friends of the Constitution? When the Assembly session began on the morning of 28 January, everything combined to assure the success of the Jews of the Southwest's self-centered venture.

THE BORDELAIS' VICTORY

Talleyrand opened the debate on behalf of the Committee on the Constitution. His presentation was straightforward: for more than two centuries the Jews of the Southwest had enjoyed all the rights of *regnicoles*; they paid the same taxes as other Frenchmen; they participated in electoral assemblies and, finally, "they currently serve in the national militias, holding commissions and fulfilling duties without regard to any day of the week." (This was a response to Abbé Maury's argument claiming that Jews could not fulfill their military duty on the Jewish sabbath.) Talleyrand concluded: "They do not ask to be allowed to participate in the rights of citizenship, but rather to be sustained in the enjoyment of these rights." He therefore proposed on behalf of the committee that "the Jews whom these previous laws acknowledged as citizens... preserve that status, and accordingly may be active citizens if they satisfy other existing quali-

---

31 "Pétition des Juifs établis en France, adressée à l'Assemblée nationale le 28 janvier 1790, sur l'ajournement du 24 décembre 1789," in *La Révolution française et l'émancipation des Juifs*. Vol 5: *Adresses, Mémoires....*

fications demanded by decrees of the Assembly."[32]

The Assembly immediately erupted in commotion.[33] On the left, Rewbell, implacable adversary of the Jews, wished to take the floor, but he was interrupted by protests. Vicomte de Noailles interceded in favor of the Bordeaux Jews "who have given proof of strongest patriotism..."[34] Heckling rang out. Finally Rewbell managed to make himself heard. He restated arguments developed during December's debates,[35] adding: "Exception for the Jews of Bordeaux will soon lead to the same exception for the other Jews in the kingdom." Then, calling attention to the tensions in Alsace, he cried out: "After your decree, they will say that there exists a confederation of Jews and speculators who want to lay their hands on all properties."[36]

But it was now no longer an issue of Alsace's Jews. The nation was on the verge of municipal and departmental elections, and Bordeaux's deputies in the Assembly had no reason to lose their Jewish electors' votes in order to mollify Alsace's fears. De Sèze, one of Bordeaux's deputies, a moderate monarchist and future attorney for Louis XVI during his trial, declared himself "the champion of an unfortunate people, long oppressed by your laws..." With eloquence, he repeated Talleyrand's arguments and concluded: "If the Jews did not hold municipal office in Bordeaux..., it is because reason had still not dissolved all prejudices and because the Rights of Man were misunderstood."[37]

Several members requested that Le Chapelier read aloud from *lettres patentes* confirming the "Portuguese" Jews' rights. Abbé Maury protested that whereas the letters granted only revocable privileges, the Assembly was being asked to render "an eternal decree" that would make it impossible to resist the demands of the Jews of Alsace and Lorraine.[38] Therein lay the heart of the debate.

---

32 *Archives parlementaires de 1787 à 1789. Première série (1789 à 1800). Recueil complet des débats législatifs et politiques des Chambres françaises.* Jules Mavidal and Émile Laurent, eds. 32 vol. (Paris: P. Dupont, 1862-1888), 11:364.

33 "This motion caused lively objections," ibid.

34 Ibid.

35 Ibid. "The Jews gathered themselves to exist as a nation separate from the French. They have never enjoyed the status of active citizens..." Nothing was more inaccurate concerning the Jews of Bordeaux.

36 Ibid.

37 Ibid.

38 Ibid.

Le Chapelier, deputy from Rennes and a moderate *patriote*, sensed a trap. When he rose to speak he replied to Abbé Maury, "It is merely a matter of preserving established rights...," and cleverly turned Maury's argument against him: "We cannot make the status of the Jews of Bordeaux depend on that of the Jews of Alsace."[39]

François, marquis de Beauharnais blundered in presenting a motion "proposing to preserve the privileges granted the Jews of Bordeaux by Henry II."[40] The *patriotes* immediately retorted: " 'Privileges'? Who these days talks of 'privileges'? 'Privileges,' when it is a matter of rights?... Are we French because we have 'privileges'?" Use of the term "privilege," wrote Duquesnoy, "aroused the greatest protests."[41] Beauharnais decided to substitute the word "rights" for "privileges," but retained the reference to Henry II's letters. The left then erupted in furor. De Sèze, when he rose to speak, proposed to issue a decree stating that the Jews of Bordeaux would continue to exercise the rights of active citizens. The left calmed down. Bon-Albert Briois de Beaumetz suggested extending the motion to include the Jews of Bayonne.[42] Abbé Grégoire, who had been silent until that point, demanded the same rights for the Jews of Avignon[43] and, ever mindful of the interests of the Jews of the East, asked the Assembly

---

39 Ibid.

40 Ibid., 11:365.

41 Adrien-Cyprien Duquesnoy, *Journal d'Adrien Duquesnoy, député du Tiers état de Bar-le-Duc, sur l'Assemblée constituante, 3 mai 1789–3 avril 1790*. Published for the Société d'histoire contemporaine by Robert de Crèvecœur. 2 vol. (Paris: Alphonse Picard et fils, 1894), 330. The marquis de Beauharnais was a distant relative of the vicomte de Beauharnais. The latter, guillotined 23 July 1793, was the husband of Josephine [who later married Napoléon Bonaparte.—TRANSL.].

42 Bon-Albert Briois de Beaumetz (1759–1809) was a deputy of the Nobility from Artois and a supporter of the Constitution. He emigrated in 1792; after reaching the United States, he went to the West Indies, where he died.

43 It concerned Avignonnais Jews living in France. The century-old hostility between Avignon and Carpentras would influence the condition of the Jews residing in the papal territories. Avignon, a commercial city, sought reunion with France in order to expand its trade. Following the election of a new municipal government in April 1790, its Christian and Jewish residents socialized and civil equality was attained. On 12 January 1790 the commune's General Council rejected the pope's authority [over the city] and appealed for unification with France. The Jews of Avignon, as a result of the National Assembly's decree of 28 January 1790, immediately gained all civil and political rights. In Carpentras, on the other hand, hostility against the Jews remained strong. In June 1790, the Comtat's representative assembly refused to recognize their status as citizens. In November 1790, when the requirement that Jews wear a yellow hat was abolished, residents reacted by roughing up Jews in the street. It was only in the spring of 1791 that visible signs of discrimination disap-

to set a date to debate the topic, in order, he said, to refute "the faulty reasoning of Abbé Maury and others…"[44] To bring the debate to a close, Louis-Michel Le Pelletier de Saint-Fargeau, a *patriote* who had been won over to the cause of Jewish emancipation, proposed a text that recognized the "Spanish," "Portuguese" and Avignonnais Jews' rights as active citizens.[45]

Then the Assembly's right-wing deputies flew into a rage as a vote was taken amidst continuing tumult sustained by legislators opposed to the motion. The first canvass, in which deputies voted by standing or remaining seated, appeared inconclusive. Another vote was taken—in vain. The tumult grew. Several members requested a roll-call vote. Immediately, Duquesnoy reported, "Forty to fifty people—Abbé Maury, M. d'Esprémenil,[46] the comte de Montboissier and other, similarly minded deputies immediately dispersed throughout the hall, making a frightful din, crying, 'Point of order! Wait until tomorrow! The hour is too late—they want to kill us with hunger!' There is no trick too contemptible to which they did not resort in order to prevent a vote."[47] According to the *Courrier de Provence*, "the anti-Jewish party itself recalled the image of the synagogue."[48] Another journalist observed: "The party-of-God's zeal and the hatred of the Jews produced a holy fury in these pious men."[49]

peared. Cf. R. Moulinas, "Les Juifs d'Avignon et du Comtat Venaissin," in Patrick Girard, *La Révolution française et les Juifs* (Paris: Robert Laffont, 1989), 149–160.

44 *Archives parlementaires*, 11:365.

45 Louis-Michel Le Pelletier de Saint-Fargeau (1760–1793) was president of the Parlement of Paris. Extremely wealthy, he was a deputy of the Nobility of Paris, a *patriote*, and an author of the penal code of 1791. A deputy to the Convention, he authored a plan to organize public education. He voted for the king's death and was killed by a member of the royal bodyguard. His remains were interred in the Panthéon.

46 Jean-Jacques d'Esprémenil (1745–1794) was an advisor to the Parlement of Paris and a leader of the parliamentary opposition to royal power. Elected by the Nobility of Paris, he became a fierce enemy of the Revolution and was executed during the Terror.

47 Duquesnoy, 328. According to the *Archives parlementaires*, 11:365, "there gathered, in a section of the hall to the right of the president, a group of deputies who forcefully opposed the vote, asking that it might be put off until another session."

48 Cited by Léon Kahn, *Les Juifs pendant la Révolution* (Paris: P. Ollendorff, 1899), 72. [In Christian iconography of the era, the Jews were often depicted as a blindfolded female figure, representing the "blindness" of the Jews in refusing to accept the Christian faith. Thus, the *Courrier de Provence*'s commentator was criticizing "blind" opposition to Jewish emancipation.—TRANSL.]

49 Ibid., 78.

A full hour passed in confusion. The duc de La Rochefoucauld-Liancourt,[50] indignant, tried in vain to call the troublemakers to order: "It is the Assembly's duty and honor to delay the roll-call vote no longer." But the right wing had apparently decided to prevent the vote on the motion. Some deputies, standing in the chamber, demanded adjournment "on the ground that, the hour being very late, several prelates and priests had left the session ..."[51] Exasperated, the *patriotes* held firm and refused to adjourn before a vote was held on the motion.

At last, "after much debate...,"[52] the roll was called. Talleyrand voted "yes." Some aristocrats booed him but the galleries applauded. "When the name of M. de La Fayette—who voted 'yes'—was called, there was repeated applause."[53] When Mirabeau's name was called, he was absent. By a vote of 374–224, the Assembly decreed, at last, that "all Jews known as Portuguese, Spanish or Avignonnais continue to enjoy the rights which they have enjoyed until now—and accordingly enjoy the rights of active citizens... "[54]

The session finally adjourned for the evening at eight o'clock. It had lasted more than ten hours. Their mission accomplished, the Bordeaux delegation, present throughout the debate, rejoiced: "We at once sent a letter to announce this welcome news to the Jews of Bordeaux, whom we represent." When news of the decree reached Bordeaux, there were several incidents of no great consequence,[55] and more demonstrations of support than hostility. "The decree in their favor," a witness reported, "was read that evening in a café where more than eight hundred people had gathered. Everyone took an oath of loyalty to the National Assembly's decrees and promised

50 François-Alexandre-Frédéric, duc de La Rochefoucauld-Liancourt (1747–1827) was grandmaster of the King's Wardrobe, a deputy of the Nobility to the États Généraux, a constitutionalist and member of the Club des Feuillants. He emigrated after 10 August 1792, returned to France during Bonaparte's rule, and was made a peer of the realm by Louis XVIII. He was a philanthropist and a member of the Academy of Sciences.

51 *Archives parlementaires*, 11:365.

52 Duquesnoy, 328.

53 Ibid.

54 "Journal de la députation...," 74.

55 "Several young men gathered at the Bordeaux Bourse in a cabal against the Jews. They demonstrated that evening, even at the celebrations, but all this unpleasantness ended there. The next day the Jews had the satisfaction of receiving apologies from several of their enemies." *Archives parlementaires*, 11:520.

to look upon the Jews as brothers..."[56]

In Metz, however, Abraham Spire noted dejectedly in the *Journal révolutionnaire*, which he had published since 1789: "This resolution constitutes an affront to the Jews of the other provinces... We fear the opposition of the people here. They do not feel that they should help our descendants benefit from this fortunate era. Our hope rests in divine intervention."[57]

---

[56] Ibid.

[57] Abraham Spire, *Le Journal révolutionnaire d'Abraham Spire*. Introduction and translation by Simon Schwarzfuchs (Paris: Institut Alain de Rothschild; Lagrasse: Verdier, 1989), 82.

CHAPTER 7

A LONG WAIT

In the winter of 1790 the Jews of the East remained alone in their disappointment. A year after hopes had been raised by the king's call to convene the États Généraux, and six months after the National Assembly adopted the Declaration of the Rights of Man and of the Citizen, they could see no gains from the Revolution. During the summer of 1789 they had endured a wave of hostility and violence more intense than any during the Ancien Régime. They had been denounced as usurers and aliens in registers of grievances and in the Assembly by deputies of the eastern provinces. On two occasions the Assembly had sidestepped taking action just when it had been on the verge of acknowledging their status as citizens. If the Assembly hesitated it meant that the body believed it had reason to doubt that the Jews of the East could be citizens. In deferring a decision the Assembly had given the Jews' adversaries an important victory.

Even worse, when the Assembly acknowledged that the Jews of the Southwest and Midi were full citizens, it had drawn a dividing line between France's Jews: on one side, the Sephardim, integrated and fully French; on the other, the Ashkenazim of the East, an odd or suspect population. In going their own way the "Portuguese" Jews, led by the skillful Bordelais, had played their game well. But they had also reduced the chances of their "brothers" of the East to obtain immediate recognition that they were citizens.

The Jews of the East had no other choice but to increase their political activities. They knew that they had the force of principle behind them: if the Assembly were called upon to decide about their citizenship, it would be unable to refuse without repudiating the Declaration. But many negative factors worked against the Jews of the East, and the most significant one was the indifference of a majority of deputies, for whom the issue appeared minor. The political struggle for emancipation thus became primarily a battle to set the Assembly's agenda. Supporters of Jewish emancipation knew that the Assembly had promised to revisit the matter of citizenship and believed that were the matter put to a vote, they would be assured of success. Their adversaries' goal, on the other hand, was to postpone any such debate indefinitely.

The Jews of the East were able to count on Paris's small Jewish community as an ally. No explicit decision had been made about the status of the city's Jews. But the decree of 28 January 1790, which acknowledged all "Portuguese, Spanish and Avignonnais" Jews as citizens, benefited the Sephardim living in Paris. The Parisian community now turned toward settling the status of the several hundred Ashkenazic Jews in the capital. Paris's Jews, represented by a very active committee, enjoyed the support of liberal noble deputies of Paris, such as Clermont-Tonnerre, Du Port and the duc de La Rochefoucauld; within the Paris Commune, they had support among very influential figures, notably Brissot and Condorcet. Most valuable of all, they had a passionate defender within the city's government: Jacques Godard.

A young attorney in the Parlement of Paris, Godard lived on the rue des Blancs-Manteaux, in the heart of the Carmelites district, where many Ashkenazic Jews lived. He knew their problems, was interested in their situation, took a lively interest in Jewish emancipation and would become its chief advocate in the capital. Intellectually inquisitive,[1] Godard maintained constant close contact with Berr Isaac Berr, of Nancy, and Théodore Cerf-Berr, of Strasbourg,[2] who provided documents and translations of Jewish writings on religious law and social ethics. He took part in editing the address presented to the National Assembly on 26 August 1789; had edited the new address of 24 December at the time of the debate on citizenship for the Jews,[3] and took part in drafting the Jews of the East's petition of 28 January 1790. Elected in September 1789 to the Paris Com-

---

1 Cf. David Feuerwerker, *L'émancipation des Juifs en France de l'Ancien Régime à la fin du Second Empire* (Paris: Albin Michel, 1976), 337.

2 Ibid., 332–336.

3 On 23 October 1789 the marquis du Pastoret, a renowned jurist and writer, sent him his work, *Moïse considéré comme législateur et moraliste*, published in 1788, with greetings "for the good cause that he will defend and which is so worthy of him." In Feuerwerker, *L'émancipation...*, 337.

mune's representative assembly, Godard concluded that the city's in-
tricate political structure, with its many small pockets of municipal
rule,[4] provided an ideal arena in which to advance the Jews' cause.
During July 1789 many Jews had performed their duties in the
National Guard; others made important patriotic contributions:
Zalkind Hourwitz gave the nation a quarter of his salary; Cerf-Berr
sent a portion of his silver dining service to the mint.[5] Parisians thus
looked upon the Jews without disfavor and this became an important factor several months later, during the winter of 1790, when
Parisians and supporters of Jewish emancipation began organizing
for long-awaited elections to municipal and departmental offices.
These elections presented Paris's Jews and Godard an opportunity
to raise once again the central question of the necessary eligibility requirements to be a voter and officeholder, and the Paris Commune's
official support for the cause of Jewish citizenship would provide important, strong backing in the National Assembly.

On 28 January 1790, when the Assembly was debating the citizenship of the Jews, a delegation of Parisian Jews visited a gathering
of the Commune's representatives as they were sitting in session at
the Hôtel de Ville.[6] Godard rose from his seat, placed himself at the
head of the Jewish delegation, and then read a speech in which "he
expanded upon their claim with all possible nobility and eloquence."[7]
Recalling the civic contribution of Jews in the National Guard, and
citing "the fine Hourwitz" as an example, he invited the Commune's
legislators to declare "the irrevocable proscription of all prejudices
which most dishonor the French nation."[8] Abbé François-Valentin
Mulot, the presiding officer, responded warmly to the Parisian Jewish delegation "that he will be the first to applaud that which will
be favorably decided for your nation."[9] "As the first evidence of our

---

4 The districts' primary assemblies drew up decrees and motions. Their commit-
tees exercised police powers. In this way they appeared to be centers of local democ-
racy. Cf. Sigismond Lacroix, ed., *Actes de la Commune de Paris pendant la Révolution.*
1st and 2d series. 15 vol. (Paris: L. Cerf, 1894-1914), 3:109.

5 Léon Kahn, *Les Juifs de Paris pendant la Révolution* (Paris: P. Ollendorff, 1899),
153.

6 François-Louis Bayard, *Journal de la mfunicipalité et des districts de Paris,* no.
46: 380.

7 Lacroix, 3:605.

8 Ibid., 3:606.

9 "Your request aims to banish all the vices of which people take pleasure of ac-
cusing your nation, to make blossom the virtues which you cultivate in secret, and

brotherhood," he invited the delegation to attend the meeting. The legislators applauded, scheduled a discussion on 30 January and ordered that Godard's and Mulot's speeches be printed.[10]

The next day, again at Godard's initiative, the local assembly of Paris's Carmelites district, "which holds in its bosom the most Jews [among the city's residents],"[11] met and unanimously adopted a motion "so that the Jews, whose good conduct and wholehearted devotion to public matters we vouch for, from now on enjoy the rights of active citizens."[12] That motion was quickly submitted to the Commune's assembly: "If the Jews settled in Paris are not yet French," declared the district delegation's spokesman, "believe us, gentlemen, they deserve to be. Shall I dare make a confession? They are already in our midst. The Carmelites district has no wish to make distinctions among citizens. They are received in our meetings; they share the honors and fatigue of military service."[13] Abbé Mulot congratulated the district's delegates: "Your district which, as well known, encompasses several streets, almost all of whose residents are Jews, is a great weight when it speaks in their favor."[14] Another priest, Abbé Antoine-René-Constant Bertolio, fervently spoke in favor of the Jews' cause,[15] expressing indignation that the disabilities under which they lived were cited as reasons to deny them the status of citizens.[16] At his request the assembly voted that "the Jews of Paris be given a public and authentic account of the good behavior they have always demonstrated, of the patriotism of which they have given proof…"[17] The assembly then decided to invite all of Paris's districts to express

to unlock for the State new sources of wealth," in Lacroix, 3:607.

10 François-Valentin Mulot (1749–1804) was a representative of the Paris Commune. A *patriote*, he was sent in May 1790 as a conciliator to the Comtat Venaissin. A deputy from Paris to the Legislative Assembly, he was imprisoned in 1794 as a suspect. Under the Consulate he was secretary general of the prefecture of the Seine.

11 Ibid.

12 *Archives parlementaires de 1787 à 1860. Première série (de 1787 à 1799). Recueil complet des débats législatifs et politiques des Chambres françaises.* Jules Mavidal and Émile Laurent, eds. 32 vol. (Paris: P. Dupont, 1862-1888), 10:761.

13 Ibid., 10:760.

14 Ibid.

15 "It is in vain that one would like to speak of Heaven and the Christian religion in order to continue to deprive the Jews of the rights of man. Our religion recommends nothing of the sort." Ibid., 10:762.

16 "The long duration of their woes is only a more urgent reason to end it. Let us hasten to make them forget the crimes of our ancestors…" Ibid., 10:762.

17 Ibid., 10:763.

an opinion about their citizenship. Godard warmly thanked the assembly in the name of the city's Jews, and concluded with emotion, in the fashion of the day: "Let us bless the Revolution that will make us all brothers…"[18]

He then made a whirlwind tour of the capital's sixty districts. Accompanied by a delegation of Parisian Jews, he spoke before each district assembly, reading aloud the speech of the president of the Carmelites district. The speech was persuasive because, except for the Carmelites district and that of Sainte-Geneviève, all the others had hardly any Jewish residents. All the local assemblies declared in favor of citizenship for Jews, except that of Mathurins, the neighborhood of second-hand dealers, who feared their competition.[19] On 20 February 1790 Godard reported to the Commune's legislators the nearly unanimous sentiments of the district assemblies. On 24 February he submitted to the Paris Commune a proposed address to the National Assembly, which he had composed with three rapporteurs—Abbé Claude Fauchet,[20] Abbé Bertolio and Jean-Claude-Antoine de Bourge[21]—in which he referred to the precedent the Assembly had set on 24 January when it recognized the citizenship of the "Portuguese" Jews.[22] Godard's address was immediately and unanimously adopted.[23]

The next day, a delegation from the Commune, led by Abbé Mulot, solemnly went to the National Assembly to present the address in favor of Paris's Jews. Talleyrand chaired the meeting, and responded to the petition in promising terms: "Gentlemen, the National Assembly has undertaken a sacred obligation to restore to all

---

18 Ibid.

19 Philippe Sagnac, "Les Juifs et la Révolution Française (1789-1791)," RHMC [Revue d'Histoire modern et contemporaine] 1 (1889): 227.

20 Claude Fauchet (1744–1793) was the king's preacher and a member of the Paris Commune. Chaplain-general of the National Guard, he created the Circle sociale in 1790, a *patriote* group. Bishop of Cäen in 1791, he was elected to the Legislative Assembly, then the Convention, from Calvados. Denounced as a conspirator in Marat's murder, he was executed 31 October 1793.

21 Jean-Claude-Antoine de Bourge (1747–1825) was an attorney, a member of the Paris Commune, deputy to the Convention, a member of the Council des Anciens, and finally a magistrate.

22 "You will not allow," he wrote, "that in Paris, where 'Portuguese' Jews live alongside 'Germans,' the first group will have heaped upon it the nation's favors and the second group its contempt. Neither reason nor liberty can long tolerate such an unequally monstrous distinction." In Feuerwerker, *L'émancipation…*, 356.

23 *Archives parlementaires*, 11:698.

men their rights...It is in this spirit that we will examine with fairness the arguments you put forth in favor of the Jews, and in such
moving fashion."[24] The Assembly applauded; Talleyrand then invited
the delegation to take a place at the front of the chamber, and the
Commune's address and the Assembly's response were ordered to be
printed.

Sensing a favorable climate of opinion, partisans of emancipation attempted to press their advantage. On 26 February Jews from
Lunéville and Sarreguemines submitted a new memorandum in
which they declared their solidarity with the Jews of Paris.[25] That
same day, as the agenda for the session was being set, the duc de La
Rochefoucauld-Liancourt asked the Assembly to set a date by which
it would decide the civil status of the Jews. Target, who presided over
the session, opposed the request, noting that the question of the Jews'
rights affected "only a portion of men,"[26] whereas the Assembly had
to decide upon how the judicial system, the army and finances were
to be organized, "which affects all the realm."[27]

The question was again postponed. Godard's offensive failed.
But the Paris Commune's declaration in favor of granting citizenship
to the Jews had an impact: when a list of electors and eligible voters
in Paris was drawn up in 1790 a number of Jews appeared on it.[28]
From then on the Jews of Paris exercised their rights as citizens.

PERSUADING PUBLIC OPINION

On 22 March 1790 the question of the Jews of the East was
again raised in the Assembly with a request that the next week's session be devoted to the issue. After discussion, the duc de Choiseul-
Praslin asked for a postponement, to which the body agreed.[29]

---

24 Ibid. Cf. Brissot, addressing the assembly of the Paris Commune's representatives: "This *adresse* was received with applause that deserves your zeal to defend
humanity and equal rights." Lacroix, 5:593.

25 "Nouveau mémoire pour les Juifs de Lunéville et Sarguemines; Présenté à
l'Assemblée Nationale, le 26 Février 1790," in *La Révolution française et l'émancipation
des Juifs*. 8 vol. (Paris: Edhis [Éditions d'Histoire Sociale], 1968). Vol 5: *Adresses, Mémoires et Pétitions des Juifs, 1789-1794*.

26 *Archives parlementaires*, 11:710.

27 Ibid.

28 Cf. Kahn, *Les Juifs...*, 119–120.

29 *Archives parlementaires*, 12:70.

With that decision, the Jews of the East realized that their adversaries' strategy was to delay in order prevent the Assembly from
holding any debate about their citizenship. As one of their opponents,
a deputy named Jean-Adam Pflieger, wrote: "It will be the duty of
future legislators to grant, if it happens, the petition of the Jews of
Alsace..."[30] The Jews of the East had to rally public opinion to their
cause if they were to capture the Assembly's interest and compel it to
take action.

The Jews of the East intensified their efforts to mold opinion.
Their well-argued petition of 28 January 1790 was widely distributed and used as a reference document.[31] Other eloquent voices were
raised on their behalf.[32] Thus Abbé Lamourette, a friend of Mirabeau,
replied to Abbé Maury and reminded the Assembly of the principles inherent in the Declaration of the Rights of Man: "You can no
longer," he declared, "refuse them civil status without causing the
foundations of your political edifice to totter."[33]

Most significantly of all, the Jews of the East turned their efforts
to winning over popular opinion in their home provinces. A "Letter
of an Alsatian on the Jews of Alsace," published in February 1790,
refuted Rewbell's argument in the National Assembly that "to give
Alsatian Jews the right of citizenship was to declare their death war-

---

30 Jean-Adam Pflieger, *Réflexions sur les Juifs d'Alsace, par M. Pflieger* (Paris:
Devaux, 1790), 16.

31 "Pétition des Juifs établis en France, adressée à l'Assemblée Nationale, le 28
janvier 1790, sur l'ajournement du 24 décembre 1789," in *La Révolution française et
l'émancipation des Juifs*. Vol. 5: *Adresses, Mémoires...*

32 Godard developed the main argument: "The Jews are not at all aliens in
France. They are subjects of this empire; and consequently they are and ought to be
citizens." To deprive the Jews of their rights would be to admit that "in France the
Jews could not be men." He added: if some Jews are "debased," this is "the work of
people who have given them refuge..., the product of institutions which had been
given to them." Neither the Jews' religion nor their religious holidays were obstacles
to their citizenship. Far from injurious to the eastern provinces, emancipation would
be profitable to them, for the Jews, freed from their shackles, would abandon usury
and make commerce and handicrafts prosper. The petition concluded eloquently:
"Illustrious representatives of the Nation: You are human; you will therefore put an
end to the Jews' sufferings. You are just; you will restore to them the status and rights
which they demand. Hasten only the era of your justice..." *Archives parlementaires*,
12:733. The petition was signed by the six representatives of the Jews of the three
provinces, and by Cerf-Berr, former syndic-general of the Jews.

33 [Antoine-Adrien Lamourette], "Observations sur l'état civil des Juifs, adres-
sées à l'Assemblée nationale par l'abbé L***," p. 19, in *La Révolution française et
l'émancipation des Juifs*. Vol. 8: *Lettres, Mémoires et Publications diverses, 1789-1806*.

rant." "[T]o suppose the possible massacre of several thousand people, and to announce these fears publicly," the "Letter" declared, "is, in a way, to prompt a massacre."[34] In Strasbourg the Society of the Friends of the Constitution voted on 27 February to adopt a report concerning the condition and status of Alsace's Jews.[35] While it made favorable reference to the principles of the Declaration of the Rights of Man, the report's main thrust was to persuade Alsatians that they would benefit, rather than be harmed, if Jews were emancipated. Confronting rumors spread in the countryside that recognition of the Jews' citizenship would immediately lead Jews to call in debts that farmers owed, the report responded that, on the contrary, once Jews were granted access to all occupations they would be a source of prosperity for Alsace. Moreover the report contended that Alsatians were being defamed by those who claimed that Alsace's Jews would be massacred if the Assembly granted them equal rights. The report was then forwarded to the Society of Friends of the Constitution in Paris "as expressing its feelings and opinions on this matter, and requesting that it be presented before the National Assembly."[36] It was a politically skillful step to have Strasbourg *patriotes* refute arguments advanced by the Alsatian *patriote* Rewbell.

In Lorraine young Lion Goudchaux published a letter responding to Abbé Maury.[37] Berr Isaac Berr replied to Bishop La Fare, who had published his speech opposing citizenship for Jews. In his public letter Berr quickly recapitulated all the arguments of the 28 January address in favor of emancipation.[38] He also advanced a surprising

---

34 "Lettre d'un Alsacien sur les Juifs d'Alsace, à M. Reubell, député de cette province à l'Assemblée nationale," pp. 23–24, in *La Révolution française et l'émancipation des Juifs*. Vol. 8: *Lettres, Mémoires...*

35 "Rapport lu à l'Assemblée de la Société des Amis de la Constitution, Le 27 février mil sept cent quatre-vingt-dix, sur la question de l'état civil des Juifs d'Alsace," pp. 14 and 15, in *La Révolution française et l'émancipation des Juifs*. Vol. 8: *Lettres, Mémoires....*

36 Ibid.

37 "Lettre du Sr Lion Goudchaux, Juif de Nancy, à l'abbé Maury, député à l'Assemblée nationale, sur la motion pour l'inadmission des Juifs au droit de cité, du 5 mai 1790," in Feuerwerker, *L'émancipation...*, 371.

38 "After the National Assembly decreed the inalienable rights of man, without distinguishing between Christian and Jew, after it decreed that Portuguese, Avignonnais, etc. Jews are included in the decree of the Rights of Man, it cannot, without categorical contradiction, decree the contrary for the Jews living in other parts of the kingdom." "Lettre du Sr. Berr Isaac Berr, négociant à Nancy, Juif naturalisé, en vertu des lettres patentes du Roi, à Monseigneur l'évêque de Nancy, député à

proposal: the Jews would renounce their right as citizens to vote and hold elective office in return for the right to "remain a private community and to have amongst them and to bear the costs of, rabbis and leaders, as much for civil as for religious law"[39]—in other words, in return for the right to maintain their community structures and the judicial authority of their rabbis. Moreover he declared that he spoke "for all Jews living in the provinces of Lorraine, Alsace and the Trois-Évêchés, [and guaranteed] to make them agree to and subscribe to this sacrifice."[40] To be sure the great majority of Jews in the eastern provinces were mainly concerned about exercising all the civil—as distinguished from political—rights of citizens: the rights to be able to marry, buy property, engage in commerce and freely establish a domicile. They were indifferent insofar as political rights were concerned because in 1790 few, if any, among them envisioned being elected mayor of a village or district judge. But from the viewpoint of principles, Berr Isaac Berr's proposal was unacceptable. It accepted that Jews might live as citizens with inferior rights, compared to Christians and even to the Jews of the Southwest. Indeed, Berr Isaac Berr's nephew, Jacob Berr, protested his uncle's extraordinary proposal.[41] The Lorraine syndic's offer expressed the bitterness, indeed the weariness, that engulfed the Jews of the East's representatives. "Who," observed Berr Isaac Berr, "would have said that in the month of April 1790 the Jews would again wear slavery's chains?"[42]

ATTACKS AGAINST THE JEWS

Despite such efforts, prejudice and hostility against the Jews did not abate in the eastern provinces. In Nancy Jews asked the municipality to support their efforts to persuade the National Assembly to grant them citizenship, as had the Paris Commune. Nancy's officials delayed responding—and decided finally on 1 June that it was not necessary to discuss the request. In Alsace, Easter commemorations revived incidents of what Mirabeau's newspaper, *Le Cour-*

l'Assemblée nationale," p. 18, in *La Révolution française et l'émancipation des Juifs*. Vol. 8: *Lettres, Mémoires...*

39 Ibid., 19.

40 Ibid.

41 Jacob Berr, "Lettre à Mgr. l'Évêque de Nancy. Nancy, le 25 avril 1790," in Feuerwerker, *L'émancipation...*, 368.

42 Berr Isaac Berr, 5. [See fn. 38, above].

rier de Provence, denounced as "popular fanaticism."[43] Cerf-Berr's residence in Strasbourg had to be protected by the army. Captain Foissac, the National Guard commandant in the city of Phalsbourg and author of anti-Jewish writings before the Revolution, published "An Appeal in Behalf of More than a Million Citizens Against the Disastrous Scourge of Jewish Usury," in which he called for a "new Titus" to destroy the Jewish race.[44]

The harshest attack was launched in Strasbourg. The city had asked in its registers of grievances submitted to the États Généraux that measures against usury, which had been incorporated in the *lettres patentes* granted to Alsace's Jewish communities on 10 July 1784, be strengthened. In an attempt to mollify their opponents, Jewish leaders issued, in February 1790, an address to the people of Alsace confirming that Jewish money lenders would respect the Sovereign Council of Colmar's decree of 1787, which imposed a moratorium on repayment of their loans. The address humbly promised that Alsace's Jews would be "regenerated"—"Ah, do not despair of seeing a salutary revolution take effect in our morals…"— if they were granted equal rights, as had been the Jews of Bordeaux.[45] Nonetheless, their opponents in Strasbourg remained determined to mobilize a vast swell of opinion against them and to force a broad, popular referendum on the Jews' citizenship: "In fifteen assemblies composed of equal representation of all estates, all were unanimously opposed to this acceptance."[46] The municipality adopted an address to the National Assembly, setting forth a severe indictment of the Jews. In Lorraine, it declared, "one hundred and eighty Jewish families received from Stanislas the blessing of civil status, and yet, since 1751…, scarcely five or six of these families engage in respectable or legitimate business…";[47] similarly, in the period since the *lettres patentes* of 1784 had been issued, "the Jews have thrived on the favors granted them. They have paid no attention to

---

43   *Le Courrier de Provence*, vol. 7, no. 122: 407.

44   De Foissac, *Plaidoyer pour plus d'un million de citoyens contre le fléau désastreux de l'usure des Juifs* (n.p., n.d.); cf. Feuerwerker, *L'émancipation…*, 363–364. [Titus Flavius Vespasianus (39–81 C.E.) was a Roman military commander who razed Jerusalem in 70 C.E. during the course of suppressing a Jewish revolt in Palestine. He reigned as Rome's emperor from 79–81 C.E.—*TRANSL.*]

45   "Adresse des Juifs alsaciens au peuple d'Alsace," p. 4, in *La Révolution française et l'émancipation des Juifs*. Vol. 5: *Adresses, Mémoires…*.

46   *Archives parlementaires*, 12:711.

47   Ibid., 12:713.

the means which enable them to merit these favors."⁴⁸ The address drew
what its authors deemed an obvious conclusion: "Experience…should
make us fear that the vices of which we blame them are inherent in their
distinctive character and perhaps in a constitution which they are hiding
from us."⁴⁹

After making reference to a secret Jewish pact the Strasbourg
Commune declared that there was no place for Jews in the city because the Jews would never be regenerated. Agriculture was economi-
cally unrewarding and, moreover, the Jews scorned it; manual trades
did not provide enough work for Christian workers, let alone Jews;
the arts only flourished in times of prosperity and economic crisis now
reigned; commerce "requires honesty" and "no one was unaware that
Jewish commerce only lives by other means." The only economic pursuits remaining for the Jews were usury and the second-hand trade.
Again the conclusion was obvious: "If what you wish is our happiness, we believe it to be firmly linked to the nonadmission to our city
of the Jews as citizens."⁵⁰ (The municipality of Strasbourg also submitted a supplementary request: that permission allowing Cerf-Berr
and his family to reside in the city be rescinded.)⁵¹

The address, signed by Strasbourg's mayor, Frédéric Dietrich,
and fifteen elected municipal officials, was submitted to the National
Assembly in April 1790. The issue of Jewish citizenship was scheduled to be taken up at an evening session on 16 April. True to the
strategy emancipation's opponents had adopted, Abbé Maury suggested that debate be postponed. He intended, Maury said, to submit
a memorandum concerning the Jews, and it would be only fair if they
were acquainted with its contents so that they could respond to it.
Rewbell went further, asking for an adjournment until organization
of the government was completed—in other words, until the Assembly had adopted a Constitution for the nation.

Then the duc de La Rochefoucauld d'Enville,⁵² whose views car-

---

48 Ibid. Infuriated by these assertions of Strasbourg's municipal authorities, the
Jews of Lorraine issued a vigorous reply. In it they recalled that they were forbidden
to engage in crafts and professions, unable to own the houses in which they lived,
and were crushed by taxes. Cf. Feuerwerker, *L'émancipation…*, 370.

49 *Archives parlementaires*, 12:714.

50 Ibid.

51 Ibid., 13:69.

52 Louis-Alexandre, duc de La Rochefoucauld d'Enville (1743–1792) was a friend
of Condorcet and La Fayette, deputy of the Nobility of Paris, and a *patriote*. President

ried great moral authority in the Assembly, intervened, asking the Assembly to set a definite date by which it would decide the question regarding the Jews of the East. He called attention to the threats against them, noting that tensions would only be alleviated with a definitive decision, and added as evidence to support this assertion that "even in Alsace, people are so prepared to expect to see them declared citizens that certain villages have already set aside their share in the division of communal property."[53] The Assembly was content to refer the matter to the Committee on the Constitution.

Disquieted by these successive postponements, which kept alive a climate of anti-Jewish hostility, Théodore Cerf-Berr sent a letter on 16 April to the president of the Assembly on behalf of the Jews of the East, spelling out the "threats and worries" they suffered in Alsace, and especially in Strasbourg. He asked the Assembly to remind the municipalities to respect its decree of 28 September 1789, which placed Alsace's Jews under the law's protection. Rœderer responded by proposing a decree "ordering the municipalities and the National Guard to protect with all their ability the persons and goods of the Jews."[54] The Assembly immediately adopted it. Two weeks later, however, when the Assembly revisited the conditions required to be French and to enjoy active citizenship in the context of a discussion regarding departments, frontiers and maritime cities, the body as a whole was careful to avoid a decision regarding citizenship for the Jews of the eastern provinces. Indeed, the decree was approved with a clause noting that nothing in it was to be taken as "prejudging anything on the question of the Jews, which was and remains postponed."[55] Supporters and opponents of emancipation had set forth all of their arguments before the Assembly. All that remained was for the Assembly to resolve the question of the Jews' status. The Assembly, however, continued to avoid confronting the matter.

If the Assembly hesitated it was because legislators were en-

---

of the Directory of Paris under the Legislative Assembly, he was massacred by a mob in September 1792.

53 *Archives parlementaires*, 13:69. The duc de La Rochefoucauld, however, was badly informed. The Alsatian municipalities to which he alluded protested vehemently. One municipality replied: "Given that our wish is that the Jews may never be able to become active citizens in our community, this could be a definite blow that could lead to our ruin..."

54 Ibid., 13:76–77.

55 *Le Courrier français*, vol. 5, no. 121.

gaged in a wide-ranging political debate, into which opponents of
the Revolution skillfully injected fears about alleged consequences of
Jewish emancipation. During the winter of 1790 steps to sell Church
property were halted. The monarchist press, which shared Maury's
virulent anti-Judaism, circulated rumors that, were Jews to become
citizens, they would en masse bid to acquire ecclesiastical properties at very low prices. Charging that the "deicide people" were
going to become owners of God's houses, adversaries of emancipation attempted to incite outrage against sacrilegious purchases, as
well as jealousy regarding lucrative transactions. A journalist depicted the Jews as "ready buyers, waiting for their prey to be delivered
to them."[56] In Paris, another journalist wrote, "the descendants of
Aaron, Moses and Elijah are going to seize the tranquil and sunny
retreats of the disciples of Saint Bruno, Saint Benoît, of the seraphic
Saint Francis...Where you see uncircumcised monks, you will see
foreskinless usurers...A group of Jewish capitalists in Paris offered
800,000 livres for the site of the Chartreux in Paris, from which we
can conclude that it is worth twice as much..."[57]

Others went further still. An Alsatian deputy who represented the Clergy declared to his constituents: "You are going to be,
through the sale of ecclesiastical property, reduced to begging; the
Jews will purchase the properties you work."[58] The monarchist press
also launched charges that the Jews had corruptly purchased the
votes of *patriote* deputies who supported emancipation. *L'Orateur
du Peuple* described "Bailly, Le Chapelier, La Fayette, Malouet,
Barnave and other deputies attending to the Jewish matter in return
for 72,000 livres of silver."[59] Following the Assembly's debate on 28
January, which resulted in recognition of the citizenship of the Jews
of the Southwest, a monarchist caricature depicted Talleyrand crying
out in front of a Jew who presents him with a sack of gold: "King
of the Jews, you have gained the upper hand..."[60] Abbé Grégoire,
too, was a favored target of such slanders. The *Journal de la Cour*

---

56 *Gazette Universelle*, no. 142 (30 January 1790).

57 *L'Observateur de Feydel*, 27 February 1790. [The "site of the Chartreux" is that
of a monastery affiliated with a contemplative religious order founded by St. Bruno
in 1084.—*Transl.*]

58 Sagnac, 230.

59 Cf. Kahn, *Les Juifs de Paris...*, 57. [Jean-Sylvain Bailly (1736–1793) also served
as mayor of Paris from 1789 to 1791. He was executed during the Terror.—*Transl.*]

60 *Le Rôdeur français*, no. 26 (6 February 1790).

called him the "Judaic prelate," and *L'Ami du Roi* referred to him as
"Rabbi Grégoire."[61] Grégoire, recalling in his memoirs these accusations of corruption, wrote with a touch of sarcasm: "I could have
collected...millions [from the blacks], which, combined with other
millions from the Jews, would have placed me on a par with Croe-
sus..."[62]

THE ASSEMBLY'S EVASIONS

Debate in the Assembly during May 1790 regarding the status of Paris gave advocates of Jewish emancipation an opportunity
to seize the initiative. A representative of the Paris Commune, de
Bourges, sent a letter to the Assembly's Committee on the Constitution asking immediate recognition of the right of citizenship for
Jews. He also delivered copies to a gathering of the Commune's
delegates, where three members who supported emancipation—
Condorcet, Brissot and Robin—were designated to make a report.
On 21 May 1790 Brissot read the report to the Commune's assembly:
"It is worthy," he wrote, "of a commune, in whose heart *philosophie*
shines, even under despotism, to take in hand the cause of these victims of ignorance, when another commune, led astray by fanaticism,
seeks to persecute them."[63] A representative of the Commune, André
Rousseau, who came from Alsace, protested: "The Jews would fare a
better fate if the National Assembly did not support them; it is to be
feared that the farmers, who have a fanatical hatred of them, might
slaughter them."[64] Other members, including Abbé Mulot, fervently stood up for the Jews. The Commune voted to send the address
proposed by Brissot, Condorcet and Robin to the Assembly. The Assembly remained unmoved. On 13 June the Jews of Alsace sent a new
petition to the Assembly. It was read aloud to the Assembly. It was
immediately referred to the Committee on the Constitution.

Nevertheless certain issues related to the situation of the Jews of
the East could not be left in limbo. In the summer of 1789 the Jews

---

61 Cf. Kahn, *Les Juifs de Paris...*, 63–64.

62 Henri-Baptiste Grégoire, *Mémoires de Grégoire, ancien évêque de Blois, député à
l'Assemblée constituante et à la Convention nationale, sénateur, membre de l'Institut.* Introduction by M. H. Carnot. 2 vol. (Paris: Ambroise Dupont, 1837), 1:393. [Croesus, king of
Lydia during the sixth century B.C.E., was legendary for his wealth.—*TRANSL.*]

63 Lacroix, 5:585.

64 Ibid., 5:596.

of Metz had asked the Assembly to abolish "this right of protection of 20,000 livres per year, granted as a gift to the Brancas family, which has no legitimate basis either in the rights of families or of the realm."[65] The issue seemed to have been settled by decrees voted during the night of 4 August when the Assembly had abolished all special privileges, taxes and rights. The duc de Brancas himself, in January 1790, had published a denial of statements made by Metz's Jewish community relating to this tax of 20,000 livres per year;[66] at the same time, however, he went to court, seeking this amount as a payment of arrears.[67] The Assembly's Committee on Properties had decided to look into the matter.

On 20 July 1790 the committee's rapporteur, M. de Vismes, presented its conclusions:[68] because the Jews of Metz were French the Brancas tax was not in the same category as the *droit d'aubaine*, which permitted confiscation of the estates of foreigners who died on French soil. The "grant" made to the Brancas family was therefore "purely a monetary expression of thanks"[69] since, in the wake of the abolition of feudal privileges, no right of "protection" could be imposed on anyone. The Committee on Properties therefore recommended abolition of this tax, as well as abolition without indemnification of all special taxes levied on the Jews. The Assembly immediately adopted the committee's proposal.[70] Rewbell, the "fearsome enemy of the Jews,"[71] was the sole deputy to raise his voice against the decree. An

65 "Mémoire particulier pour la communauté des Juifs établis à Metz, rédigé par Isaac Ber-Bing, l'un des membres de cette communauté," p. 24, in *La Révolution française et l'émancipation des Juifs.* Vol. 5: *Adresses, Mémoires....* Cf. *Archives parlementaires* (14 April 1790), 12:733.

66 *Mercure de France* (16 January 1790), 135.

67 *Archives parlementaires*, 12:732, note 1.

68 Ibid., 17:215.

69 Ibid., 17:217.

70 Ibid., 17:219. However, abolition of the Brancas tax did not at all settle all of the financial difficulties which overwhelmed the community in Metz. It had been obligated to borrow some very sizeable sums—490,000 livres—in order to cope with taxes and charges that weighed upon it. All members of the community were responsible for its settlement. This generated fears among the community's notables that they would have to utilize their own resources to settle a sizeable debt if the Jews left Metz, thanks to their newfound rights. The Assembly, in taking up the matter, submitted it to its Committee on Finances, which in turn proposed to refer to Metz's revolutionary directorate all disputes that arose. The Assembly issued a decree to this effect on 20 May 1791. Cf. Feuerwerker, *L'émancipation...*, 417.

71 In the words of Adrien-Cyprien Duquesnoy, *Journal d'Adrien Duquesnoy, député du Tiers état de Bar-le-Duc, sur l'Assemblée constituante, 3 mai 1789–3 avril 1790.* Published

important chapter in the former status of France's Jews was closed when the Assembly ended the special taxation system that had crushed them throughout the Ancien Régime.[72]

It was one thing to abolish the special taxes imposed upon the Jews; it was quite another to declare them citizens, and a majority in the Assembly was in 1790 still not prepared to take the decisive step of proclaiming that Jews were the equals of Christians. On 12 August 1790 the National Assembly promulgated "Instructions" regarding elections for administrative posts. The first article stated: "Among the Jews, it remains only those known as Portuguese, Spanish and Avignonnais Jews who may be active and eligible citizens, according to the decree of 28 January 1790."[73] Similarly, when the Assembly declared on 11 September 1790 that, with respect to reorganization of the judicial system, non-Catholics could assume all judicial posts, the legislature stated, in the text of Jacques-Guillaume Thouret's report, that "it did not intend any judgment with respect to the Jews, upon whose status it [the Assembly] reserved a decision."[74]

In this uncertain situation, Jews who during the Ancien Régime had obtained *lettres patentes* of naturalization which declared them to be French and subjects of the king, set out to gain acknowledgment of their citizenship. David Silveyra, who represented the "Portuguese" Jews of Paris and was well known among the Assembly's deputies, took the issue to the Committee on the Constitution, whose members included Talleyrand, Le Chapelier, Rabaut de Saint-Étienne and Target,[75] all of whom supported Jewish emancipation. On 28 October 1790 the committee issued a "decision" explaining that "the National

---

for the Société d'histoire contemporaine by Robert de Crèvecœur. 2 vol. (Paris: Alphonse Picard et fils, 1894), 330.

72 Rewbell returned to the attack on 21 July 1790. According to him, the Jews in the three provinces paid only for the rights of protection, habitation and toleration. To exempt them from these payments, he declared, was in reality to exempt the Jews from all taxes, contrary to the principle of equality proclaimed by the Declaration of the Rights of Man. The argument was fallacious. A discussion then began on the consequences of the decree, during which Du Port, Regnault and Briois de Beaumetz spoke, rejecting Rewbell's requests. The Assembly then finally approved the decree's text, abolishing all taxes imposed on the Jews. *Archives parlementaires*, 13:219.

73 Feuerwerker, *L'émancipation...*, 379.

74 Ibid., 380. Cf. Sagnac, 232.

75 Guy-Jean-Baptiste Target (1733–1807) was an attorney and a deputy of Paris's Third Estate. An author of the 1791 Constitution, he refused to defend Louis XVI. He served as a judge of the Appeal Tribunal from 1797 until his death.

Assembly no longer wants to concern itself with the status of the Jews. But it is dedicated to the principle that all those who, under the former government, had legally received the status of citizens, should continue to enjoy it. Therefore there is no doubt that Jews who have specific *lettres patentes*, as do the Portuguese, Spanish and Avignonnais Jews, may cite the decree of 28 January."[76]

Despite these limited gains the cause of emancipation had not progressed to a decisive conclusion since 1789. Indeed, on 28 January 1790 the Assembly had acknowledged to the "Portuguese" Jews only the rights they had already enjoyed under the Ancien Régime. Some subjects no doubt became citizens; but this change merely reflected a general change taking place in the nation: if Jews had gained rights, it was less because these rights were accorded to Jews than because some Jews were acknowledged as being French. As for the basic issue of acknowledging the citizenship of the Jews of the East, the National Assembly continued to avoid making a decision.

Contributing to this stalemate were deep personal and political divisions among the *patriotes* who supported emancipation. Adrien Du Port, a member of "the Triumvirate" along with Barnave and Alexandre de Lameth, exercised growing influence over the Assembly. However, La Fayette, whose popularity was at its zenith, was jealous of their ascendancy; and Mirabeau, who was now providing covert advice to the royal court, fought the "Triumvirs" and detested La Fayette. More serious yet was the ideological conflict among the *patriotes* over extending rights to people of color. Barnave, who owned slaves and plantations in Saint-Domingue, and was a friend of Alexandre de Lameth and his brother, Charles, appeared to be a supporter of the colonists and opposed not only abolition of slavery but also recognizing citizenship for people of color—a cause dear to the most committed *patriotes*, especially members of the Society of Friends of the Blacks—Abbé Grégoire, Condorcet, Brissot, La Rochefoucauld—as well as to progressive democrats such as Robespierre and Pétion.

At the same time that *patriote* supporters of Jewish emancipation were riven by differences over freedom and rights for people of color, opponents of emancipation were gaining significant support from the Catholic Church, which was increasingly hostile

---

76 In Feuerwerker, *L'émancipation…*, 381.

to the Assembly's policies. Sale of Church properties had already given opponents of the Revolution opportunities to mobilize secular anti-Judaism by depicting a stampede of Jews seeking to buy Church estates. Recognition of the citizenship of Protestants in December 1789, then that of the Jews of the Southwest in January 1790, worried the Church, which saw in it the beginnings of separation of church and state within the French kingdom. The anti-revolutionary press led a violent campaign based on the theme of "all rights for Protestants and Jews, none for the Church, which they are despoiling, or for Catholic priests, whom they are enslaving." "Your kings, O my people," wrote the *Journal of Louis XVI*, "deny to ministers of the state religion the tolerance, the peace of mind granted to the Jews, the Lutherans, the Calvinists..."[77] The *Journal de la Cour et de la Ville* added: "Do you want to place Calvinism, Judaism, Lutheranism on the throne? But at least, for pity's sake, deign to tolerate this suffering Catholic religion!"[78] In the fashion of the era, the Jews' "triumph" was denounced in verse:

> By order of fateful decrees, O Christians,
> We must become Jews in order to be citizens,
> We will have Judean usurers for priests,
> And impudent sophists, Protestants, atheists.[79]

This growing conflict, which set the Church against the *patriotes,* paralyzed any conclusive action on behalf of the Jews and explains the Assembly's repeated delays in taking up the issue of the Jews' citizenship.

The Assembly's vote on 17 July 1790 to establish the Civil Constitution of the Clergy made progress toward emancipation even more difficult. The Civil Constitution provided for election of bishops and priests by assemblies of "lay electors" who were to be designated by active citizens among eligible citizens, and the law did not require that these "electors" be Catholic. This raised the possibility that were the Assembly to acknowledge the Jews' citizenship, Jews would be

---

77   Kahn, *Les Juifs de Paris pendant la Révolution,* 48.

78   *Journal de la Cour et de la Ville,* 18 January 1791.

79   Ibid. ["*Par de fatals décrets, ô chrétiens, / Il faut judaïser pour être citoyens, / Pour prêtres, nous aurons l'usurier de Judée, / Le sophiste impudent, le protestant, l'athée.*"]

allowed to participate in choosing these electors—and to be chosen
as electors of priests and bishops. The prospect that Jews might be
able to play a part in determining the careers of the Catholic Church's
priests only further agitated the Church's faithful. All debate on Jewish emancipation ground to a halt for the moment.

Emancipation's most resolute advocates refused, however, to give
in to discouragement. Abbé Grégoire was designated to assume the
presidency of the National Assembly between 18–30 January 1791.
The moment appeared ripe to attempt to extract, surreptitiously, a
decree on behalf of the Jews. On 18 January, during the usually less
well-attended evening session, Louis-Simon Martineau, a deputy and
member of the Committee on Ecclesiastical Affairs, proposed to the
Assembly that it decide immediately that the "decree of 28 January
1790 applies without distinction to all Jews, of whatever kind and
whatever denomination, who have obtained *lettres patentes* of naturalization."[80] This would have endorsed the decision of 28 October
1790 by the Assembly's Committee on the Constitution. Martineau
then added "that all those who combine, moreover, the qualifications
required by the law ought to enjoy the rights of active citizens."[81] This
would be general emancipation. Since the question of Jewish rights
was not on the session's agenda, opponents of emancipation were
aroused. Prince de Broglie rose to speak against "all this intrigue
hatched long ago by four or five powerful Jews in the *département*
of the Bas-Rhin," and denounced "one of them, among others, who
had acquired an immense fortune at the expense of the State and for
a long spread considerable sums in this capital in order to procure
protectors and supporters." These were obviously remarks aimed at
Cerf-Berr, but they cast suspicion on all partisans of emancipation.
Then, calling attention to the tension in Alsace, "the city of Strasbourg in ferment," prince de Broglie asked that Martineau's motion
be sent back to the Committee on the Constitution, and that the session return to the agenda.[82] Another deputy, M. de Folleville, who
had stood in vain as a candidate against Grégoire for president of
the Assembly, treacherously emphasized that referring the proposal

---

80 *Archives parlementaires*, 22:318. Louis-Simon Martineau (1754–1835) was deputy
of la Vienne to the Legislative and the Convention. A Girondist, he voted for the
king's execution and to indict Marat.

81 Ibid.

82 Ibid.

back to committee impressed him all the more since, "if we adopted Martineau's bill under the presidency of Abbé Grégoire, we would draw from it malicious conclusions against him…"[83] To Grégoire's great displeasure the demand to refer back to committee passed by a strong majority.

In May 1791, despite Barnave's efforts, the Assembly granted political rights to mulattos born of free fathers and mothers. The *patriotes* ended by splitting up their votes. Nonetheless the measure's enactment restored hope among advocates of emancipation. Moreover, creation of electoral lists in Paris, in preparation for forthcoming elections to the Assembly as provided in the new Constitution, gave Paris's Jews an opportunity to resume their lobbying. On 16 May 1791 an address they had drafted was read in the National Assembly. In it they emphasized that the legislation enacted to date regarding the Jews was inconsistent: in Paris, in the same dwellings, and sometimes within the same families, depending upon whether they were from Bordeaux or Alsace, Jews either enjoyed or were deprived of the right to vote. The Assembly simply referred the address to the municipal authorities of Paris for information. On 26 May 1791 Paris's Jews wrote to the National Assembly urging it "to extend formally to the Jews of the capital the consequences of the salutary principles that it has just confirmed regarding liberty of religious opinions."[84] These efforts, too, were in vain.

On 21 June the king and his family left Paris secretly in an attempt to flee the country. Halted at Varennes, near the German border, on 25 June, they were taken back to the Tuileries Palace under heavy guard. In the tempest aroused by the sovereign's flight, the citizenship of the Jews of the East mattered little to the Assembly's deputies.

---

83 Ibid.
84 In Feuerwerker, *L'émancipation…*, 385.

CHAPTER 8

AT THE LAST MOMENT

All that is unjust cannot last.
Adrien Du Port

O<small>N</small> 17 J<small>ULY</small> 1791 L<small>A</small> F<small>AYETTE AND</small> J<small>EAN</small>-S<small>YLVAIN</small> B<small>AILLY</small>, <small>MAYOR</small> of Paris, ordered troops to open fire on a crowd that had gathered on the Champs-de-Mars to support a petition opposing Louis XVI's reinstatement after his attempt to flee France. The fusillade sealed the split among the *patriotes* and supporters of Jewish emancipation. Clermont-Tonnerre, a liberal monarchist, now issued a critique of the Declaration of the Rights of Man, hoping that political rights might be reserved for those who could prove not only their status as property owners, but also that they had been "permanently in the country for a specific number of generations..."[1] Abbé Grégoire was absorbed in the struggle for the rights of men of color. The National Assembly engaged in revising the Constitution throughout the summer without the subject being mentioned. The cause of Jewish emancipation seemed definitively abandoned.

On 3 September the Assembly concluded debate on the Constitution. On 14 September the king accepted it. The Constituent Assembly seemed exhausted.[2] "It had, in two and a half years, lived several centuries," wrote the historian Jules Michelet. "It had sated itself and passionately longed to adjourn." On the right, numerous

---

1 Charles Du Bus, *Stanislas de Clermont-Tonnerre et l'échec de la révolution monarchique (1757-1792)* (Paris: F. Alcan, 1931), 463.

2 [The National Assembly was proclaimed on 17 June 1789, following the decision by representatives of the three orders of the États Généraux (Clergy, Nobility, and the Third Estate, or commons) to vote as individuals rather than by blocs comprising members of each estate. On 9 July 1789 the Assembly designated itself to be *l'Assemblée nationale constituante*, or the Constituent Assembly, to indicate that its primary focus was the drafting of a Constitution for the nation. Following Louis XVI's ratification of the Constitution on 14 September 1791, the Assembly, on 1 October, became *l'Assemblée national legislative*, indicating that its primary task was henceforth to be consideration of laws to govern and administer the nation. —T<small>RANSL</small>.]

I believe that freedom of worship no longer allows that any distinction may be made among citizens' political rights on the basis of their beliefs. And I believe equally that the Jews cannot be the only exception to enjoyment of these rights, when pagans, Turks, Muslims, even the Chinese—people of all sects, in a word—are admitted.

— ADRIEN DU PORT

conservative monarchists either resigned their seats or emigrated; on the left, democrats were silent after the fusillade of 17 July; republicans were subjected to prosecutions. These developments allowed the "Triumvirate" of Du Port, Barnave, Lameth and their associates, to regroup as members of the Club des Feuillants and to take control of the Assembly.

On 27 September the question of the Jews' citizenship unexpectedly resurfaced. At its morning session, the Assembly adopted a decree forbidding citizens "from assuming in any way titles or privileges that have been abolished, to dress their household servants in livery, or to affix coats of arms to their coaches."[3] Adrien Du Port rose to ask permission to make "a very brief observation." After paying homage to equality he reminded the deputies that the Constitution, which had just been promulgated, "determined the qualifications necessary to become French citizens, and then for French citizens to become active citizens." Since the decree postponing consideration of the Jews' status was inconsistent with these general arrangements, he proposed that "the Assembly revoke the decree, and that Jews become active citizens if they fulfill the conditions prescribed in the Constitution." "I believe," he added, "that freedom of worship no longer allows that any distinction may be made among citizens' political rights on the basis of their beliefs. And I believe equally that the Jews cannot be the only exception to enjoyment of these rights, when pagans, Turks, Muslims, even the Chinese—people of all sects, in a word—are admitted."[4]

Jean-François Rewbell immediately demanded the floor to speak against Du Port's proposal. Michel-Louis-Étienne Regnault de Saint-Jean-d'Angely opposed the request, declaring that "to oppose Du Port's proposal is to oppose the Constitution itself."[5] The president, Thouret, immediately ended debate and called for a vote. And "the Assembly adopted M. Du Port's proposal amidst applause." Rewbell then observed with irony that the Assembly, in its haste, had voted

---

3   *Archives parlementaires de 1787 à 1860. Première série (de 1787 à 1799). Recueil complet des débats législatifs et politique des Chambres françaises.* Jules Mavidal and Émile Laurent, eds. 32 vol. (Paris: P. Dupont, 1862-1888). 31:372.

4   Ibid.

5   Ibid. Michel-Louis-Étienne Regnault de Saint-Jean-d'Angely (1761–1819) was an attorney, deputy of the Third Estate and a moderate *patriote*. Later ennobled as a count under the Empire, he served as president of the Council of State's section on interior affairs.

a decree without having a final text placed before it. Acknowledging the point to be well taken, Thouret invited Du Port to put his motion in writing. And so it was immediately decreed: "The National Assembly, deeming that the necessary conditions to be French citizens and to become active citizens are fixed by the Constitution, and that all men who, satisfying the aforesaid conditions, take the civic oath and undertake to fulfill all duties that the Constitution imposes, are entitled to all advantages that it offers, revokes all postponements, reservations and exceptions inserted in preceding decrees relative to individual Jews who take the civic oath."[6]

An hour of debate had sufficed. All French Jews had become citizens.

Nonetheless the deputies of the eastern provinces renewed their opposition the next day, 28 September. At the reading of the report of the previous day, Prince de Broglie interceded. He conjured up visions of the disastrous response the decree would arouse in Alsace. Had not the Jews attained the rights of French citizens while still preserving the benefit of their laws and special institutions? Seeing that the Jews had been admitted to citizenship, they at least ought to abandon their special status in return. Prince de Broglie then proposed that "the taking of the civic oath on the part of Jews be regarded as a definite relinquishment of civil and political laws to which Jewish individuals believe they are subject."[7] One deputy observed that, as the civil laws of the Jews were, in effect, their religious laws, they could not be asked to renounce their religion. The observation appeared fair. A draft of a decree was drawn up, modifying the text adopted the previous day, clarifying that the civic oath "will be regarded as a renunciation of all privileges and exceptions previously instituted on their behalf."[8] The Assembly adopted the decree. It wanted Jewish emancipation, but it also wanted the Jews integrated as citizens. Having granted the first, it intended to carry out the second.

Everything seemed to have been said, when Rewbell once again asked for the floor for several reflections on the wording of the decree. Murmurs arose from the Assembly, its members impatient to be done with it. Rewbell immediately raised the accusation of the Jews' corrupt influence: "If you refuse to hear all discussion, may you

---

6 Ibid.

7 Ibid., 31:441.

8 Ibid.

be persuaded that in my region, the enemies of the public good will make its inhabitants believe that the usurers have found powerful protectors in Paris."[9] Then he exclaimed in dramatic tones: "If the Assembly does not wish to be informed, I hold it accountable for all trouble that yesterday's decree may create in Alsace, at a time when nonjuring priests are redoubling their fanatical intrigues!"[10]

Tired of resisting, the president gave him the floor. Rewbell immediately turned to issues of money. He conjured up "the numerous and unfortunate class who live under the usurious oppression of the Jews." Peremptorily, he declared that "the Jews are at this moment creditors in Alsace of twelve to fifteen million [livres] owed by this class of Alsatians." He added: "If we consider that all of these debtors, together, do not possess three million [livres], and that the Jews are not the type to lend fifteen million on the basis of three million worth of secured valuables, one will be persuaded that there is at least twelve million worth of usury based upon these claims..." Rewbell asked, therefore, that in Alsace all Jews be required to furnish to local administrations relief of their claims on Christians. The authorities would determine whether these debtors were able to discharge their debts, and it was up to the new Legislative Assembly to make helpful decisions. "Act," Rewbell declared, "so that we may finally say to our fellow citizens that you had kindly come to their aid, and that the National Assembly is no less well-intentioned toward them as toward the Jews!"[11]

What Rewbell wanted, in reality, was to prevent the Jews from obtaining repayment of their loans, which he presumed to be usurious and, at the same time, to strengthen his own political credit in Alsace. His stratagem was clever because it would have been difficult for the Assembly to refuse to protect Christians from Jewish usurers at the same time that it acknowledged the Jews' status as citizens. The Assembly therefore passed Rewbell's proposed decree. Paradoxi-

---

9 Ibid.

10 Ibid. [Nonjuring priests were members of the Catholic clergy who refrained from or refused to take an oath to support the Constitution adopted by the National Assembly. Clerical opposition to the Constitution stemmed from enactment, in July 1790, of a law called the Civil Constitution of the Clergy. Its provisions included the principle that the Church in France would not be subject to any foreign authority, and that vacancies in the clergy, from parish priest to bishop, were to be filled by popular election. —*TRANSL.*]

11 Ibid.

cally, the struggle for the Jews' emancipation concluded with a final measure of defiance against them.

The next day Madame Elisabeth, the king's sister, wrote to a friend: "The Assembly crowned all of its follies and irreligion by giving the Jews the right to be admitted to all employment."[12] The press, however, was indifferent. After the tensions of that summer, the country longed for calm, awaiting the Constitution to bring political peace. All eyes were turned toward the Legislative Assembly, scheduled to convene on 1 October. Hardly any newspapers, whether moderate or *patriote*, mentioned that the Jews had been acknowledged as citizens.[13] Even in Strasbourg the news was received without making "the sensation that good *patriotes* had feared."[14] The passions that Jewish emancipation had aroused during the past twenty months had finally subsided.

WHY?

In these last moments in the life of the Constituent Assembly, what considerations had led Du Port and his friends to get the Assembly to declare that the Jews were citizens? Du Port had probably always supported the cause of emancipation. A former attorney at the Parlement of Paris, a jurist who was at once bold and rigorous, he could not resign himself to the fact that the Assembly, which had voted the Declaration of the Rights of Man and had acknowledged the citizenship of the Jews of the Southwest, evaded, in an obvious contradiction, granting those same rights to the Jews of the East. Practical political considerations also reinforced these juridical consideration. Laws voted during the summer of 1791 had markedly increased financial requirements necessary to be named a second-degree elector.[15] Given the impoverished circumstances of the Jews of the East, only an exceptionally few notables were capable of partici-

---

12 Ferdinand Dreyfus, "Comment les Juifs sont devenus citoyens français," *Revue politique et parlementaire* 25 (July-September 1900): 588.

13 Cf. Kahn, *Les Juifs pendant la Révolution* (Paris: P. Ollendorff, 1899), 112.

14 *Le Mercure universel*, 17 October 1791.

15 The voting system of the 1791 Constitution, based on a poll tax, established several categories of active citizens. Active citizens who comprised the *primary assemblies* paid a direct contribution equal to the value of three days' labor. Those designated second-degree electors comprised the *electoral assemblies*, which named by means of election all civil servants, judges and deputies.

pating in the electoral process of appointing deputies, civil servants and magistrates. Emancipation, in reality, was tied to integration. Morally satisfactory, emancipation no longer presented political difficulties.

Perhaps another, more personal motive inspired Du Port and his friends. Several days earlier, debate had resumed on the status of France's colonies. The planters and their allies had never accepted the liberal decree of 15 May 1791 regarding the civil status of free people of color. Given that Barnave and Lameth, along with Du Port, commanded the parliamentary majority, the moment appeared ripe to rescind the decree and to enact a law securing the colonists' power. After a long and emotional debate on 23-24 September, despite opposition by democrats such as Abbé Grégoire, Robespierre and Pétion, the Assembly enacted a text granting colonial assemblies control over "the personal status of unfree persons and the political status of men of color and free blacks." This placed their status in the hands of the colonists. Moreover, on 28 September, the day after the Jews were emancipated, the Assembly decreed that all persons living in metropolitan France were free, whatever their race. Slavery, however, was retained in the colonies. The Massiac Committee, the colonial planters' lobby, had won its victory and had prevailed over the friends of the blacks. Two years after having proclaimed that all men were born free and equal in rights, the Assembly bowed its head before the planters and their allies, sanctioned slavery—an absolute negation of the Declaration of the Rights of Man—and abandoned men of color to the power of the colonists. Such ideological capitulation, such renunciation of their ideal by the men who had described the Declaration as a "national catechism," probably called up, in the minds of the best among them, a kind of moral compensation: if their coalition broke apart at the moment when they sacrificed blacks, at least they had liberated Jews.

Was Abbé Grégoire, who had campaigned on behalf of both with equal ardor and generosity, able to consider himself pleased on 27 September? The most oppressed group of mankind remained imprisoned in its chains at the same time that the Jews saw theirs struck off, because they were closer at hand, and because they were white.

AUTHOR'S ACKNOWLEDGMENTS

I ESPECIALLY THANK M. JEAN FAVIER, DIRECTOR GENERAL OF France's Archives nationales, and his colleagues, whose friendly and enlightened aid turned out to be, in this instance as in so many others, irreplaceable. I thank, too, Mme Lucie Roux, chief curator of the Archives de la region Lorraine; M. Jacques d'Orléans, chief curator of the Archives du Bas-Rhin; M. Jean Valette, chief curator of the Archives de la Gironde; M. Jean Cavignac, curator of services of the Archives départementales de la Gironde; M. Hubert Collin, director of services of the Archives de Meurthe-et-Moselle, and their colleagues who greatly facilitated my research.

I express my gratitude to M. Jean Becarud, chief librarian of the Bibliothèque du Sénat; Mme Françoise Bermann, librarian of the Bibliothèque nationale; Mme Monique Pouliquen, chief librarian of the Bibliothèque historique of the Archives nationales; Mme Yvonne Levyne, librarian of the Alliance israélite universelle, and to their colleagues for their patient assistance.

To Patrice Gueniffey, for his enlightened and cordial assistance; Jean-Denis Bredin, for his fond attention; and Micheline Amar, for her friendly aid, I express my gratitude.

Finally, I thank Bernhard Blumenkranz, enlightened historian of French Judaism, whose critiques and suggestions were very valuable to me; as well as Gérard Nahon.

—Robert Badinter

TRANSLATOR'S ACKNOWLEDGMENTS

For some unexplained reason, spouses and significant others seem always to be mentioned last in authors' acknowledgements. As translator of this work, I am not bound by that tradition, and so I thank my wife, Janette, for supporting me wholeheartedly and enthusiastically in seeing this project through. Janette was with me to share my joy when I turned a corner in a gallery of the Musée Historique Lorrain in Nancy and found myself standing before its life-size portrait of Abbé Grégoire, sitting at his writing desk and beaming beneficently at his onlookers. Janette also indulged me in Bordeaux on 11 September 2001 when I set off in search of the site of the Gradis mansion on what is now a busy commercial street in the city's center. Along the way during our travels through France, we have always found a warm welcome, and Janette has come to share my delight with its people and culture.

Odile Contassot is the best instructor of French any Anglophone could ever hope to encounter and befriend. I met her at the Alliance Française in Manhattan during one of her sojourns in New York. There she helped me dredge up—and add to—the French I had learned but left unused since I graduated from college the year she was born. Later, a good friend, Odile helped to untangle sentences I could not then render, read through the first draft of this translation, and saved me from a host of errors. Those that remain are mine alone, introduced in the course of multiple revisions.

Larry and Eve Yudelson, proprietors of Ben Yehuda Press, are exactly the editors and publishers you want for a project such as this. When I suggested the idea of this translation to Larry, his immediate response was, "Sure, let me see it. I don't know much about Jewish emancipation in France during the French Revolution, but I'm sure I'll learn something." And that, after all, is what editing and publishing are all about (or should be).

The late Arthur Hertzberg did not live to see this translation. I made his acquaintance through *Present Tense* magazine, which he attempted valiantly to save. After it folded, he honored me with an invitation to join an informal Talmud seminar he led for a small group at New York University. A Conservative rabbi, he combined deep Orthodox knowledge of traditional Jewish texts with Reform liberalism regarding contemporary social and political issues—a trifecta rarely matched in the American rabbinate. No doubt he would have disagreed—vigorously—with much of my introduction to this book. Nonetheless I believe he would have done so in the spirit honored in *Pirkei Avot*: "Any controversy waged in the service of God shall in the end be of lasting worth...."

A number of friends and colleagues have read and offered comments on earlier drafts, and all provided encouragement at critical times: Murray Polner and Seymour Lachman, editor of *Present Tense* and director of Wagner College's Hugh L. Carey Center for Government Reform, respectively; and Janice Scheetz, Naomi Winter Cohen and Jeff Mittleman, at United Israel Appeal. I was unable to share the manuscript with the late Sister Ann Gillen, SHCJ, executive director of the National Interreligious Task Force on Soviet Jewry, but she remains in memory as my own Abbé Grégoire.

Finally, I owe a great debt of gratitude to my late father and my mother, Harold and Vera Simms, who taught me to persevere—though at times they must have regretted having done so when their eyes glazed over while I shared with them my immersion in the intricacies of Jewish emancipation during the French Revolution. Most of all, I wish to acknowledge my maternal grandparents, Abraham and Molly Goldstein, who made their way to America after taking the bold step of uprooting their growing family from Kishinev following a pogrom in 1903. In a circuitous way that makes the author and translator of this book *landsmen*. This world, especially the Jewish corner of it, is small, very small, indeed.

—Adam Simms

BIBLIOGRAPHY

BOOKS AND ARTICLES

Anchel, Robert. *Les Juifs de France*. Paris: J.-B. Janin, 1945.

——— . "Les lettres patentes du 10 juillet 1784." *Revue des études juives* (1932).

——— . *Napoléon et les Juifs*. Paris: Presses Universitaires de France, 1928.

Archives parlementaires de 1787 à 1860. Première série (de 1787 à 1799). Recueil complet des débats législatifs et politiques des Chambres françaises. Edited by Jules Mavidal and Émile Laurent. 32 vol. Paris: P. Dupont, 1862-1888.

Aulard, François-Alphonse. *Histoire politique de la Révolution française*. Paris: A. Colin, 1901.

Barrière, Pierre. *L'Académie de Bordeaux, centre de culture internationale aux XVIIIᵉ siècle, 1712-1792*. Bordeaux: Bière, 1951.

Benot, Yves. *La Révolution française et la fin des colonies*. Paris: La Découverte, 1988.

Berr, Berr Isaac. *Réflexions sur l'enregistrement de l'édit des noncatholiques au parlement de Metz, 10 mars 1788, et projet pour rendre les Juifs plus utiles et plus heureux en France*. Archives nationale, 154, AP 2.

Blumenkranz, Bernhard. "À propos des Juifs dans les cahiers de doléances." *AHRF* [Annales historiques de la Révolution française] 130 (1967).

——— . *Bibliographie des Juifs en France*. Toulouse: Privat, 1974.

——— , ed. *Histoire des Juifs en France*. Toulouse: Privat, 1972

——— and Albert Soboul, eds. *Les Juifs et la Révolution française. Problèmes et aspirations*. Toulouse: Privat, 1976.

Bredin, Jean-Denis. *Sieyès, la clé de la Révolution française*. Paris: Fallois, 1988.

Brette, Armand. *Recueil de documents relatifs à la convocation des États généraux de 1789.* 4 vol. Paris: Imprimerie nationale, 1894-1915.

Butel, Paul and Jean-Pierre Poussou. *La Vie quotidienne à Bordeaux aux XVIIIᵉ siècle.* Paris: Hachette, 1980.

Cahen, A. "L'émancipation des Juifs devant la Société royale des sciences et des arts de Metz." *Revue des études juives* 1 (1880).

———. "Les Juifs de Metz, budget de la communauté." *Mémoires de la Société d'archéologie lorraine* 3d ser. (1875).

Cavignac, Jean. *Dictionnaire du judaïsme bordelais aux XVIIIᵉ et XIXᵉ siècles: biographies, généalogies, professions, institutions.* Bordeaux: Archives départementales de la Gironde, 1987.

Chassin, Charles-Louis, ed. *Les Élections et les cahiers de Paris en 1789.* 4 vol. Paris: Jouaust et Signaux, 1888-1889.

Chevalier, Yves. *L'Antisémitisme: le Juif comme bouc émissaire.* Preface by F. Bourricaud. Paris: Cerf, 1988.

Clément, Roger. *La Condition des Juifs de Metz sous l'Ancien Régime.* Paris: Henri Jouve, 1903.

Cloots, Anacharsis. *Lettre sur les Juifs à un ecclésiastique de mes amis, lue dans la séance publique du Musée de Paris, le 21 novembre 1782, par M. le B. d. C. D. V. D. G.* Berlin: n.p., 1783.

Dictionnaire universel françois et latin, vulgairement appelé Dictionnaire de Trévoux. 6th ed. 8 vol. Paris: La Compagnie des Libraires Associés, 1771.

Dohm, Christian Wilhelm. *De la réforme des Juifs.* Preface by Dominique Bourel. Paris: Stock, 1984.

Dreyfus, F. "Comment les Juifs sont devenus citoyens français." *Revue politique et parlementaire* 25 (July-September 1900).

Du Bus, Charles. *Stanislas de Clermont-Tonnerre et l'échec de la révolution monarchique (1757-1792).* Paris: F. Alcan, 1931.

Duquesnoy, Adrien-Cyprien. *Journal d'Adrien Duquesnoy, député du Tiers état de Bar-le-Duc, sur l'Assemblée constituante, 3 mai 1789–3 avril 1790.* Published for the Société d'histoire contemporaine by Robert de Crèvecœur. 2 vol. Paris: Alphonse Picard et fils, 1894.

Expilly, Jean-Joseph (abbé). *Dictionnaire géographique, historique et politique des Gaules et de la France.* 6 vol. Paris: Desaint et Saillant, 1762-1770.

Feuerwerker, David. *L'émancipation des Juifs en France de l'Ancien*

Régime à la fin du Second Empire. Paris: Albin Michel, 1976.

———. "Les Juifs en France. Anatomie de 307 cahiers de doléances de 1789." *Annales E.S.C.* [Économies, sociétés, civilisations], 1 (1965).

Ginsburger, Moses. *Cerf-Berr et son époque. Conférence faite à Strasbourg le 17 janvier 1906*. Translated into French by E. Ginsburger. Guebwiller: J. Dreyfus, 1908.

———. "Les familles Lebmann et Cerf-Berr." *Revue des études juives* 59 (1910).

———. "Samuel Lévy, rabbin et financier." *Revue des études juives* 65-66 (1913).

Girard, Patrick. *La Révolution française et les Juifs*. Paris: Robert Laffont, 1989.

———. *Pour le meilleur et pour le pire. Vingt siècles d'histoire juive en France*. Paris: Bibliophane, 1986.

Godechot, Jacques. "Les Juifs de Nancy de 1789 à 1795." *Revue des études juives*. 86 (1928).

———. "Les professions des Juifs nancéiens aux XVIIIᵉ siècle." *Revue juive de Lorraine* 2 (1926).

Grégoire, Henri-Baptiste (abbé). *Essai sur la régénération physique, morale et politique des Juifs*. Preface by Robert Badinter. Paris: Stock, 1988.

———. *Essai sur la régénération physique, morale et politique des Juifs*. Preface by Rita Hermon-Belot. Paris: Flammarion, 1988.

———. *Essai sur la régénération physique, morale et politique des Juifs*. Metz: Claude Lamort, 1789. (See also: *La Révolution française et l'émancipation des Juifs*, vol. 3, below.)

———. *Mémoires de Grégoire, ancien évêque de Blois, député à l'Assemblée constituante et à la Convention nationale, sénateur, membre de l'Institut*. Introduction by M. H. Carnot. 2 vol. Paris: Ambroise Dupont, 1837.

Grosclaude, Pierre. *Malesherbes, témoin et interprète de son temps*. Paris: Fischbacher, 1961.

Harsomy, E. "Metz pendant la Révolution." *Mémoires de l'Académie nationale de Metz, années 139-140*. 5th ser. 59 (1957-1959). Metz: Éditions de Lorraine, 1960.

Hell, F.-J. *Observations d'un Alsacien sur l'affaire présente des Juifs d'Alsace*. Frankfurt: n.p., 1779.

Hertzberg, Arthur. *The French Enlightenment and the Jews*. New

York: Columbia University Press, 1968.

Hildenfinger, Paul. *Documents sur les Juifs à Paris au XVIIIe siècle. Actes d'inhumation et scellés.* Paris: E. Champion, 1913.

Hourwitz, Zalkind. *Apologie des Juifs en réponse de cette question: Est-il moyens de rendre les Juifs plus heureux et plus utiles en France?* Paris: Quilleau, 1789. (See also: *La Révolution française et l'émancipation des Juifs,* vol. 4, below.)

"Journal de la députation de Bordeaux." Registre et répertoire des délibérations de la nation juive, 1790, no. 4. Archives départementales de la Gironde.

Kahn, Léon. *Histoire de la communauté israélite de Paris. Les Juifs de Paris aux XVIIIe siècle, d'après les archives de la Lieutenance générale de police à la Bastille.* Paris: A. Durlacher, 1894.

——— . *Les Juifs de Paris pendant la Révolution.* Paris: P. Ollendorff, 1899.

Lacretelle, Pierre-Louis de. *Plaidoyers.* Brussels: n.p., 1775.

Lacroix, Sigismond, ed. *Actes de la Commune de Paris pendant la Révolution.* 1st and 2d ser. 15 vol. Paris: L. Cerf, 1894-1914.

La Révolution française et l'émancipation des Juifs. 8 vol. Paris: Edhis [Éditions d'Histoire Sociale], 1968.

Vol. 1: [Honoré-Gabriel Riqueti, comte de] Mirabeau. *Sur Moses Mendelssohn, sur la réforme politique des Juifs.*

Vol. 2: [Claude-Antoine] Thiéry. *Dissertation sur cette question: Est-il moyens de rendre les Juifs plus heureux et plus utiles en France?*

Vol. 3: [Henri-Baptiste] Grégoire. *Essai sur la régénération physique, morale et politique des Juifs.*

Vol. 4: Zalkind-Hourwitz. *Apologie des Juifs en réponse de cette question: Est-il moyens de rendre les Juifs plus heureux et plus utiles en France?*

Vol. 5: *Adresses, Mémoires et Pétitions des Juifs, 1789-1794.*

Vol. 6: *La Commune et les Districts de Paris. Discours, Lettres et Rapports, 1790-1791.*

Vol. 7: *L'Assemblée Nationale Constituante. Motions, Discours et Rapports. La Législation nouvelle, 1789-1791.*

Vol. 8: *Lettres, Mémoires et Publications diverses, 1789-1806.*

Latrice, P. "L'Abbé Grégoire, Ami de tous les hommes," and "La régénération des Juifs." *Mélanges de science religieuse* 36, 3 (September 1979). Lille: Facultés catholiques.

Lemalet, M. "L'émancipation des Juifs de Lorraine à travers l'œuvre de Berr Isaac Berr," in Daniel Tollet, ed., *Politique et religion dans le judaïsme moderne: des communautés à l'émancipation. Actes du colloque tenu en Sorbonne les 18-19 novembre 1986.* Paris: Presses de l'université de Paris Sorbonne, 1987.

Léon, Henry. *Histoire des Juifs de Bayonne.* Paris: A. Durlacher, 1893; Marseilles: Laffitte Reprints, 1976.

Lettres patentes du Roi, confirmatives des privilèges dont les Juifs portugais jouissent depuis 1550, données à Versailles au mois de juin 1776. Paris: Imprimerie Destoupe, 1781.

Levylier, Roger. *Notes et documents concernant la famille Cerf-Berr, recueillis par un de ses membres.* 3 vol. Paris: Plon, 1902-1906.

Liber, Maurice "Les Juifs et la convocation des États Généraux." *Revue des études juives* 63-66 (1912-1913).

Lignac, [?] "Les Juifs et la convocation des États généraux." *Revue des études juives* 64 (1912).

Malesherbes, Chrétien-Guillaume de Lamoignon de. *Mémoire sur le mariage des protestans, en 1785.* [n.p., n.d.]

——— . *Second mémoire sur le mariage des protestans, en 1786.* London: n.p., 1787.

Malino, Frances. *Les Juifs sépharades de Bordeaux, assimilation et émancipation dans la France révolutionnaire et impériale.* Translated by Jean Cavignac. *Les Cahiers de l'I. A. E. S.* [Institut Aquitain d'Études Sociales], no. 5 (1984). [Originally published in English as *The Sephardic Jews of Bordeaux: Assimilation and Emancipation in Revolutionary and Napoleonic France.* University: University of Alabama Press, 1978].

Malvezin, Théophile. *Histoire des Juifs de Bordeaux.* Bordeaux: C. Lefebvre, 1875.

Marlin, François. *Voyages en France et pays circonvoisins depuis 1775 jusqu'en 1807.* 4 vol. [Title appears in Bibliothèque nationale de France card catalog entry as: *Voyages d'un Français depuis 1775 jusqu'en 1807.*] Paris: Guillaume, 1817.

Marx, R. "La régénération économique des Juifs d'Alsace à l'époque révolutionnaire et napoléonienne," in Bernhard Blumenkranz and Albert Soboul, eds., *Les Juifs et la Révolution française. Problèmes et aspirations.* Toulouse: Privat, 1976.

Maupassant, Jean de. *Les Armateurs bordelais au XVIIIe siècle. Abraham Gradis et l'approvisionnement des colonies (1756-1763)*. Bordeaux: G. Gounouilhou, 1909.

Mémoire remis par les députés juifs de Bordeaux à Monsieur de Malesherbes, Ministre d'État. Introduction and notes by Jean Cavignac. Bordeaux: Archives départementales de la Gironde, 1988.

Mercier, Louis-Sébastien. *L'An 2440, rêve s'il en fut jamais; suivi de l'Homme de fer; Songe*. [n.p.], 1786.

Mendelssohn, Moses. *Lettres juives du célèbre Mendelssohn, Philosophe de Berlin, avec les remarques et les réponses de M. le Docteur Kölble et autres savans hommes*. Frankfurt and The Hague: n.p., 1771.

Michælis, Johann David. *Orientalische und exegetische Bibliotek*. Frankfurt: Johann Gottlieb Garbe, 1782.

Michelet, Jules. *Histoire de la Révolution française*. Edited by G. Walter. 2 vol. Paris: Gallimard "Bibliothèque de la Pléiade," 1952.

Mirabeau, Honoré-Gabriel Riqueti (comte de). *Sur Moses Mendelssohn, sur la réforme politique des Juifs*. London: n.p., 1787. (See also: *La Révolution française et l'émancipation des Juifs*, vol. 1, above.)

Moulinas, René. "Les Juifs d'Avignon et du Comtat Venaissin," in Patrick Girard, *La Révolution française et les Juifs*. Paris: Robert Laffont, 1989.

———. *Les Juifs du pape en France. Les communautés d'Avignon et du Comtat Venaissin aux XVIIe et XVIIIe siècles*. Preface by Claude Mossé. Toulouse: Privat, 1981.

Nahon, Gérard, ed. *Les Nations juives portugaises du Sud-Ouest de la France (1684-1791)*. Paris: Fundaçao Calouste Gulbenkian, 1981.

Pfister, Christian. *Histoire de Nancy*. 3 vol. Paris: Berger-Levrault, 1902-1909.

Pflieger, Jean-Adam. *Réflexions sur les Juifs d'Alsace, par M. Pflieger*. Paris: Devaux, 1790.

Pluchon, Pierre. *Nègres et Juifs aux XVIIIe siècle: Le racisme au siècle des Lumières*. Paris: Tallandier, 1984.

Poliakov, Léon. *Histoire de l'antisémitisme*. Vol. 3: *De Voltaire à Wagner*. Paris: Calmann-Lévy, 1968.

Procès-Verbal de l'Assemblée nationale, imprimé par son ordre. 75 vol. Paris: Baudouin, 1789.

Reuss, R. "L'Alsace pendant la Révolution française." *Revue d'Alsace*, new ser., 3 (1879).

Rials, Stéphane. *La Déclaration des droits de l'homme et du citoyen*. Paris: Hachette "Pluriel," 1989.

Rœderer, Pierre-Louis. *Œuvres*. 8 vol. Paris: Firmin Didot Frères, 1853-1859.

Roubin, N. "La vie commerciale des Juifs comtadins en Languedoc au XVIIIᵉ siècle." *Revue des études juives* 34-36 (1896-1897).

Rousseau, Jean-Jacques. *Œuvres complètes*. 5 vol. Bernard Gagnebin and Marcel Raymond, eds. Paris: Gallimard "Bibliothèque de la Pléiade," 1969.

Sagnac, Philippe. "Les Juifs et la Révolution Française (1789-1791)." *RHMC* [Revue d'Histoire moderne et contemporaine] 1 (1889).

Seligmann, Edmond. *La Justice en France pendant la Révolution*. Paris: Plon-Nourrit, 1901.

Sévigné, Marie de Rabtin-Chantal (marquise de). *Madame de Sévigné. Correspondance*. 3 vol. Edited by R. Duchêne. Paris: Gallimard "Bibliothèque de la Pléiade," 1972-1978.

Spire, Abraham. *Le Journal révolutionnaire d'Abraham Spire*. Introduction and translation by Simon Schwarzfuchs. Paris: Institut Alain de Rothschild; Lagrasse: Verdier, 1989.

Szajkowski, Zosa. *Jews and the French Revolutions of 1789, 1830 and 1848*. New York: Ktav, 1970.

———. "La délégation des Juifs de Bordeaux à la commission Malesherbes en 1788 et à l'Assemblée nationale de 1789." *Zion* 18 (1951).

Thiéry, Claude-Antoine. *Dissertation sur cette question: Est-il moyens de rendre les Juifs plus heureux et plus utiles en France?* (Paris: Knapen Fils; Delaguette et Fils, 1788). (See also: *La Révolution française et l'émancipation des Juifs*, vol. 2, above.)

Tocqueville, Alexis de. *L'Ancien Régime et la Révolution*. 2 vol. Paris: Gallimard, 1953.

Tribout de Morembert, Henri. "Considerations sur le concours de l'Académie royale de Metz en 1787 et 1788." *Mémoires de l'Académie nationale de Metz*. 6th ser. (Metz: Le Lorrain,

1974.)

——— . "Les Juifs de Metz et de Lorraine, 1791-1795," in Bernhard Blumenkranz and Albert Soboul, eds., *Les Juifs et la Révolution française. Problèmes et aspirations.* Toulouse: Privat, 1976.

Turgot, Anne-Robert-Jacques (baron de Laune). *Œuvres de Turgot et documents le concernant.* Edited by G. Schelle. 5 vol. Paris: F. Alcan, 1913-1923.

Voltaire. *Œuvres de Voltaire.* Edited by Adrien-Jean-Quentin Beuchot. 72 vol. Paris: Werdet et Lequien fils, 1829.

Weill, G. "Un texte de Montesquieu sur le judaïsme." *Revue des études juives* 49 (1904).

Wessely, Naphtali Herz, *Instruction salutaire adressée aux communautés juives de l'Empire, par le célèbre Hartwic Weisly, Juif de Berlin; traduite en François, en l'année 1782. Nouvelle édition, Augmentée de Notes, d'une Lettre à M. l'Abbé Maury, Député à l'Assemblée Nationale, par l'Éditeur, et de la réponse de l'Abbé Maury.* Paris: Belin, 1790.

Weyl, Robert and Jean Daltroff. "Le cahier des doléances des Juifs d'Alsace." *La Revue d'Alsace* 109 (1983).

NEWSPAPERS (AND EDITORS)

L'Ami du Peuple ou le Publiciste parisien (Marat).

Courrier de Provence, pour servir de suite aux Lettres du Comte de Mirabeau à ses Commettants (Mirabeau).

Courrier de Versailles à Paris et de Paris à Versailles; from 20 October 1789: *Courrier de Paris dans les provinces et des provinces à Paris*; from 3 August 1790: *Le Courrier de Paris dans les LXXXIII Départements*; from 1 March 1791: *Le Courrier des LXXXIII Départements* (Gorsas).

Courrier français (Poncelin de La Roche-Tilhac).

Gazette de Paris (Du Rozoi).

Gazette Universelle, ou Papier-Nouvelles de tous les pays et de tous les jours (Boyer et Cerisier).

Journal d'État et du citoyen (Mlle de Kéralio).

Journal de la municipalité et des districts de Paris (Bayard).

Journal de Paris (Garat, Rœderer).

Journal de Versailles, ou Affiches, announces et avis divers

(Regnault de Saint-Jean-d'Angély).

Journal des Débats et des Décrets (Gaultier de Biouzat).

Journal générale de la Cour et de la Ville (Brune et Gautier).

Mercure de France, dédié au Roi (Mallet Du Pan).

Mercure universel (Tournon).

Moniteur universel.

L'Observateur de Feydel (La Reynie).

Le Patriote français (Brissot, Girey-Dupré).

Le Point du Jour, ou Résultat de ce qui s'est passé la veille à l'Assemblée nationale (Barère).

Révolutions de France et de Brabant (Desmoulins).

Révolutions de Paris (Loustalot, Chaumette, Maréchal, Fabre d'Eglantine).

Le Rôdeur français (de Villenave).

INDEX

Economic status: in Alsace 14
Edict of Nantes 5, 5n10, 55
Electoral qualifications 91
Electors, categories of, 1791 152-153, 152n15
Elizabeth, Madame 152
Encyclopédie (on Jews) 28
Esprémenil, Jean-Jacques d' 123, 123n46
États Généraux 1, 1n1, 48, 62, 63, 75, 78; and Alsace 66-67; and Bordeau 63-65; and Bourg-Saint-Esprit 65-66; and Cerf-Berr 68. *See also:* Registers of grievances
Executioners, citizenship rights of 96
Expulsions of Jews: from Bayonne 8; from France 63; from Lorraine 22; by Bordeaux Jewish community 7-8

Fauchet, Abbé Claude 131, 131n20
Froissac, Captain de 136
Franco-Judaism xxvi-xxvii
Frederic II ["the Great"] (King of Prussia) 36
Frederic William I (King of Prussia) 36
Fréteau de Saint-Just, Emmanuel-Marie-Philippe 89, 89n50
Furtado, Abraham (*l'aîné*) 58, 58n73, 61, 62, 65n8, 114

Garat, Joseph (*l'aîné*) 115, 115n11
"German Jews" 7, 12-13, 24, 25, 58, 59n76, 61, 61n81, 66
Godard, Jacques 117, 119-120, 128-132, 133n32
Goudchaux, Lion 134
Gradis, Abraham 6
Gradis, David 7, 65, 65n8
Gradis, Moïse 58
Gradis family 8n24
Grégoire, Abbé Henri-Baptiste 42, 47, 48-52, 48n46, 56, 67, 74, 83, 84, 89,115, 117, 118, 122-123, 139-140, 143, 145, 146, 147, 153; on anti-Jewish violence 77; Bordeaux Jewish leaders' open letter to 77, 78, 78n10; and Dohm xvi; illustration 50; on moneylending 51, 51n48; "Motion in Favor of the Jews" 92-93; National Assembly debate, December 1789 104; National Assembly speech 85-86; Royal Academy of Sciences, Metz xvii-xviii; on the Talmud 51-52

Haskalah (European Jewish Enlightenment) 36
Hebera 9
Hell, François-Antoine-Joseph 14, 14n51, 18, 39, 84, 97; National Assembly debate,